The Greatest *Five* Years of Your Life

by

MARGUERITE CARTER

and

ALAN CARTER

Historical Research and Photographs

by

Alan R. McConnell

Published by

ALAN McCONNELL AND SON, INC.
546 S. Meridian St., Rm. 602, Indianapolis, Ind.

Library of Congress Catalog Card Number: 64--2440

Marguerite Carter's predictions are not to be considered personal in any way, as a forecast for an individual requires the time of birth, the place, month, date and year. The prophecies written here of world affairs and for the birthsigns are taken from rules laid down in the text books of long ago and rewritten to apply to our modern way of life by Miss Carter. The intention is to show "trends" as these planetary influences in general, aspect the various birth periods and those individuals who come strongly under their own birthsign through a concentration of planets at their birth. Those who were born in any month when the major planets were "scattered" are apt to find the predictions do not apply as fully because of a lack of planetary strength!

The Greatest Five Years of Your Life

We sincerely believe that the coming five years can be the greatest of your life! Nothing is ever static. There is always growth and change. At this particular period in the evolution of humankind, more and greater changes appear to be taking place than in any relatively short period for hundreds of years. Judged upon almost any basis of knowledge, the five years immediately before us seem to promise great developments.

We believe that the only way any human being comes to be a part of any unhappy condition or tragic development is *as a result* of becoming *first* a part of those conditions within himself, which is expressed in that which he allows to go on in his mind.

All the negative, destructive FEAR thoughts to which humanity gives way and which are very easy to accept and dwell upon, tend to ally the individual with their like in the world of so called reality.

We know that YOU *can* make this in actual reality —

"THE GREATEST FIVE YEARS OF YOUR LIFE!"

TABLE OF CONTENTS

FOREWORD BY MARGUERITE CARTER

It is not at all outside the realm of probability that I have seen and judged your chart of birth, for I have looked upon the birth charts of uncounted thousands. There have been times unnumbered when my heart was anguished in the wish, to reach *out* in mind to some lone struggling mortal whose chart I held and studied, that I might console him in his anxious hours and point out the way I could so clearly see, for him.

Often it has been a really simple thing to tell him fully what I knew was true. Force of circumstances never intervenes and thus I could express to him, the meaning which would take him to his dearly cherished ends. Repeatedly there has been clear indication of the closeness of a veiled and shadowed happy outcome, which but a little turn within himself would bring to sure reality.

Always I am sure that I can see the HIDDEN REASON for unhappiness and the certain means to its avoidance — and that means can be expressed in words which reach the understanding of the one who needs it though it is, in part, a means of mind, of *soul*, and I can surely help him reach that state where understanding comes — and happiness *within that state can never be denied.*

So I rejoice for him and know his hands are loosed from forces which, although unseen, have bound him to the limitations which have been his lot. I can tell him of the turn events will take and I can tell him how to plot his course and guide his mind from those deep channels of unhappy failure into which it has, by gradual process, grooved itself. I *know* his trials *will end* for now he learns the real, the true. He will not fail to choose the way which leads, unswerving, to his every, dearest wish. That way is his free choice and his alone.

I have the words to reach his ears. I know my warnings will be heeded. I seek to find my way within his mind to turn it from the contemplation of destruction which, though he is not aware of it, is leading to a blinded passing by of all the good which lies beside his hand. So I suggest the summoning of courage and the donning of his shield and buckler, the fronting of his course of life with serene *faith*. He now accepts the meaning thus expressed and tragedies, as always, go — depart, becoming only shadows, fleeing to the dark from whence they came.

He wishes me to tell him how to act in his perplexity and that I find the way to do, yet no one can escape his fate behind closed doors. To caution him against the danger might be to work him harm, for hiding from the danger, or seeking elsewhere in the realm of earthly things, is but to bring his mind to greater harmony with that evil which he fears. But now he sees the *good* and grasps it closely to his heart. That good is *ever there* for those who know the truth.

Another seeks to know what action he may take to reach success. I look within his chart and know that there within his reach lies all the fullness of success for which he yearns. He wishes me to tell what acts will take him surely to achievement. His desire is for me to plot his course in actions which will take him to his goal. I *can* point out those steps and I know the telling will be heeded for this ONE will listen with his heart and I know his fate is marked there clearly *through his heeding.* NEVER has a blind and heedless destiny enforced unhappy ends. They come to any man because he walks the way, *of his own choice,* which brings him to those ends.

I know my telling him the steps to take in action will be fruitful. He will heed the telling which so many fail to do. For him to reach success, his MIND must be conditioned to the goal. Though I speak the truth to others full a thousand times, they WILL inevitably think of something else, for mind must be conditioned to receive that truth. I have seen information placed before a human being — one who was in dire need of money. The information thus presented was completely adequate and would, if followed, have with certainty assured a large return, almost at once. But was that being benefited. No! He did not recognize the truth and NO ONE EVER WILL, though it pertains to health — or money — or to happiness, *unless* his mind is *ready to receive it!*

For this ONE, I possess the means to aid him on his way. I have the power which will stem the tide of his reverses. I KNOW THE WAY, for it is clearly marked to those who have discernment in the things of spirit. I have a means by which I can *convey the truth* to him. I know that I can tell him what the working out of cosmic law portends. He will receive the plotted course I have for him as truth and make it doubly sure. Thus — I *know* success for him *is certain!*

My heart is lifted to a surge of glad rejoicing for I have found a chart of birth which shows a danger road and yet is marked by *willingness* to heed and recognize the truth. I tell that person lightly of the danger and I POINT THE WAY for him to act — but principally I show him how to *face* his threat with *inner calm and courage.* HE WALKS THROUGH IT UNSCATHED and thus my cup is filled and I am glad of having lived and played a part in God's great plan.

And so I send this forth — my part of a sincere and earnest effort made, to shed a little light upon the path for you who find the going rough, and I shall find a joy in aiding you to place *your* feet upon that way!

Marguerite Carter

IT IS WRITTEN IN THE STARS
by Alan R. McConnell

Whenever you encounter a skeptic — to the belief that the planets exert an influence upon our lives here on earth, *you can be certain that* individual has *never* gone deeply enough into this subject to ATTAIN REAL KNOWLEDGE of it's verity!

Many scientists are no longer skeptics for many of the TRUTHS which were taught by the ancients have recently been scientifically proven!

We do NOT live in a wholly material, physical, factual world, though some of our modern-day scientists would have us believe so. Many forces outside our own little earth affect us in UNSEEN WAYS!

Sir Francis Bacon is credited with having really founded our modern-day laboratory science; although, *he was also a believer in astrology!*

During the explosion of new scientific knowledge which occurred after the idea really took hold, the tiny fragments tended to multiply endlessly, requiring an ever-increasing number of people to examine the evidence, and ever-increasing specialization, so that the tendency has been to *center everyone's attention* on *material* problems, material wealth, and the absolute authority of experts trained in scientific method. The present goal of modern science is to explain everything *through the physical* and deny everything existence which cannot be explained on its own terms. Science *has* accomplished miracles. Yet there is still an inner hunger in the midst of plenty which is not yet satisfied. When this hunger is upon us it is time to go outside and watch the stars. There in the sky is the inspiration for the most ancient wisdom of all. The sky is so vast that past, present, and future may be seen at a glance, because those stars which were overhead before are still in view and those which will be overhead in the future are there to be seen, too.

As the housewife has put away the old cookbook, so science has put away the old books too. New books have been written, new encyclopaedias and text books, from which the older wisdom of which I speak has been excluded. There is a tremendous body of knowledge still in existence today concerning the ancient art of the stars, more than could be read in a lifetime, yet these writings for the most part remain untouched. Many great and noble thoughts are there enshrined as well as evidence to intrigue the scientific mind. Aged astrological records have been shown to contain great accuracy and have provided the key to many historical monuments. (Religious shrines in Europe contain astrological motifs which picture the sky at the exact time that an important event took place.)

It has been shown that the greatest centers of ancient civilization *lived* by the stars. In this respect the word Astrology is used here rather than Astronomy because the modern definition of Astronomy limits this science to describing the physical characteristics of the stars.

The word Astrology is composed of two Greek roots — the first (astro) meaning *star*, the second (logos) meaning *word* or *explanation.* Since older civilizations lived by the stars, men of that day would not have had much interest in information about the stars which was of no *earthly* use to them. Words sometimes change in meaning as a result of direct manipulation. (There is a very interesting explanation of this after the word adulteration, as referred to words, in the foreword of the dictionary of the Encyclopaedia Brittanica.)

The word Logos is defined in today's unabridged dictionaries as the *cosmic reason* giving order, purpose, and intelligibility to the world (universe). Therefore Astrology referred to the *art* or *practical application* of Astronomy which provided the *reason* for studying the stars all through history.

In spite of the way that materialism seems to be sweeping all before it, there are still many who believe in ways of reaching truth which although not denying the physical — go beyond it. Among them are creative artists, philosophers, and those who rely on their faith in a superior intelligence. From what has been said before it may be seen to which system of ideas Astrology is dedicated.

The historical pathways of the seven liberal arts all lead back to Astrology as a source of knowledge and authority. Although the Greeks as a whole are usually given credit, special histories show that the greatest thinkers among early Greeks studied in Egypt or the East. The number seven itself is astrological — symbolizing the four phases of the moon, each of *seven* days duration; the *seven* stars of the ancients — the sun, moon, and five planets; and the four cardinal points plus the trine. In accordance with this the seven liberal arts were separated into two categories — the quadrivium and the trivium, based on the astrological numbers four and three.

According to Astrology as well as those who believe that there is more to man than meets the eye there is *within you* a tremendous hidden world of possibility which if searched diligently will lead you to great reward and the silencing of the voices of doubt and limitation which seek to lead you downward to an entirely material and lonely existence. In the hope that you will be helped to understand the deeper meanings which *lie behind* the descriptions concerning *you* which are to be found elsewhere in this book I would like to tell you about the background of Astrology and some of the great minds who have been deeply concerned with it. As one who stands beneath the open sky sees the stars completely encircle him so that from his standpoint he occupies the center, so this outline of astrological history will begin in the present, at the point of observation.

Astrologically 2,000 years is the period of an age, which is identified with one particular sign of the zodiac. Ancient astrologers placed the age of Aquarius near the present time. Momentous events occur during periods of change from one age to the next. Astrologically these changeover periods cover several hundred years and it is believed that we are now in a transitional period between Pisces and Aquarius. In counting back from the present, the beginning of the Piscean age would have coincided with the beginning of the Christian era; the age of Aries would have begun

2,000 B.C.; and the Taurian age 4,000 B.C. Modern astronomical calculation shows that during the aforementioned periods the signs in their order as given were actually on the eastern horizon at the spring equinox. From a descriptive standpoint, so much of history is similar to the outstanding characteristics of those particular signs and the changing periods from one sign to the next that the actual trend of history will be compared, in this outline, to the description of the zodiacal signs associated with previous ages.

MODERN — (c.1750 — c.1950 A. D.)

From this standpoint, all of *modern* history would astrologically fall within a changing period, from Pisces to Aquarius, and the period would reflect a *combination* of the dominant characteristics of each sign. Aquarius is described as masculine, self-assured, energetic, progressive, competitive, inventive, and impatient with old ideas. It is also an air sign and has been regarded as having a nature which is at once magnanimous and electrical. Dominant characteristics of Pisces have been described as feminine, sensitive, emotional, artistic, self-concerned, secretive, psychic, and sentimental. It is also regarded as watery, mystical and enigmatic.

During the relatively short period of change from one kind of world to another in modern times, new ideas have struck men with the force of thunderbolts, changes have been truly electrical — the age old attempts of man to fly have been accomplished, the Earth has been explored to its furthest limits, adventures in space have become a reality, and a host of other developments have taken place which are typically Aquarian as described above. On the other hand, the Piscean characteristics have continued to be reflected in literature, art, and religion, in a tenacious holding on to old ideas and possessions for *emotional* reasons, periodic feelings of loneliness, and tendencies toward apathy.

The comparison of entire periods of history in which people of all birthsigns were involved, with the major characteristics of just one or two zodiacal signs may seem a ridiculous oversimplification, yet, for example, the typical activities of the *majority* of people during the solar year are remarkable in their similarity to the dominant characteristics of the signs.

For instance, during September, in Virgo — dominant characteristic, concern with detail — school begins; during December, in Sagittarius — dominant characteristic, impulsive generosity — Christmas buying is exceptional; during January, in Capricorn — dominant characteristics, practicality and cautiousness — people budget, plan, pay bills, etc. It is amusing to note that during the time that income tax was due in March (during Pisces) never were so many people so *"pitiful"* at once. Self-pity is a likely habit of sensitive Piscean natives. When the payment date was moved forward into Aries, a very fierce and aggressive sign, the trend changed completely to *stiff resistance* against being pushed beyond what they felt was right, and the battle really began!

The beginnings of the United States were based on strongly Aquarian concepts but not without strong resistance. As always there were many who would have preferred greater restriction in the law for the preservation of special advantages already in existence for the benefit of a few people. It is interesting to note that two of the three most famous presidents were strongly Aquarius, while the *first* was a combination of Aquarius—Pisces, a very complicated person who presented characteristics of both signs strongly throughout his life.

Exploration and adventure, outstanding Aquarian tendencies, have led to a fantastic expansion of knowledge of geography when considered from the standpoint of the few short years in which it has been accomplished, compared to the tremendous span of years preceding it during which such knowledge remained fairly constant. A place called Thule was mentioned by ancient Greek writers, indicating that distant places were better known then than in succeeding years. The period which lay between the exploration of America by water and the transcontinental railroad, and which was represented by the stage coach and the pony express, was so short it hardly counted as more than the wink of an eye.

The Aquarian tendencies have certainly created a new world, but in the frantic rush to make everything conform to the new outlook *some* things were inevitably trampled. The tendency in the United States has been to teach from *new* books so that the older books have passed through many editions, and either the contents must be very dull or written in such a way that they are very difficult to change, in order to avoid being censored.

It is true that a tremendous body of astrological knowledge exists in older libraries and private collections, very little of which is in the United States. The eventual thoroughgoing investigation of this source of knowledge will undoubtedly lead to a *new* historical viewpoint. Even though the attempts to *exclude* all knowledge of an astrological nature have been extreme, some has slipped through the net, although it is generally ignored.

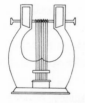 In western music there are *seven* notes in a scale enclosed within a *twelve* tone structure, just as the "planets", originally seven, were enclosed within twelve zodiacal signs. The music scales were constructed by Ptolemy, an Alexandrian astrologer. Most of the illustrations in encyclopedias of the ancient lyre picture a seven-stringed instrument.

The symbols used in Astronomy to designate the planets would be meaningless as to structure if it were not for their astrological meaning. From the *circle* is derived the principle of generation, and it is used to represent the creative principle in the symbols of the planets, while the *cross* represents matter, conflict, and the physical. The symbol for the benign planet Jupiter has a portion of the circle superior to the cross (♃), whereas Saturn, a malefic planet, has the cross superior to a portion of the circle (♄). All of the other symbols are based on similar astrological meanings.

Rudyard Kipling gave a speech before the Royal Society of Medicine in London in 1928 on Astrology in which he put forth such astrological concepts as those having to do with influences, emanations, and the "pneuma", and showed how similar these ideas are to the facts of electricity, radio waves, magnetism, cosmic waves, and the treatment of diseased tissue by the "influence of an influence" (radium). He then posed the question, "Haven't we been driven to abandon our conceptions of life, motion, and matter? In the upheaval didn't men each carry off his own cherished possession and camp by it?"

Many great names in modern history have held ideas sympathetic to the basic concepts of Astrology, but rarely are they presented from that standpoint. As an illustration, Ralph Waldo Emerson said — "but one blood rolls uninterruptedly, an endless circulation through men, as the water of the globe is all one sea, and truly seen, its tide is one."

Modern "reasoners" have continually referred to Astrology as illogical. Science writers have frequently referred to the behavior of atomic particles as *illogical*. Also, a basic concept of a famous modern school of philosophy, existentialism, is that the *universe* is illogical. If these ideas are right, perhaps the present prevailing concepts are insufficient and Astrology is closer to the truth than is generally believed.

It has been popular among some historical writers to identify Astrology with back-alley fortune telling, charlatanry, and with men of evil design who led astray simple-minded kings and members of the aristocracy. This is a completely distorted view. During the years between the discovery of America and the revolutionary war, the subject of Astrology was studied seriously and written about by most of the great men of science and philosophy of the age. For many years prior to the revolutionary war in America, Benjamin Franklin published an astrological almanac which was so highly regarded that in thousands of homes it was the only reading matter other than the Bible.

Astrology had held a central place in the greatest universities of Europe for hundreds of years and its origins were traced directly to ancient sources which formed the basis of *all* formal knowledge during the medieval and renaissance period.

RENAISSANCE — (c. 1500 — c. 1750 A. D.)

The years after the discovery of America were years of upheaval in Europe, particularly in matters pertaining to education and religion. These years marked a breaking away from *tradition* and *authority* and Astrology represented a part of the authority which was being challenged. Various men who wrote against Astrology were actually attacking authority in the church and were defending man's right to freedom of thought.

There were three basic concepts *attributed* to Astrology which were argued endlessly and are still brought forth to disprove Astrology. The most central problem which involved the leading minds was *whether the Earth occupied the center*, physically. This was part of church dogma and those who even hinted at other beliefs were likely to be burned at the stake. The book of Copernicus, which deals with his system, was not removed from the list of books which were banned *until 1835*. So you can see how *much* heat the argument generated!

However, Aristotle's viewpoint on this was very reasonable and the fact that he had given a specific opinion 1500 years before proves that the problem *was not new!* He said — "But we should rather suppose the same to be true of the whole world as is true of animals, namely that the center of the animal and the center of the body are not the same thing. For this reason there is no need for them to call in a guard for its mathematical center; they ought rather to consider what sort of thing the true center is, and what is its natural place."

The second important challenge to tradition, also a religious tenet, involved the *nature of the stars* as being eternal, perfect, and immutable. The new knowledge certainly caused a great emotional wrench but it did not destroy the divine plan. It simply showed that man's ideas were too rigid and limited, a failing which has not been cured through advancement in modern science. One modern writer (Franz Cumont), referred to almost everywhere as an authority on Astrology from the strictly modern standpoint, said — "We who in our northern towns scarcely perceive the light of the stars, continually veiled in fogs and dimmed by smoke, *we* to whom *they are merely bodies in a state of incandescence moved by mechanical forces, we* can hardly comprehend the strength of the religious feeling which they inspired in the men of old." This is a good example of the way materialistic ideas have dimmed the eyes of many of the modern men of intellect to the beauty and majesty of the stars.

The third challenge to Astrology was based on the contention that it *robbed men* of *free will*. Even though Ptolemy had, over 1000 years before, said — "The stars impel, they do not compel" — the idea that Astrology teaches a hopeless subjection to fate is still in evidence today.

The great men of the period who were sympathetic to Astrology, defenders of it — or outright supporters, although being in many cases men of science, *had* deep philosophical insight but they were *not materialists*. They were men caught between two worlds (the Piscean — Aquarian) with the courage to speak out in support of new ideas, but still supporting the ideas of value which existed in the spiritual thoughts which had come down from ancient sources.

Among those favorable to Astrology were Sir Walter Raleigh, who wrote his views in his *History of the World*, Sir Francis Bacon, and John Donne. Some of those who *defended* Astrology were Sir Christopher Heydon, G. E. Leibnitz (who invented differential and integral calculus), and Jerome Cardan — mathematician, physician, and astrologer. Albertus Magnus, an astrologer, the teacher of St. Thomas Aquinas, was canonized by the church in the 20th century. If a list were made of the *great* minds of the period it would be found that by far the *majority* were defenders of Astrology to some degree.

The Medici family, which dominated Italy during the Renaissance, was directly responsible for many masterpieces of creative art through their patronage of the great artists and scholars, and various outstanding members of the family were guided by astrologers during their most active and successful years. It was during these years that Constantinople, the great center of Byzantine power, center of the Greek Orthodox church, and repository of the writings of ancient knowledge, fell to the Turks. Many Byzantine scholars took refuge in Italy and were welcomed into the homes of the Medici family. This fortunate circumstance of wealth and power in the hands of those who were sympathetic, willing, and able to provide a refuge for men of imagination and knowledge, contributed greatly to the eventual reawakening of interest in learning throughout Europe. Marsilio Ficino, who was astrologer to Lorenzo Medici, was credited with translating the first works of Plato in Europe. Many great poets of the period were known as astrological poets. In most of the great households during this period, Astrology was regarded with great respect and astrologers were considered among the most influential people of the European courts, in which were to be found those of highest enlightenment.

Gaurico, a famous astrologer in Italy during the last half of the 15th century, made many accurate predictions concerning various noted people of the illustrious Italian families. His prediction that Alessandro Farnese would become pope led to his being knighted and eventually becoming a bishop. Alessandro Farnese became Pope Paul III. Gaurico was later court astrologer to Catherine de Medici, who was the wife of King Henry II of France, and whose children were Francis II, Charles IX, Henry III and Queen Margaret. Among other astrologers at this court was Nostradamus. In the latter half of the same century, John Dee was astrologer to Queen Elizabeth I of England, during whose reign England enjoyed tremendous expansion and development as a sea power. The Spanish Armada was destroyed in 1588, a *very* fateful year as foretold a century before by Regiomontanus, an astrologer.

In the literature of England, one of the favorite works of the centuries has been the story of King Arthur. Although many modern editions have been censored concerning Merlin — or the facts obscured, he was (in the story) an astrologer who advised King Arthur throughout life, who arranged many of his greatest triumphs, and who occupied a key position in the arrangements which led to Arthur's birth.

This period of history was very much a reflection of Piscean and Aquarian characteristics, the mysticism of Pisces being reflected in most of the art of the period, and the interest in new ideas of Aquarius being developed everywhere.

MIDDLE AGES — (c. 250 — c. 1500 A. D.)

After the end of the Roman Empire in the 5th century A. D., a cloistered, secluded, and solitary way of life evolved throughout Europe and the words *secret* and *mysterious* gradually came to be descriptive of life, not only in the monasteries, but also of the lives of almost everyone during those centuries.

The guilds which developed then maintained complete secrecy with great vigilance, in order to keep outsiders from discovering their methods. Various fraternal orders were *sworn* to secrecy and organizations which were not of these classes also practiced secrecy as a way of life. People of all circumstances engaged in secret and mysterious rites, most of which were magical to some extent, and the movements and intentions of most people were *cloaked in secrecy* even though they were many times doubtlessly engaged in a harmless, ordinary activity. The words secluded and isolated could be equally well—applied to the non—Christian world as well. As an example, the Barbarians engaged in secret rituals in the depths of the forest. The often—expressed poetic reference to the "maid in the tower" has come down to us as almost a *symbol* of the Middle Ages. The *secretive, mystical,* and *sensitive* nature of Pisces dominated the age.

During most of the period Astrology was known and practiced by the most famous names of history, but as in all ages of limited knowledge, Astrology was also limited by the concepts of those who used it. To the extent that people were superstitious or credulous, ideas of a similar nature crept into *all* branches of learning. There were astrological advisers to monarchs or others who had gained power and a few of these had studied in the East but, in accord with the secretive mood of their times, most of them have continued to be shadowy characters in the "play of history".

Most of the knowledge of the Middle Ages came from early Christian sources, but some of the men who were considered as absolute authorities were non—Christian. *The Natural History of Pliny* (who believed in Astrology) was the great encyclopedia of the Middle Ages, and the works of Claudius Ptolemaus of the Alexandrian school, an astrologer, were the final authority on the stars. One of the authorities of the early Middle Ages was Julius Firmicus Maternus, a Christianized Roman whose belief was astrological as well as Christian. He attempted to bring together the Christians and the believers in the older faith.

It was comparatively late in the Middle Ages before the highly advanced philosophical ideas of Aristotle and Plato became known. One of the famous centers of medieval learning was established in Italy at Padua about the time that Aristotle's teachings became known during the early 13th century. An interesting historical fact concerning this city is that it had *seven* gates, representing the seven liberal arts of of the ancient Greeks no doubt, but *originally* an astrological number. Modern road maps of Italy still show seven highways leading into Padua.

Many of the ideas of the age are still with us today, but mostly as remnants of Piscean concepts. In the center of Europe today many people may be seen working in the fields using tools and methods which were of the medieval age. In many parts of Europe, the traditional dress of the Middle Ages is still in use. The art of the medieval period to a great extent was expressive of loneliness and mysticism, usually containing hidden and secret meanings *more important* than the casual observer would perceive. The meanings were so devious that sometimes an important person might have occasion to view a work of art in which *he* appeared in some obscured manner, and not be aware that he was "part of it".

A great many comments have been made concerning the animals pictured in the astrological art of the Middle Ages. The source of these ideas was Greek as well as oriental. The oriental concept was entirely concerned with representing ideas of nature, wisdom, and religion in substantial form. The Greeks, however, had concepts which resulted in unequalled beauty in the representing of similar knowledge.

The animals pictured usually had biological peculiarities, behavioral characteristics or similarities with ideas they wished to represent. The horse was swift, the goat scaled the high places, the crocodile had no tongue, the mole was blind, the hawk flew into the sun, the vulture was seen before battles and was believed to have foreknowledge, etc. Many of those who were responsible for the astrological art of the Middle Ages had very little knowledge of the hidden meanings and, as a result of their own concepts, tended to transform the art into a wilderness of myth. The knowledge of the period is no criterion by which to judge men of wisdom, who have seldom recorded their deepest thoughts in a way which could be easily discovered by the uninitiated. As it has been said, since ancient times, "Let wise man tell wise man, the fool shall not behold it."

A great variety of outstanding events throughout this period were religious in nature. The symbol of early Christianity was the fish and, as part of ritual, it still maintains a central place in the customs of the Christian religion. The astrological symbol of Pisces contains two fish swimming in opposite directions, signifying the inner nature of Pisces, one of which represents the tendency to resist the main currents of life, and the other representing the wish to just drift with the current and, in such passive ways, to dream.

The Middle Ages were pastoral with long interludes of quiet, but with sudden emotional upheavals, in which people were caught up and swept into strange places and sometimes a different solitude.

The age which began 2000 years B. C. and continued until the beginning of the Christian era was astrologically the Arian period. The outstanding characteristics of Aries are described as masculine, aggressive, ambitious, energetic, combative, martial, inclined to command, and self-assertive. It is also described as fiery and is associated with the mind and intellectual interests.

TRANSITIONAL PERIOD
ARIES – PISCES (c. 250 B. C. – c. 250 A. D.)

The period of transformation between the ages of Aries and Pisces contains the years of greatest expansion and contraction of Rome, and the gradual decline of Greece as a center. This, as it is today, was an age of change which, however, reflected a combination of the characteristics of the signs Aries and Pisces, instead of Pisces – Aquarius. It was a time of great military activity but coincided with the genesis of a great new religion which finally absorbed the remnants of the ancient world in Europe and instituted a form of government on earth which was intended to reflect divine will.

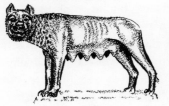 The age of the Roman Empire is like a set of scales with the point of balance resting at the beginning of the Christian era, the generation in Aries on one side, balancing the decline in Pisces on the other. The preceding age had been dominated by the military attitude and Rome had its genesis in that age, which was Arian in its attitudes. As the empire declined, the Christian way gradually absorbed the minds of men, but during the centuries near the beginning of the Christian era there was constant turmoil – especially as related to intellectual opinions and religious

ix

beliefs.   There were Jewish Christians, Egyptian Christians, Roman Christians, Greek Christians, Gnostic Christians, and many others.   There were Orthodox Jews and pagans (whatever that word means).   Today, it refers mostly to *ancient* pagans, but Plato (who is considered a *pagan* by some), taught the concept of a supreme God! There were many divisions among all these groups, as there were many other religions, so that, of the outstanding men of the age who were considered authorities by later scholars, one might be a pagan Greek associated with the school in Alexandria, or a Christian Greek, or a pagan Roman, or a Jewish Christian, or any other combination.

Plotinus who has been considered the greatest Neo—Platonist by some, wrote in the 3rd century A. D.   So inspired were his concepts that it is said his teachings are still important in the thought of today.   In his major work, Plotinus said, "We might therefore liken the stars to letters, at every moment flung along the heavens, and which after having been displayed, continued in ceaseless motion, so that, while expressing another function in the universe, they would still possess significance."

Iamblichus, another Neo—Platonist who lived in this period, taught the importance of astrological philosophy as did Proclus who lived somewhat later, but both of whom were quoted extensively by European scholars of the succeeding centuries. The most famous of all astrologers of this Alexandrian or early Christian period in the first several centuries after Christ was Claudius Ptolemaeus, or Ptolemy, whose system of the planets and whose mathematics were accepted as the final authority for over 1000 years.   The results of his methods compare very favorably with modern computations.

 As Rome bridged the changing age between Aries and Pisces, so did the greatest cultural center of that time in Alexandria, Egypt. The gathering of great minds in Alexandria, known as the "Alexandrian school", began near the end of the Arian age, continuing through the years that Jesus was on Earth, and on into the Piscean age.   It gradually declined in importance and ceased to exist after the pillage of the city by the Arabs.   Extreme interest in the intellectual is a dominant characteristic of Aries.   The early teachers at Alexandria were men of science and literature.   Most of the latter were critics of older creative thinkers of the Arian age.   Men of science who studied there were Appollonius of Perga, Euclid, and Archimedes.

Later on, just *before* the birth of Christ, the emphasis became philosophical. During the years following the birth of Jesus, Philo Judaeus taught a philosophy which contained elements of the Jewish faith, Astrology, and Christianity.   He was afterward considered a mediator between those who held these different concepts. Among later philosophers at Alexandria were gnostic Christians whose philosophy was astrological in concept.

This transitional age was very much a mixture of the Arian characteristics exemplified by aggressiveness and intellectual interests, and the Piscean temperament which is considered mystical, emotional, and sensitive.   Astrological concepts were an important part of life during the entire period, having been taught by the leading philosophers at Alexandria, in Greece, by the Stoics (most of whom were from Asia), in Rome, and among the Jews, and these concepts later became part of Christian tradition. Many of the most highly educated men of the period, even though known later as mathematicians, historians, or scientists, had studied with Eastern masters, or Egyptians, whose knowledge was *based* on Astrology.

THE ARIAN AGE — (c. 1750 — c. 250 B. C.)

The Arian age, which began near 2000 B. C., was the period during which the art of warfare was developed. In this period weapons, both offensive and defensive, armor, and new tactics were created. The horse began to be used to pull chariots in warfare during the early part of the Arian age. This was the period of Egypt's "golden age" in maturity, and the age of the great Greek philosophers and poets. It was the age of Homer, Thales, Archimedes, Plato, Aristotle, Aristophanes, Solon, Ptolemy I (who was responsible for the creation of the Alexandrian library), and the intellectual men of Egypt and the East.

Plato, in his *Timaeus*, which was written when he was old and full of wisdom, said, "Thus much let me say however: God invented and gave us sight to the end that we might behold the courses of intelligence in the heaven, and apply them to the courses of our own intelligence which are akin to them, the unperturbed to the perturbed; and that we, learning them and partaking of the natural truth of reason, might imitate the absolutely unerring courses of God and regulate our own vagaries."

Near the beginning of this period, Egypt was invaded from the East by armies which used the horsedrawn chariot. In the Middle East there was scarcely a peaceful time during the 1500 years, which marked the center of the Arian age, so that a fairly complete history could be written just on the basis of warfare. Cities, countries, and sometimes whole peoples disappeared, and it was recorded that at one time Palestine was severely depopulated.

The Assyrian civilization had its greatest growth during the middle of the Arian age, and its decline at the end of the period. This nation of people is remembered as the most war-like of all history. However, all major powers of the period felt the impetus toward military activity. Much of the conflict written in the Old Testament took place during this period.

The symbol of Aries is the ram or the horns of the ram. The rise of the god Ammon—Re in Egypt coincided with the end of the transitional period from Taurus to Aries, and ancient records of this god show his headdress embellished with huge ram horns. All during this period, in the Old Testament, in historical records, and archaeological remains, are evidences of the ram as a religious symbol and ritual sacrifice. The meaning of this symbol may be found in the astrological description of Aries.

Most of the priests of this period were learned and were famous for their intellectuality. The Assyrians had a tremendous library. Kings were usually members of the intellectual group during the period; were, in many cases, of the priestly class and cultivated intellectual pursuits. Isaiah, Micah, Solomon, Ptolemy — all intellectuals, lived during this age. The development of iron implements and new inventions took place in Aries and an increase in trade between nations was brought about through ambitious action. The major characteristics throughout were aggressiveness and intellectuality.

The Taurian age began near 4000 B. C. Astrologically, Taurus is characterized as calm, enduring, steady, having great strength, and is described as *massive* — especially in concept, as in architecture and the creative arts. This sign is also described as *earthy* and is considered as practical, dependable and of fair demeanor.

TRANSITIONAL PERIOD
TAURUS – ARIES – (c. 2250 – c. 1750 B. C.)

The period from about 2250 to 1750 B. C. marked a change from the concepts of Taurus to those of Aries and reflected a combination of the characteristics of both signs. The symbol of the bull was gradually replaced by that of Aries. In some places over the world, the old symbols have continued on to a limited extent in religious concepts and art. Cattle are still considered holy in India and this ancient belief existed until recently in China, also. Arian symbols are still found among some peoples of the East.

From about 2250 to 2000 B. C., in Egypt, a struggle occurred among ruling families and this is known as the intermediate period. Hammurabi lived during the years near 2000 B. C. His reign combined the characteristics of Aries and Taurus. In some ways it marked a return to the solidity of the Taurian age, but was remarkable for the code of Hammurabi, an intellectual (or Arian) concept.

THE TAURIAN AGE – (c. 3750 – c. 3250 B. C.)

The massive monuments of Egypt and Babylonia, especially the pyramids and ziggurats, are typical of the Taurian concepts. They reflect permanence, stability, and massiveness. The period in which they were conceived and built transpired during the very middle of the age of Taurus. The ziggurat was an astrological structure of gigantic size built in Babylonia during this period as an edifice for the high priest of Astrology. Later monuments during the Arian period, which imitated this type of construction, were copies of the older ideas of Taurus and were intended to *recapture* the substantial and stable way of life which existed during the Taurian age. As late as the Christian era, there were records which expressed a desire to return to the ways of the older people who lived during that time.

Descriptions of this age are found in the Bible, in Homer, and in the works of many other later writers. It was the age of the patriarchs of old, the ante-deluvian kings and, as a whole, it represented an age of peace and wisdom.

During modern times it has been proved that the story of the flood was recorded by the Sumerians, an older non— Jewish people who lived during this age, and archaeological evidence of a flood has been found, which indicates that this story had been handed down by this older people. The astrological and cultural knowledge of the Sumerians was absorbed by their neighbors, but evidence shows that they already possessed this kind of knowledge when they settled, during the Taurian age, in the area later known as Babylonia.

Throughout the world, the symbol of the bull became known so that eventually religious rites were practiced from China to Europe involving the bull. There are records of a practice in early Scotland of driving cattle between two fires during the spring festival in May. Gigantic statues of bulls were used to guard the gates of palaces and temples in Sumerian and Babylonian cities. The first and last letters of the Hebrew alphabet were *Aleph* and *Taw*, signifying the beginning and the end in Taurus. The ancient Greek symbol for the first letter of the alphabet, *Alpha* (A), was derived from the ancient astrological symbol for Taurus, the bull's head (☒) — modern astrological symbol (♉). The corresponding Chinese symbol has been compared by Dr. Hugh Moran, a specialist in the origin of the alphabet, with the ancient Jewish and Greek signs for Taurus, the meaning and character of which were identical. The characteristics of Taurus are to be found everywhere during this early period.

CONCLUSION

There are many evidences of yet older periods which were similar in concept and symbology to the signs of the zodiac which follow Taurus — Gemini, Cancer, and Leo. An ancient Chinese zodiac shows the constellation of Taurus placed on beyond by approximately five signs from its present position, as it would appear on the same relative day of the year. This is not offered as scientific evidence of greater age but merely indicates the probability that very ancient people also had a knowledge of events which had occurred in times past, having meaning for them, and were thus recorded.

The ancient people used a lunar calendar based on the constellations near the pole. The moon wanders back and forth across the path of the sun 12 times in a lunar year of 354 days. Ancient calendars sometimes alternated between 12 and 13 months per year. The number 40 which appears all through the Old Testament, derives from the lunar zodiac and phases of the moon, and in the New Testament it was written that Jesus faced 40 days of temptation. The birth of cattle takes place near the end of a period represented by 40 phases of the moon, and the number was significant as a period of suffering, withdrawal, or penance. Periods of slightly shorter duration deriving from a different way of observing the moon, would result in a span of approximately 9 months, which is equal to a major unfavorable aspect, astrologically.

In Yucatan, where the Mayans lived, the pyramids and temples are very similar to those in Egypt and the East. One of the most important numbers there, which was used in the actual structure of the pyramids, is 52. There are 52 steps on the facade of the great pyramid in Chichen Itza in Yucatan, as there are 52 steps in each great step in the pyramid to the sun at Teotihuacan in Mexico. The "52" referred to a 52 year cycle, the same as in the East and was one of the many evidences showing a common source of knowledge. It is said that the older Mayan civilization was peaceful and did not practice human sacrifice as the later Indians did. There was the tradition of an older period here, also, as in the East which was looked back upon as an age of wisdom. Although the archaeologists have at this time dated the major ruins in Yucatan at a much later date, the concepts of the people were truly Taurian as reflected in their gigantic monuments and symbols. The story of a *great flood* and a story similar to the one about the *tower of Babel* were recorded here, too. It is interesting to note that the word May, which is of very ancient origin and which coincides with the sign of Taurus, is embodied in the word Maya. The ancient word *Ma* is encountered everywhere as a *universal* word for mother.

It is the intent of this message to show how there has been *continuity* of knowledge stemming from an older wisdom — in spite of everything. There are those who say Astrology always changes itself to conform with *past* events. If so, it is the one valid source of true historical perspective which does not depend upon human authority and human records which have been altered by later men, but since there is great evidence of the origin of the alphabet itself in the stars as shown recently by Dr. Moran, the record of our beginnings remains beyond the reach of man and is truly *written in the stars!*

EXPLANATION

The dates used in the foregoing historical outline are those which are in general use with the beginning of the Christian era as the central point of time. However the transit of the first point of Aries through the major star of the constellation Aries occurred about 250 B.C. so that the beginning of the Christian era coincided with the beginning of the Piscean era at the end of the astrological cusp period. Since an astrological age is near 2150 years and the change of the first point of Aries into Pisces is calculated as near 250 B.C. the change into Aquarius would have occurred near the beginning of this century, the change from Taurus to Aries would have been near 2200 B.C. and the change from Gemini to Taurus near 4460 B.C. The dates in the outline should be adjusted accordingly for further comparison and the descriptions of individuals born under these signs as given further on in this book may be thought of as dominant characteristics of the historical ages given above.

THE VALUE OF ASTROLOGY

Astrology can be of extraordinary value to people who have a desire to think about the subject in an abstract fashion and who would like to try to understand it in order to be able to *apply* the basic meanings in dealing more effectively with individuals with whom they are associated, and not only with individuals but with people in general. An understanding of the birthsign characteristics will to a surprising degree reveal what human beings as a whole are likely to do when they are affected psychologically by a birthsign, or during a period which is traditionally ruled by or symbolized by a particular birthsign. There is no question but that this volume gives more extensive analysis and description of all the birthsigns than anything which has previously been written. Human beings, of course, are individuals. No two people are exactly alike; consequently, individuals express the qualities or characteristics of the sign in which they were born *in varying degrees*. The fact that Astrology has been of absorbing interest to so many people throughout the centuries (whereas other means of approaching character analysis have never taken such a hold of people) is unquestionably for the reason that the orthodox descriptions of the birthsigns fit so many people in so many ways. Human beings instinctively recognize great and lasting truths in Astrology.

There are many considerations which are applicable to individual human beings other than the birthsign itself. The solar influence which is significant of a birthsign in changing cycles, traditionally has to do with the individuality of people who were born in that sign. Sometimes, people seem to have few if any of the characteristics of the birthsign for the reason that their personality, or the face they turn to the world, seems to express something vastly different. In understanding human beings, however, one must consider whether they have the *basic qualities* of their birthsign — tending to look upon life in a way *similar* to others who were born in the same sign. This is indisputably the case — they do. A rising sign which is determined only by the exact *time* of birth, has long been considered to symbolize the personality. An individual's rising sign, as explained elsewhere, may be quite different than the birthsign and may change the way that person seems to think or expresses himself.

Philosophy is the intent of mankind to understand and explain by various means the mysteries associated with human life, in fact, with all life. Men have attempted through philosophy to explain why things are, what they mean, and to suggest solutions in many cases. As far as we have any record of human thought or human events, philosophy has been divided into two main branches. One of these has understood and expressed a belief in the fact that this is a *cause—effect* world and that *ultimate* truth may be discovered in the study of *matter,* exclusively. Another main branch of philosophy has believed, and expressed in the strongest terms, that the universe is of *divine origin* and that many of the phenomena of life are not explainable by means of sense perception. A very large proportion of the outstandingly great men of history, in all ages, have believed in the latter branch of philosophy.

If one, as an individual, accepts the fact that the universe is of divine origin there are many things which have happened and do happen which are not measured or even understood in the ordinary material way. This may be said of much that has been used in connection with Astrology. Whether or not the reasons for many results can be *understood* fully by technological means is of little consequence. The fact that they *work* for humanity here upon earth is sufficient. The *value* of science to humanity — in any of its branches, lies in *application,* not in mere understanding of technological meanings. One of the ways an individual without intensive study can gain an insight, at least into the probability of great truths, is by a *thorough* understanding of the various birthsigns. One who is interested in an abstract fashion and who is inclined to wonder about people and what they have done in past ages (and what they may do in succeeding ones) will unquestionably receive considerable enlightenment by reading carefully the descriptions of the birthsigns and then associating that knowledge with various periods in history.

Bringing the matter down to the modern-day world and to dealing with other human beings is the fact that regardless of their own birthsigns, human beings as a whole tend to act in certain ways generally while a particular sign of the zodiac is functioning, as dated in the descriptions of the individual birthsigns in this book. Individuals who were born in a sign tend to look upon the affairs of life, and to be within themselves, as their birthsign indicates *all the time,* but all human beings *during the period when the sign is functioning* tend to take on the qualities of that particular sign and to express those qualities in their actions and the things they do.

For example, in September school begins. The basic quality of the sign Virgo which is from the 23rd of August to the 23rd of September, is *discrimination.* Secondarily, it is *analysis.* This sign is associated with recording, with registering, with beginning. It is not coincidental that this period will not to any considerable extent be active in *study,* but mainly concerned with *admission* to school and the whole psychological meaning of such a beginning. Further reading of the description of the sign will show the analogy between the beginning of school and the Virgo qualities or characteristics.

The 24th of September to the 23rd of October encompasses the sign Libra. In general, the basic qualities of Libra are *deliberation* and *justice.* Secondarily, is *diplomacy.* Libra is not aggressive, and imparts qualities of seeking harmony and pleasant surroundings in associations. In October, people as a whole are not aggressive. It is a period which tends to bring a certain drifting, a quieter and more diplomatic approach to associations, and a desire for peace and harmony. Extensive examination of the qualities of the birthsign illustrate the tendency of all people to express these qualities during this time.

Scorpio begins the 24th of October and continues to the 22nd of November. The basic quality of Scorpio natives is *single-minded purpose.* Secondarily, it is *obligation*, which means a sense of obligation to which the individual subscribes and it imparts a tendency to demand fulfillment of duty by others. October-November is an aggressive period which is reflected in the yearly normal upswing in business affairs and it extends to aggressiveness in merchandising and in other fields where human beings are more clearly definite and positive. This is closely associated with the things which take place at this time of year. Insurance statistics indicate that a greater number of people are born in July - August than at any other time. This is approximately nine months after the period of Scorpio, which has always been associated astrologically with the generative processes.

The next sign is Sagittarius, extending from the 23rd of November to the 21st of December. A basic quality of Sagittarius is *generosity*. Secondly, it is *honesty*. The approaching Christmas season comes at this time and the natural joviality and generosity of Sagittarius is strongly apparent.

The succeeding sign is Capricorn from the 22nd of December to the 20th of January. The outstanding quality of Capricorn is *conservatism*. Secondarily, it is *management*. The Christmas season is immediately followed by a tendency on the part of all people to budget, to evaluate, to form new resolutions for a more consistent, conservative and constructive attitude as well as actions. People in general are not at all inclined to plunge at this time.

The next sign is Aquarius, from the 21st of January to the 19th of February. The outstanding quality of Aquarius is *humanitarianism*. Secondly, it is *inventiveness*. There is an immediate change in people as a whole when Aquarius comes into prominence. Even those who are not inclined to be inventive or to accept new ideas in the ordinary course of events are likely to lay out new plans, to have a strong desire to improve the conditions which surround them (as usually takes place in household and business at the beginning of a new year), and to make alterations which aim at improvement of one kind or another.

The next sign is Pisces, from the 20th of February to the 19th of March. This sign as has been expressed is symbolic of the Christian era. The dominate characteristic of Pisces is *sensitivity*. It is not an aggressive sign. During this period the old adage about the left hand not knowing what the right hand does is very typical of great numbers of people. The tendency to "hedge and hoard" is strong, but the inclination to emotional impulse is strong also bringing to many a period of self-deception.

The following sign, from the 20th of March to the 20th of April, represents the vernal equinox; the sign is Aries; the dominate characteristic is *aggressiveness*. When income tax became payable in April, people no longer submitted mildly, merely offering protest, but they often fought in court, and were actively and militantly opposed to many of the things which were represented by the collection of such tax. It is a period of action, a period in which people in general are more likely to *demand their rights* and to go to court in order to defend what they consider their rights.

Next is Taurus, from the 21st of April to the 22nd of May. This sign is a fixed sign, representing placidity and a tendency toward dreaming. The basic quality of the sign is *technicality*. Secondarily, *compatibility*. Unless opposed, all people who were born in this sign are companionable, hospitable and compatible with associates. People in general at this time of the year are much more likely to daydream and not to be actively aggressive, but to go along in a steady routine, visualizing the future. The condition often known as "spring fever" exists to a considerable extent during this time of the year, when people do not feel like driving themselves unnecessarily, and when there is greater enjoyment of the pleasures and the good things of life in general.

Gemini comes next, from the 23rd of May to the 22nd of June. The outstanding qualities of Gemini are *restlessness, taking chances, changing*. This is traditionally the month of marriages. It is also the month of taking chances in general. People are much more receptive to new ideas and much more likely to accept them quickly.

The next sign in order is Cancer, from the 23rd of June to the 21st of July. The outstanding quality of Cancer is *domesticity*. There is greater interest in homes, and in building of homes, and the acquisition of homes during this period than at any other time of the year. The second quality of Cancer is *consistency,* which means particularly that people who were born in the sign do not change readily, in occupation or otherwise. People in general, during this period, are not as easy to sway from that which they desire to achieve, are not inclined to alter their opinions, and much less likely to take up new ideas or plans which are not traditional.

Leo comes next, from the 22nd of July to the 22nd of August. The outstanding quality of Leo is *expansiveness*. Secondarily, it is *leadership*. All people at this time of year are likely to have ideas for expansion, ideas which are much larger in scope, and are much more likely to take chances than they would ordinarily.

There are many other things which are applicable to every sign of the zodiac and a close reading of the qualities of each sign will play up the extent to which all people can, during the period of each sign, express the inner qualities of that sign. The tendency of most people to insist upon specific individual examples relative to the description above makes it imperative that one consider these tendencies only from the standpoint of large groups of people. Many exceptions may be noted at once, including those people who are not subject to the same routines as we are in the western world. The tendencies as described may still be apparent, however, and the reader may discover many for himself by reading the descriptions in this book of the signs other than his own and considering the tendencies of masses of people during the periods throughout the year when the sun is in each sign.

METHODS OF SELF-HELP
IN
UNITOLOGY

One who desires to study his own planetary influences should, for his own welfare, understand that there is nothing inevitable and unavoidable in ANY influence. It has been avowed by students of the subject that the stars "impel but do not compel". That is completely true although the meaning is not generally understood.

The truth is that planetary influences are of the *same nature* as human thought. Changing periods of cosmic vibration through which you as an individual pass, are purely psychological or mental, but through the processes of your thoughts which "tune in" upon vibrations of the universe emanating from the planets, inevitably they affect material affairs, measurably. During a period when Mars is considered "unfavorable" by students of cosmic vibration, the individual who is *attuned* to those influences is much more likely to decide recklessly or to be aggressive to an excessive degree; in other words to make decisions which readily lead to accidents.

Men judge other men by outward appearances, by methods they may seem to use in the conduct of their affairs, by their actions and mannerisms – while *divine law* judges them in the most minute degree, by what they are WITHIN!

It is an accepted fact that anything worth working for at all is worth *striving* for; and the most *important objective* toward which anyone can strive is *attainment of skill* in his thinking processes so as to *harmonize* with CONSTRUCTIVE forces.

The unseen vibrations which come from the planets, producing these psychological effects upon mankind, actually are like an oscillating current in electricity. They vary in intensity and in direction. At one particular time a vibration is positive or of constructive nature, tending to bring generally beneficial things into being or to strengthen all that which is in harmony with its positive force. At another time the vibration is negative and of such a nature as to tend toward removal from this plane of existence, those things which in themselves are similar in their vibrations. Thus does cosmic or divine law function. *All* people are affected in mass by *major cycles,* and *each* is affected by changes in vibrations to which *he alone* is attuned.

That these influences are real, that the planets do influence human beings is unquestionably a fact. Knowledge of the amazingly complicated system is limited in our day, but we have some vision of its scope.

One who thinks seriously about the trials and sorrows of life which are the lot of mankind in its present state of evolution (and who does not think of these, having encountered them) – such a one seeks earnestly for some solution of his problems. That solution actually does lie in the religions of the world!

The temptation toward negatives of fear (which is the arch destroyer of faith), anger, hatred, and greed are always present; but there are times when the cosmic forces of the universe tend to bring these inner thought forms into being – or action, and as like is always associated with like, the reflection of those thoughts is manifested in the life of *he who thinks them*.

It has recently become a recognized fact that sun spots definitely accompany business cycles, recurring in waves of depression, those depressions being mental — produced therefore, entirely by thoughts in the minds of people. The sun spots are merely significators of the same influences or powerful forces which affect the lives of people bringing about in their affairs, that which they have previously allowed their thoughts to express — and nothing or less.

It is absolutely a fact, which you can prove, as can any other human being, that the solution of your problems, of bringing about in your life — happiness, prosperity, joy, and the full satisfaction of reaching constructive objectives, lies entirely within *your own* power of mind. One who is in an undeveloped state of evolution and development cannot, or WILL not, accept this as being true. To say, therefore, that it *is possible* for him to accomplish any given thing is based upon first — his *acceptance of these truths* (providing his thoughts are not already geared to CONSTRUCTIVES): and secondly — upon his *willingness to strive* for the skill necessary to *direct* his thought processes so as to *produce the result!* Education is not here referred to, but constructive thought — which anyone can learn to have by *cultivating* it.

If one *refuses* to cultivate the proper mental outlook — in seriousness, and his processes of thought are of negative quality to an extensive degree, his acts can never result in anything excepting frustration and failure. There is absolutely no question that a kindly, all-embracing and infinite power is at work in the universe, yet a power which regulates life by inexorable law.

The study of planetary forces becomes extremely destructive when *fear* of "unfavorable" influences enters in. Then its every possible benefit is nullified. There are repeated periods in the life of every man, when encouragement and help are needed. To aid specifically at such times is the real purpose of Unitology. It attempts to anticipate those periods when he will accept discouragement, or when previously harbored thoughts of discouragement are likely to express themselves in his life — inevitably bringing their like into his own affairs, and to tell him definitely and specifically *what to do about it!*

Unitology is not a creed nor does it oppose or seek to change any man's religion. Truth has many faces and understanding the universe and God is based upon the conditions of a man's evolution, his circumstances of life, his race, and the mode of thought he is born into; consequently, while his understanding may differ from that of of any other man and therefore appear controversial, actually it becomes clear that such is not the case.

Fundamental requirements are necessary. All religions convey them for him whose understanding is reached. One requirement is FAITH, a definite force in itself. The rest may be expressed in one word, LOVE — the most powerful vibration of all in its every manifestation.

Because of individual man's continued associations with the present imperfect state of life, his observation of the purely physical in everyday existence, the sorrows and the tragedies, it becomes difficult for him to widen the scope of his vision to see beyond them and the little sphere in which he grows. Yet the knowledge of its application to the here and now has never been lost. It is only allowed to sleep for a time. The essence of truth is still clear to a few, who hold it for the benefit of all.

Many do not get a balanced benefit from interpretation of their birth charts, for the reason that understanding the influences under which he was born, and which express *him,* requires (on the part of any man), an earnest desire to comprehend their real meaning. To a considerable extent the light of truth is a personal discovery. One makes the discovery himself. The great value of one's individual chart of planetary positions at birth is to be gained only by real effort on the part of the individual, to understand the various meanings in the stars.

A student of planetary influences can be correct in his judgment of the chart of another, only when he is able to estimate accurately the state of evolution which that person is in and is thereby able to judge correctly the capability of a changed viewpoint and mental attitude, which can alter indications in the chart completely, but which would not be apparent in a purely material and wholly scientific judgment of planetary positions.

There is absolutely *nothing* to be afraid of *at any time* — in any planetary influence, and unless one can approach the subject with *full belief in* and *understanding* of that fact, it is much better to avoid it completely. The specific prediction of unfortunate or unhappy events in the life of any individual is definitely allied with negative forces of the universe, and they can be powerfully destructive.

The writers claim no psychic powers of any kind. The morbid is intended to be completely eliminated from consideration in this work. We believe elimination of morbid fears to be the major requirement of progress for the individual, as well as for mankind as a whole. We wish you every happiness the world affords, and we believe *fully* and with *all our hearts* that you CAN bring such happiness into your life in fullest degree. The *first* requirement is the realization that *genuine understanding* does not *bring* fear — but *eliminates* it, for there is no fear *but* fear!

The following are interpretations of influences which apply to our modern way of life, as written in text books of long, long ago; as well as descriptions of cyclic patterns which touch all living things.

May you find herein a broader concept of this wonderful world in which we live, wherein *no life* is without *meaning* and *purpose!*

CYCLES

In recent years a considerable amount of exhaustive scientific researches were made in Germany by a German scientist, Dr. Wilhelm Fliess, which proved rather conclusively that human beings go through rhythmic periods or cycles which can be determined in advance, as they will affect each individual.

The birthdate — year, month, and date of the month, are necessary to determine these cycles. This method is used increasingly in Germany to prevent accidents as well as to determine the most efficient time in the life of an individual for the performance of important tasks or the launching of a major undertaking.

It was proved quite surely that people are successful more often in their "high" periods and unsuccessful in their "low", as well as that accidents are much more likely to occur when the person responsible is passing through a negative or "low" period. At about the same time these experiments were being made in Germany, one of our greatest scientists at a leading university in the eastern part of the United States, was engaged in research along the same lines and his investigation led to the same conclusion.

Almost coincidental with these researches, another American scientist at one of our large mid-western universities was investigating the time of a baby's conception in relation to its effect upon that baby's characteristics and he quite conclusively proved that human beings are affected by the time of year at which conception occurred and that weather conditions had a marked effect.

Researches which have been made, have shown definitely that these cycles or rhythms affect animals and plants as they do human beings. It is interesting to note that the German scientist, by starting with the birthdate, used a 28 day period as the cycle for the female hormone and a 23 day cycle for the male hormone as a basis for overcoming accidents and furthering the success of large industrial firms where thousands of people are employed.

The world predictions given on pages 169 to 174 are based upon the birthdate cycles of our country and the other countries mentioned. This explanation is given with the hope that all who may read it will understand that *no* condition, however trying and difficult, is ever lasting, but *will move on!* A *new* condition will arise and a cycle of *OPPORTUNITY* always follows any negative or unhappy condition.

INNER TRUTH *by ALAN CARTER*

" Truth is within ourselves; it takes no rise
from outward things, what e'er you
may believe.
There is an inmost center in us all,
where truth abides in fulness; and around,
wall upon wall, the gross flesh hems it in,
This perfect, clear perception — which is
truth.
A baffling and perverting carnal mesh
Binds it, and makes all error; and to KNOW
Rather consists in opening out a way
Whence the imprisoned splendour may
escape,
Than in effecting entry for a light
supposed to be without. "

Browning — Paracelsus Aspires, 1st Act

All people are prophets. In all of us lies knowledge of truth and of the future but it is buried deep beneath the inhibitions of the flesh. All human beings have flashes of prophetic inner vision. They can at times *clearly* discern what events lie before them, yet their flashes of clairvoyance are unrecognized as such! But in every being lies truth, which *all* have *access to* AT EVERY MOMENT OF THEIR LIVES, in their every effort toward constructive growth!

All inspiration, in the most commonplace circumstance of life; every step which is taken toward a clear goal with sureness felt within — is a form of prophecy, for it is a revelation of that truth which lies deeply buried in us all.

In the broader vision of the seer and mystic whose inner SEEING is turned to *distant* goals, the suffering of the flesh is pitiful and yet he knows the *transient* nature of that suffering which, painful though it be at the fleeting moment of its enduring, is but a *passing phase* — yet *essential* to the need and growth of him who suffers it.

The seer whose inner vision sees the distant destiny of man strives in many ways to point the road for suffering human kind, but while the truth is clear to him he knows it IS an *inner seeing* and that the road may be full long and filled with tortuous turns and thorny by-paths for those who are his brothers and who still must find the inner path.

In this volume that path is pointed out and scientific reasons given for its being and its every devious turn, into which the world of men can walk and by the rule of thumb, test it with the instruments of calibration and of measure which will bring broad truths within the realm of here and now!

There are ROADS from nowhere and from everywhere which lead to GOD. They are as the spokes of a gigantic wheel, all meeting at one central point. Form and creed of religion have met and do meet the needs of human beings. Some of them supply the needs of few, some many. Followed in FAITH and practiced in LIVING most of them are roads which LEAD to God. There is confusion and sometimes disillusionment resulting from the seeming differences — yet those differences are man made and not important.

Often one can no longer take seriously the teachings of the religion into which he was born. Others did not receive a definite training of religious nature in childhood. The minds of such people, their finite intelligence, will not accept the surface inconsistencies of religious teachings, the frequent childishness — in seeming, yet "Suffer little children to come unto me, for THEIRS is the Kingdom of Heaven." (We might all well be as little children of simple faith and not mistake the road.)

Those inconsistencies and the childishness are not what they seem. They do provide the means by which he who reads or hears with understanding *may find a road* that leads to God. This preparation for a state of future bliss is a working plan for here and now!

But — if you cannot find the core; if you cannot happily accept a teaching from among the world's beliefs and KNOW that you have found the truth, then it is not for you. It does not mark your road; yet there IS a road which leads to peace of mind and the inner happiness we all within us seek, though frequently that seeking is unrecognized by finite concepts and emotions which are keyed to all the seeming *facts* of life.

It is not you who follow and in FAITH profess and practice your religion, to whom these words are sent. They are instead, for those without sustaining FAITH, who are exposed to worldly strife and lonely, wind-swept barrens of the soul, upon whose faces lines are biting deep, who face the parting with a loved one, whose days are filled with ugliness, beside whom shadows stalk. They know not where to turn within themselves. Their lives are filled with a hidden desperation. Their courage which must ever be alone and lonely must sustain them. There is nothing more to call upon for strength, and little hope to carry them beyond the bitter partings and a final lonely spot beneath the ground.

You who are thus; for you these words are penned. This suffering is NEEDLESS; this pain is NEEDLESS. GOD is GOOD, there IS a road for you! And life *renewed* is *ever* yours.

Alan Carter

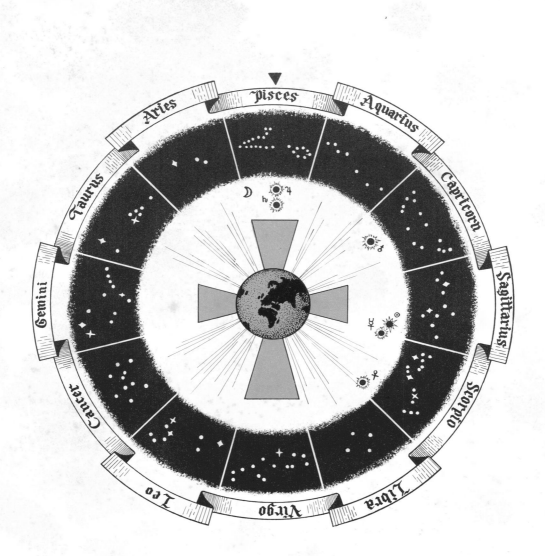

**The Heavenly Host, In Awesome, Symbolic Array,
Led Astrologers (The Magi) To Where The Christ Lay**

Additional evidence confirming the Scriptures.

explanation -- see reverse side

Explanation of Preceding Page

The chart on the reverse side of the page reveals the appearance of the sky on the evening of the day of the nearest conjunction of Jupiter and Saturn in Pisces preceding the date on which the birth of Christ is traditionally celebrated.

In the early years of the 17th Century, Kepler, an astrologer, who discovered the laws of planetary motion, remembered the prophecy of the coming of the Messiah which had been made by Astrologers in Sippar, Babylonia, centuries before the beginning of the Christian era. This prophecy stated that its fulfillment would be heralded by a conjunction of Jupiter and Saturn in Pisces. In working out the date of the nearest conjunction in time, he discovered that this would have occurred in early December, 6 B.C., according to his calculations. In the twentieth century, early Babylonian tablets were deciphered which substantiated the existence of the prophecy quoted by Kepler. Further investigation showed the date to be 7 B.C., probably in early December.

This chart shows the distribution of the planets, with Jupiter and Saturn directly at the zenith on the evening of November 28, 7 B.C. (Gregorian) and the positions of the zodiacal constellations. Anyone approaching Bethlehem from the north or northeast would have seen the conjunction of Jupiter and Saturn first in a southerly direction and then southwesterly as the evening progressed, the conjunction appearing near evening twilight and setting near midnight.

Because of extensive research in the vicinity of Babylon in recent years, ephemerides were made available in 1962 giving the apparent longitudes and latitudes of the Sun, Moon, Mercury, Mars, Venus, Jupiter and Saturn for the years from 600 B.C. to 1 A.D. Modern astronomical positions and corrections were computed at the Institute For Advanced Study and the work was completed at the research center of IBM using a modern IBM computer. This work was carried through by leading mathematicians and scientists.

The Bible states that the Magi said they had seen the star in the east. During May of the same year, the conjunction would have risen in the east just before sunrise and would have faded out shortly after the sun arose.

Intervening meetings of Jupiter and Saturn would have set faintly near morning twilight and would not have appeared nearly so southerly as the conjunction of November 28, 7 B.C. (Gregorian).

For those who are interested in the motion of the planets near the above date, preceding and succeeding positions of the planets are given below:

Longitudes below referred to equinox of date

7 B.C.	♄	♃	♂	☉	☾	♀	☿
Nov. 18	345.27	344.86	281.64	236.72	221.4	214.24℞	223.94
Nov. 28	345.38	345.33	289.43	246.92	358.2	214.12D	239.33
Dec. 8	345.67	346.12	297.22	257.13	119.4	217.67	255.21

ANCIENT CENTERS OF ASTROLOGY

Marguerite Carter has traveled to the remote corners of the globe in her study of planetary influences on our lives and the wisdom of antiquity, rich in astrological lore. Long-buried secrets of the ancients have revealed themselves from beneath the sands of Egypt, from king-priests' tombs in Yucatan, in Pompeii, the old capitals of Europe, early Greece and from the ruins of Caesar's Rome. This search for astrological artifacts and knowledge has made Miss Carter an internationally known authority. Her writings in books, magazines and newspapers both here and abroad are known to thousands.

Marguerite Carter is dwarfed by the gigantic size of 3000 year-old columns at Karnak, Egypt. Karnak is an image of vastness and monumental massiveness unequalled in all the remains of ancient Egypt. The many temples at Karnak proved to be a rich source for the history of ancient Egypt. Tablets and inscriptions tell the story of astrological study, record the reigns of kings, wars, disasters and strikingly accurate calendars much like our own. Even the great astrologer—scientists of Greece were drawn to Egypt to study their knowledge of the heavens.

Marguerite Carter breakfasts in her tent at a desert encampment in the shadow of the Great Pyramid of Khufu. Much evidence of astrological knowledge was discovered here along with inscriptions of religious significance. The symbol representing the sun and the deity, a circle with dot or cross in the center, is found here as in most pre-Christian civilizations. This symbol is estimated to be 70,000 years old with near identical interpretation in civilizations thousands of miles apart. The curious universality of religious symbols indicates that the worlds many religions are not so different as one might imagine.

The throne room of the palace of Minos (about 3000 to 2000 B. C.). This luxurious structure was as big as Buckingham Palace and contained startlingly modern appointments — drainage sumps, bathrooms, ventilation systems, ground-water conduits and waste chutes. Here, in Crete, archeologists have dedicated lifetimes to uncover the secrets of Minoan culture, but much still remains cloaked in mystery. Excavation has proved Crete to have been a cultural center. Artifacts from Africa, Egypt and other far-off lands are indicative of their cultural and commercial refinement.

The Theatre at Epidaurus (325 B. C.) in Greece. This masterpiece of architecture was so designed that an actor speaking in a normal tone could be heard in the top-most seat at the greatest distance. This area contains the best examples of ancient Greek architecture and sculpture, all of breathtaking beauty.

Many of the great and most highly respected names in history were Greek astrologer—scientists who gave us theories and formulas on which **much of our modern science is based, today!** From 600 to 400 B. C. they created algebra, calculus, geometry, and **taught** that **all things were composed of small invisible units called atoms!**

Miss Carter stands before the ruins of the "Temple of the Cross" in Palenque. From an architecturally superb adjacent building came the tablet, bearing a cross, said to be created long before the Christian era! Here, in the "Temple of Inscriptions", were found huge columns bearing astrological symbols and the tomb of a king-priest who cast the horoscopes of children brought before him! History records the Mayan civilization as a highly advanced people, builders second to none, proficient astronomer—astrologers and a gentle, deeply religious race.

Rome — its history interwoven with Astrology. Its greatest and most scholarly men used this most ancient of sciences. The cosmopolitan spirit of ancient Rome caused it to become "a center" of learning and a mart for the exchange of ideas. In this atmosphere, Astrology developed and spread throughout the empire. Here, Miss Carter was able to trace Astrology from the mighty emperors to the great universities and most of the governmental heads of Europe. The "eternal city" as well as the other major cities of Italy bear many indications of their astrological past to be found in universities, palaces, and government buildings.

Marguerite Carter in ancient Pompeii, at the foot of Mt. Vesuvius in southern Italy. The city of Pompeii was covered by volcanic ash in A. D. 79, its people and buildings frozen in time to be discovered by archeologists. The unusual manner of its demise preserved examples of its architecture, art, various shops, tools, dress and habits of its people. No other place in antiquity has afforded such an insight into the life of its inhabitants. Manuscripts of the poet—philosopher Philodemos were recovered and preserved. Many of the Greek philosophers were well versed in Astrology and responsible for its introduction to other parts of the world.

THE UNIVERSALITY OF ANCIENT KNOWLEDGE

Almost daily, as students search ancient and modern writings, it is becoming more and more evident that in olden days when very little communication existed between countries and none between certain continents, there was a UNIVERSALITY OF ASTROLOGICAL KNOWLEDGE. Examples of learning from Egypt ARE STRIKINGLY SIMILAR to those found in the culture of the Maya, separated by thousands of miles! Unless there had been at one time some direct form of communication (which has not been disproved) it appears evident that this knowledge came from "one" *original source,* and was used by every great civilization! How else can one explain the similarity from country to country — from civilization to civilization — as exemplified in the ancient ART and SCIENCE of ASTROLOGY? Comparison between the various schools of ASTROLOGY clearly shows this to be a reasoned, logical UNDERSTANDING of the interpretation of a MAGNIFICENT NATURAL LAW! It is the recognition of the SUPREME LAW which governs the Universe, and has from time immemorial!

The rise to power of Augustus Caesar was predicted by an Astrologer when the mighty Caesar was still an unknown youth. On January 17, 27 B. C., Caesar was appointed emperor by the Roman Senate and, impressed by this verification, had the coin pictured above minted (a denarius) — bearing his likeness, and on the reverse, the sign of Capricorn, under which he assumed the title of Emperor — the FIRST Roman to do so! Years of searching for this coin resulted in success for Marguerite Carter. It is believed by authorities to be the only example extant!

For centuries the imprint of this hand was preserved from the tropical Sun by the lush forest growths of Central America. It is unfortunate that as these growths have been cleared away the imprint is fading. Authorities believe this 2000 year old symbol depicts a Mayan priestly blessing. It is remarkably similar to others found around the world in widely differing civilizations (particularly India) and far distant areas. This is another example of the UNIVERSALITY OF KNOWLEDGE -- a symbol believed to be an inspired gesture!

According to many eminent authorities, the above is said to be the oldest Christian Church in Rome — and may be the oldest in the world! Imbedded in its floor is a zodiac. Scholars in studying ancient manuscripts, find more and more evidence that the early Church was closely associated in important aspects with the belief in Astrology! Astrologers predicted the birth of Christ, and for many centuries the Church not only acknowledged Astrology, but utilized it as an expression of Supreme Law!

The concepts dealt with on this page are derived from only one of many possible comparisons based on accumulating knowledge now, illustrating the **universality** of astrological wisdom in the past. The evidence of such knowledge, structures, symbols and artifacts bearing the unmistakable stamp of a common origin are found in widely separated areas of the world. The evidence dates back thousands of years and from places where it has been generally believed that men lived in tiny isolated areas of civilization, unaware of the surrounding world.

For many years, it was believed that the similarity between Egyptian (photo lower right) and Mayan pyramids (photo upper right) ended with their shape. As investigation deepened, startling resemblances in carvings and inscriptions became apparent. Some alphabetical and astrological symbols were found to be **exact duplicates** conveying the same meanings, though from opposite sides of the globe! The great degree of skill in plotting the heavens was possessed by both cultures and the use of the pyramids for observation of the heavens was common to both. One doubt remained, because it was believed the Mayans did not use their pyramids as tombs which was true of those in Egypt.

One hundred years after its discovery, a Mayan pyramid in Palenque finally revealed its greatest secret to archeologists. Deep in the pyramid's center was a sarcophagus and tomb (photo left) in the tradition of the Egyptian pyramids. The discovery ranks with that of King Tut's tomb in Egypt. It was a burial of great splendor with jewels, sculpture and other rich artifacts in the manner of the Pharaoh's tombs. The enormous stone lid of the sarcophagus was covered with intricate inscriptions of astrological symbology.

Here was another milestone in evidence of universal knowledge of the ancients. Both structures were built on astrological principles, both structures were used for astronomical observations, both contained astrological inscriptions and both contained the tombs of royal religious leaders who at the same time were believed to possess unique astrological wisdom. The Mayan King-Priest buried here cast the horoscopes of children brought before him. The Egyptian Kings used astrology to guide their affairs and frequently had the ceilings of their palaces, tombs and temples decorated with a zodiac representing their religious concepts. A reproduction of such a zodiac will be found on the reverse of this page.

THE BIRTH TRINITIES
SIGNS
AND CUSPS

Concerning birth vibrations, which are productive of *"rhythms"* in the life of individuals, there are *twelve* fundamental harmonics or major vibrations which go into the making of human character as well as operating in the working-out of cosmic law in the life of races, nations, and persons. These major vibrations are capable of mixture in any proportion. The variations which are possible reach into such astronomical figures as to be virtually incalculable.

They are intermixed with each other, imparted to and blended with the soul vibrations of an incarnating spirit or segment from the life of God, which is to be an individual. These vibration blends are affixed at birth, and the birth occurs in accordance with the orderly workings of law at a time when conditions are exactly of such nature as to *express the state of evolution* which the incoming soul has reached. The Creator, in expressions of natural law in this physical plane of existence, has naturally assured every factor to maintain steady progression in evolution and a state of BALANCE.

In this connection, consider that there have been, during the history of the world, strong and dominant hereditary strains in families. It becomes immediately apparent that if it were not for the *orderly balance* maintained by these unseen but *powerful* forces, heredity ALONE would increasingly produce human beings possessed of certain traits and abilities; and the *rest of the qualities* necessary to carry on the work of the world and to maintain a BALANCE would be *over-run* and *exterminated* by those who possessed *dominating* characteristics (such as those of conquest and aggression). However, such does not prove to be the case. People are born into the world so that EVERY duty will be performed.

The inventive and creative are never left out, as the leader or builder is never left out. If it were entirely a question of heredity — *without any factors of influence from the great cosmic forces* — the world unquestionably would, before long, come to the point of being inhabited entirely by aggressive leaders and there would be no one to originate anything or to do the work of execution. Every person, however, has his own *niche* to fill. He is fitted for *one* particular thing. In the quests of life, he finds the door is closed to him in every direction excepting the one in which he *should* go. In that direction there is smooth sailing!

We shall use a homely comparison to illustrate the admixture of qualities which mainly have to do with the inculcation of processes of thought (for unseen vibrations from the planets are of that essence) and which, working through and in complete harmonic accord with heredity — produce characteristics. There is no doubt that many *combinations of ingredients* produce a result in which many of the *separate ingredients* are unrecognizable.

As previously mentioned, the basic harmonic vibrations are twelve, comprising what are commonly referred to as "birthsigns". The birthsign which is related to the period of the year in which one was born owes the particular quality of its vibration to the position of the Earth at that time of that year. An illustration would be to compare them with varying color combinations which are productive of a wide range of shades. That, however, is *more* than an illustration as the combining of colors bears a specific scientific relationship to the various basic harmonic vibrations of the birthsigns.

Each month, the basic ingredient is different and it is blended with many other ingredients in widely-varying combinations to produce every type of being necessary to carry on the work of the world, and to fulfill *individual* destiny. Never is one born into physical life to whom is imparted the basic ingredient of the birthsign *alone,* for the individual would be quite unbalanced. One cannot bake a cake with flour alone. Other ingredients are necessary.

For that reason, investigation of science pertaining to the birthsigns only, is valueless — as the qualities imparted are psychological or of the essence of *thought,* which must be rather felt and sensed than actively measured. It is true that due to the inner factors of thought processes which are imparted, there is a tendency in each birthsign toward certain types of expression occupationally and a tendency as well to particular *reactions* in the individual, to stimuli.

Unquestionably there is a marked tendency in any group of one thousand people, all of whom were born in the same sign at birth, to respond to the experiences of life *in much the same manner.* Massive studies have clearly proved that of one thousand people who were born in the same zodiacal sign, seven hundred will respond so similarly to identical conditions of life and will generally express the same likes and dislikes as to give *unmistakable* evidence of the existence of the fundamental "ingredient" — or harmonic vibration. The interlocking qualities of the basic ingredients, the perfect simplicity and yet the extraordinary complexity, are of such nature that the hand of God must be visible to *all* who approach the subject with *open minds!*

The basic ingredients which go into forming human character are divided into *trinities.* Of these, there are *four.* The trinities comprise the major elements — *fire, earth, air, water.* All birthsigns or ingredients which are of the *same element* have certain *common qualities.*

Basically, the fire signs all bestow psychological factors and qualities of thought process which make for *leadership.* However, in the working-out of natural law, other factors are also present. Sometimes a combination of other ingredients will be fully as strong — and in *unusual* cases, stronger — than the ingredient imparted by the sun or birthsign. Among the fire signs, there is first the impatient, possessive, adventurous pioneer. He is a product of the sign *Aries.* Then there is the masterful, impulsive, emotional, spontaneous parader. This is the pure constructive essence of the sign known as *Leo.* Finally among the fire trinity, there is the frank, bluff, genial, honest, outspoken and inspiring accomplisher. That is the constructive essence of the fire sign *Sagittarius.* All people who came into the world under any of these fire signs receives a considerable amount of the psychological quality of leadership in accordance with his own division of that trinity. It must be remembered, of course, that one who was born in any other sign, although it may not be a fire sign, often receives the quality of leadership strongly from one of the fire trinity — because at the time of his birth there was *one planet or more firmly placed in a fire sign.*

Next, there is the *earth* trinity. All of these signs impart a great deal of the ingredient of thought which causes people to be able to *carry things through.* The first of these is called *Taurus.* Taurus is essentially the dogged, persistent, material, practical — but fun-loving — builder. Then there is the practical, analytical, technical, precise-thinking builder which is the basic harmonic vibration known as *Virgo.* Finally, among the earth trinity, there is the shrewd, practical, steady, conservative — but tenacious, managing builder produced by the third earth trinity, *Capricorn.*

Next among the trinities is that of *air,* and the first of these is *Gemini.* Essentially, the qualities of this sign, as all others, are interpreted in terms of action (which is only a means of expressing *individuality*). The pure essence of Gemini is alert, mentally-active, spontaneous, quick-spoken, versatile and creative. Second among the air signs is *Libra,* which is artistic, scientific, philosophical and creative. Last of the air trinity is *Aquarius*; imaginative, humanitarian, experimental and creative.

It will be observed that all three signs of the air trinity are creative and that, as with the other trinities, the qualities somewhat overlap. Again it must be stressed that these are words which *imperfectly* express the individuality which is the pure essence of the basic harmonic vibration. Understanding birthsign qualities is more a matter of *inner* perception than an analysis of words.

The last of the trinities is *water.* In one respect, all of these are alike. They are spiritual, psychic and inspirational. They respond to *unseen* forces as the strings of a musical instrument respond to the force which agitates them. First of the water trinity is the emotional, sensitive, conservative, psychic *Cancer.* Second is the intense, dramatic, magnetic, aggressive over-seer, *Scorpio.* Lastly among the water signs, there is the poetic, imaginative, inspirational, receptive and sensitive *Pisces.*

Now — consider that in every individual these basic vibrations are *mixed,* but in no two people *exactly the same.* There are no words which can completely convey the *complexities* which then exist. However, it may be stated that the *basic* ingredient of the birthsign may be recognized readily by almost anyone. The INNER QUALITY of the sign is more often than not obvious in word-descriptions of the person, recognizable without difficulty by those who know him.

These fundamental harmonic vibrations produce their like in the individual and work in complete harmony with heredity and other factors of life. Not only do they produce their like in the individuality, but they are responsible for the ebb and flow of forces in the *affairs* of life which are the personal life rhythm of the individual.

Providing your conception of astrology is "right" in the first place, that your thought processes with relation to it are *constructive* (fear of "bad" aspects is destructive), it becomes of much value for you to learn what combination of influences existed at the time *you* came into the world. The purpose in so learning about those influences from the unseen fields of vibration is not in any way to determine what is "fixed" or planned for you in the future; but for the purpose of selecting from your chart the constructive psychological patterns of thought and the *elimination* of those which are destructive. The banishing of these less-favorable thought vibrations from your mental processes *is the purpose of evolution,* and whether you learn it by repeated "suffering" or by *intelligent understanding* and BELIEF in the "goodness" of the Creator, you will one day — *learn!*

The constructive thought patterns you tend to produce, as well as the unwanted thought formations, are shown in your chart of birth. They are in exact accord and present a true picture of the state of your evolution. They are, in fact, synonymous with *conditions* in your life. Those indications in your chart which present to an occultist, the spiritual factors which make you *what* you *are,* will be read by the astrologer who regards his subject as a cold science or an equally cold art, *only* as an indication of *happenings* in your future. But *behind those happenings* are the *spiritual factors* and the KEY which will allow *you* to change indicated events which are not what you desire — *if you will!*

It has been possible for those who are students of planetary influence to predict future conditions in the lives of others, but the reason for that lies in their ability *to judge* from the chart of an individual (or a people) the state of evolution which has been reached, and to what extent in thinking processes there will be vibrations in harmony with constructive or negative forces, which bring about inevitable results.

THE BIRTHSIGNS

The next step in considering the basic harmonic vibrations is, logically, the psychological factors which a student of cosmic law can attribute to a birthsign. We shall describe the signs at length. In doing so, we shall deal with *all* the factors which are considered a part of the birthsign itself, describing them partially in the first person. As every individual is a complex mechanism, each has within his makeup many characteristics which are not obvious, as they are over-shadowed by others which have developed more fully.

There has been a measure of confusion in the minds of many regarding the reason that the changing dates between the signs appear to vary. The cause of that fact is — the changing dates *are not the same every year*. There is a variation of two or three days. The earth revolves completely about the sun every 365 days, but its position is not exactly the same each day as on the same day of the preceding year. Consequently, when we refer to a period between two dates as a birthsign in the following descriptions, it should be remembered that *arbitrary* dates are used, and that in individual cases there *might* be a variation (as one could have been born in a succeeding or a preceding sign if his birth occurred within one or two days of the changing date specified). However, the periods between the signs are known as CUSPS and they are dealt with separately. Actually, each ten degrees of every sign is somewhat different but the entire sign is *essentially* of the same fundamental quality. The greatest variation is in the period which lies near the dividing line between signs — the cusp.

Throughout recorded history, there has been an effort to convey the qualities of the birthsigns graphically, in a manner which would illustrate the spiritual meaning. It has been thought that the symbol of each sign was originally derived from the likeness of the constellation itself to the animal, or other symbol, in use. That is *not* the case, however. The fact is that the use of the symbols has always been for the purpose of conveying an understandable ILLUSTRATION of the fundamental qualities of the sign.

THE CUSPS

Those who enter the world in any of the periods which are referred to as cusps are indisputably more *complex* than those who were born in full sun signs.

The great majority of people who were born at a time when the full sun sign influence is strongest give unmistakable evidence to a practiced observer of the characteristics attributed to the sign, though not *all* do. However, one always finds it more difficult to "place" the individual who was born in one of the cusp periods.

The word "cusp" is used to designate that period which lies immediately between two signs of the zodiac. There is a time, lasting for several days in each month, when the solar vibrations tend to impart a blend of qualities. The cusp period in human affairs as a whole is likely to be one of uncertainty during which there are changes.

Individuals who are born in one of these cusp periods have reached the stage of evolution wherein a definite step is being taken and resultantly their lives are more often *unsettled*, their affairs more *complex*, and their uncertainties *greater*, than those of individuals who were born in the full sun sign. In a measure, those who were born in one of these cusp periods are given the characteristics of both signs within the influence of which they are born; yet there is sometimes a divergence. However, the native of a cusp period is to a considerable degree *capable* of developing most of the constructive or positive qualities associated with *either* sign — but is also susceptible to the negatives of *both*.

It should be borne in mind that in describing the cusp periods, individuals are not being discussed. Instead, the combination of solar vibrations which is observable in the majority of those who come into the world during one of these cusp periods is dealt with. Other planetary positions which sometimes alter the qualities are not considered.

(If you were born in one of these cusp periods — you should read BOTH signs. You will undoubtedly recognize characteristics and qualities of both in yourself — although, of course, some will be much more prominent than others. ALSO — you should read the PREDICTIONS for BOTH signs, as there is a blending in this respect as there is in the birthsign qualities.)

— and now to the twelve divisions in the Heavens —

and the cyclic interpretations —

The birthsign ARIES
March 20th to April 20th

f you were born between March 20th and April 20th your birthsign is Aries. The symbol of this sign is the Ram. In ancient Grecian legend, it was the fabled Ram with the Golden Fleece, sought by the Argonaut Jason. Your sign is the capstone of the twelve signs of the zodiac, and it has been called the *Prince of Celestial Signs*. A study of ancient history reveals the fact that a great deal of lore and legend surround it, the Chinese zodiac, for instance, referring to Aries as *The White Sheep*.

Individually, you are of the Bible tribe of Gad. Nationally, assuming you to be a citizen of the United States, you are a member of the tribe of Dan. The sign Aries is referred to as fiery, dry, equinoctial, hot, eastern, cardinal, positive, masculine, inflammatory, violent, bestial, movable, intemperate, of short ascension. It is also called fortunate. Mars is the ruling planet which means that the vibrations which were illustrated in the so-called myths of Greece and Rome in relation to the god of that name are prominent in this vibration. It is considered that the diamond and bloodstone have vibrations similar in nature to those of the pure Aries influence and that the flower which harmonizes more fully than others is the violet.

It must be clearly called to mind if one is to have any understanding of the meanings involved in Astrology, in attempting to understand one's self as well as others, that while the birthsigns are described herein at some length, people do not always outwardly conform to the characteristics of their own sign. Human beings are all complex, some extremely so. Often they do not understand themselves. Seldom are they really understood by others.

The birthsign is indicative of their fundamental inner qualities and the way that they are likely to look at life. Early environments of course, can make a difference in their attitudes, and the time of day an individual is born does unquestionably alter outward personality traits. There is indication that a considerable portion of the human race come into the world at sunrise or a little thereafter. Their own birthsign is always rising on the eastern horizon at that time of day. Our own actual researches are not sufficiently widely extended to be able to state with absolute authority the proportion of people who were born at sunrise but we are pursuing this research. It has been stated that a majority were born at that time.

References to various birthsigns, for instance your sign, Aries, as being a fire sign, dry, equinoctial, etc., have to do with deeply, spiritual, metaphysical truths. In the first place Aries is the first sign of the zodiac, and is therefore first among the fire triplicity. It is associated with the Egypt of several thousand years ago. The ram was used extensively in Egypt. The tremendous drive between Luxor on the shores of the Nile and the great temple of Luxor was lined on both sides with figures, close together, of the ram.

Aries is a cardinal sign, which means that it occupies one of the cardinal points. Aries is the east point; the cardinal point at the south being Cancer, a water sign; the third of the cardinal points on the opposite or western side is an air sign, Libra; the northernmost point being occupied by Capricorn, an earth sign. These do not refer to physical elements, they are spiritual and metaphysical. All the pyramids were built and oriented according to these four points — east, south, west, and north.

Those who were born at a time when some sign other than their own was rising (that is other than at sunrise), tend to depart somewhat from the qualities of their own birthsign in personality. They turn a little different face to the world. Those who were born at certain times, for instance when Scorpio was rising, express more of the Martial qualities of Mars and some of the qualities or characteristics of their birthsign itself are more strongly expressed. It must be remembered if you seek to understand the matter, you endeavor to comprehend others as they are *within* themselves, regardless of what they appear to be outwardly.

If you are of the pure Aries type physically, you find it difficult to accumulate money though not to obtain it. Those who approach this type of *pure* Aries are tall, well proportioned, and usually of strong physique. They are slender in early life and have high, as well as rounded foreheads. The coloring is fair, showing a tendency toward sandy hair. The interests of those who conform in physical appearance to the pure Aries type are intellectual rather than physical.

Your inclination is to be interested in public life rather than private. You are not by nature, retiring, but rather like to mingle actively with people. A great many of the world's outstanding leaders were born at a time when the vibrations from this sign were strong, which of course, most often comes about as a result of one's having been born in the sign itself or at that period of the year. You are extremely generous, and have an inherently strong desire to do good. This trait of Aries has often been referred to as *foolish generosity,* yet it expresses a powerful constructive force, excepting when given expression to for personal gratification.

A blending of Aries with some of the other signs, notably Scorpio, tends to produce a shorter type, one of stockier build and darker complexion. When there is at birth, an admixture of Aries with a sign which produces a less fair complexion, there is also a tendency to impart unusually capable business sense. Making money is comparatively easy for those who give evidence of such a blend in their physical characteristics and they achieve success in widely varied lines of commerce. An

2

Aries individual who is of this type, due to the blending of signs which produce such coloring (acting with heredity) is usually markedly impatient, headstrong, and resentful of opposition and interference. In particular he does not like criticism. This trait is, in truth, latent or active in all natives of Aries.

You are undoubtedly interested in subjects of an occult nature and the study of metaphysics intrigues you greatly. Your sign frequently imparts keen penetration along those lines, producing marked psychic and clairvoyant powers. These occasionally are, in the Aries native, phenomenally great. An admixture of water sign influences at birth will produce psychic qualities. An astonishingly large number of mind readers, spiritual advisers and psychometrics were born in this sign, receiving at birth other planetary vibrations which produce psychic perception. Individuals who were born under the solar vibration of Aries, when highly evolved, are able to penetrate many of the deeper mysteries of the universe. The state of evolution indicative of high development is, of course, revealed in planetary positions which existed at the time of birth.

It is not unusual for those who are thus highly evolved to possess remarkable telepathic powers, being able to receive vibrations from the minds of others without the exchange of words. Experiments along this line, conducted with Aries natives as recipients of such messages show them to be quite sensitive to thought vibrations. Solar forces and cosmic influences are active in the lives of Aries people. As a result of those forces, which personal development enables them to call upon, they are often able to do a tremendous amount of constructive good for others. The sign, however, is strongly intellectual and it is not unusual for natives to apply themselves so intensely as to bring about extreme mental fatigue. They have a tendency to try to carry too many things in their minds at the same time.

You are fond of dancing, music and of beauty as expressed in painting and other forms of art. If you are of a fairly pure Aries type your countenance indicates a great deal of perceptive power. You have a desire to dominate others and to command but despite this you have the ability to be extremely attractive and charming. You are noble, warmhearted, magnetic and extremely progressive, passively or actively. Should you become engaged in reforms or in political activities you would be extremely interested in the welfare of the public. You fight for your rights and you have strong convictions. It has often been said of the Aries native that he will fight in court as long as there is anything to be fought over.

You are essentially independent in everything you do and of all the signs yours is the one which produces people most likely to become irritated and resentful when there are restrictions imposed. You are fond of adventure and you are extremely determined in your ideas. When launched upon any course of endeavor you will sometimes go to great lengths to carry through, often over-riding obstacles regardless of opposition. The fact of the matter is that opposition frequently stimulates you to a greater determination.

You have, however, a tendency to become impatient when things do not move rapidly enough. In fact, it is not unlikely that you begin activities which you do not carry through because of your dislike of monotony and routine. You become quickly enthused over a new idea and as a result often lose your zest in an older one. The tendency of Aries is to long constantly for new fields to conquer. You are alert and *expectant* of adventure.

You are an excellent natural adviser and you are able to arouse confidence on the part of other people. It is however, quite likely that you make enemies. You can be bitter in anger, but it is not your tendency to be unjust or carry a grudge, even toward those who have injured you considerably. When one has done something to violate your confidence, however, it is almost impossible for him to regain it. It is among those born in the sign Aries that we find individuals who are willing to die fighting for an idea or for those of whom they are fond. You probably have warm friends and it is characteristic of you not to be able to see their faults. Those of your solar vibration are perhaps the deepest thinkers of all. They are extremely intelligent and apt scholars. You should be a very good conversationalist, being rarely at a loss for ideas.

The people of your sign are particularly noted for aggressiveness, energy, earnestness, enthusiasm, courage, originality, unusual determination (though disliking sustained, monotonous effort), fine executive abilities and the capacity for leadership, requiring quickness in thought and action. Your outstanding trait is a desire to lead. The true Aries native who cannot be at the head of things usually feels that he is in the wrong place. The sign itself is considered to rule, and consequently particularly to affect, the head. Aries indicates the bones of the skull and face. One of the marked characteristics of the sign is the tendency it imparts toward fondness for luxurious conditions in life. Those who were born under this particular solar vibration usually have a fondness for smart things, elegant surroundings and varied social activities.

As with all other signs, the virtues of Aries when carried to extremes become faults. Words expressing the positive qualities of the sign are: ambition, courage, activity, enterprise, leadership, generosity, pioneering, constructiveness, utility, thoughtfulness, productiveness, and inspiration. Words which express the negative qualities are: headstrong, impetuous, impatient, imprudent, quarrelsome, belligerent, foolhardy, jealous, disrespectful, selfish, inconstant, excitable and reckless.

The most strongly accented negative of this solar vibration is lack of patience. Often in the Aries native, the qualities of stubbornness, anger, impatience, excessive and injudicious generosity and inconstant purpose are evident. This sign is also particularly marked by egotism. It is often possessed of very strong tendencies toward jealousy. A quick temper is frequently evident although the outbursts of anger are usually soon over. Those who receive this influence strongly at birth are often sarcastic, overbearing, and *too ready* to defend their rights. A great many of the difficulties which come about in the lives of Aries people are due to the tendency of the birth vibration towards recklessness, quick temper and jealousy. The latter trait extends itself to *all* their possessions and to what they regard as their *rights* in general. A marked trait of the sign is that natives can rarely stand to be contradicted or

4

strongly opposed. They do not like to have their faults pointed out. This is characteristic of a large number of people without regard to their birthsign, but it is more consistently true of Aries natives than of others.

It is to be noted that a large number do not know the value of money. They are apt to be spendthrift without regard for consequences and to expend money lavishly on entertainment and social pleasures. This tendency toward reckless expenditure often manifests itself in a desire for display in jewels and personal adornment. Because of the self-confidence and enthusiasm of Aries, the native is apt to overestimate his capacity at times. Aries natives have a tendency to plunge into activities recklessly until they have involved themselves in debt or taken on large burdens, and then to worry excessively. Because theirs is primarily a mental sign this often leads them to the verge of nervous prostration or into the actual condition. When the native of Aries strives earnestly to eliminate the negative qualities — the faults — by cultivating the virtues or positives, he is completely assured of aid from the most powerful sources of the universe. The qualities it is most necessary for the Aries native to cultivate are *tolerance, patience, concentration, and application.*

It is a particularly good idea for the Aries individual to seek quiet places; to walk alone where there can be freedom from disturbing influences. The cultivation of a serene, tranquil, and patient mental attitude will enable the Aries native to deal in a completely constructive way with his problems. The one most important lesson for him to learn is that of *self-control.* In striving to master the conditions of life and of his surroundings it is first necessary for him to learn *mastery of himself.* The higher attributes of the sign have been pointed out. Development of those attributes enables the native to tune in upon powerfully constructive vibrations. One should recall that the physical body is part of this field of vibration and that it is subject to the control of occult and spiritual laws. The cultivation of the higher qualities of his sign is extremely necessary for the native of Aries.

It is almost an impossibility to force or drive the true native of Aries. Invariably he prefers to do his work in *his own way* and dislikes being told how to proceed. Cultivation of the intellectual abilities natural to the sign and in particular the spiritual factors which deeply underlie them invariably open a new world for him. Occult and spiritual laws should be delved into as the nature of this sign along those lines is great. The *power of intuition* is strongly marked. It is almost impossible to hide anything from the native of Aries who has developed the spiritual side of his nature. Position, honors, esteem, health — all the most desirable rewards of this earthly sphere of existence — are completely within the reach of the person who received a strong Aries influence at birth.

WOMEN OF ARIES

All women of this birthsign have an inner desire to lead. Their tendency is to be aggressive in many respects. It is a marked characteristic of those who were born in this sign, women as well as men, to wish to be in the forefront of any activity in which they find themselves. As far as the women of the sign are concerned, this extends itself to most of the conditions of their lives. While some of the other signs of the zodiac tend to like furnishings in their homes which are comfortable and not new, the Aries woman has a strong tendency to prefer things which are modernistic or certainly in the *"mode"*. When she entertains, she is likely to express smartness in her entertainment and the same thing applies to her clothes. They are likely to be extremely chic and in the forefront of prevailing styles. The true Aries woman is *sleek* and *svelte,* and she is likely to be extremely attractive in appearance.

There is a tendency among women who come into the world under a strong Aries influence to monopolize conversations. Being very intense and having their own ideas to a marked extent, they tend to talk at length about those ideas without regard for the interests of others. In common with the men of this sign, women who are born in Aries are quite inclined to be resentful and impatient when opposed or when conditions of life impose restraint. Associates of one who was born in this sign should allow her to go ahead upon her own initiative, carrying out her ideas in her own way.

The one paramount negative of the Aries influence is jealousy. This is quite likely to manifest itself to a marked degree in the woman who was born under a strong influence from the sign. Other than in this respect the character of Aries women is likely to be very fine. However, they do often encounter a great deal of difficulty as a result of the impatience which is characteristic of the sign; and quick temper, much of which comes indirectly through the tendency toward jealousy. More unhappiness has undoubtedly been brought about in the lives of women who were born in Aries through this quality than any other. On the other hand, the woman of Aries is likely to be quite gracious and charming under most circumstances.

Very few people of the sign, men or women, really like to be in menial or subservient positions. When conditions force them into such places, they sometimes become resigned but they are rarely very happy inwardly. The women of Aries are frequently exceptionally talented along musical lines. They become exceedingly capable designers, managers of institutions, hotel-keepers, and department managers. The Aries influence particularly fits one to the demands of general advertising as it has come to be practiced in recent years. Women of this sign are also capable sales-people in retail lines and are good milliners or dressmakers, having a great deal of adaptability and originality.

The woman of Aries, in common with the man of the sign, is possessed of the ability to control her thought processes and as a result, the actions to which she gives expression. The best method of doing that is by cultivating the opposite or the constructive. Those born in Aries who determine to turn their minds to a higher plane of being and to overcome the tendencies toward impatience, anger, and jealousy, can bring about in their lives the fullest degree of happiness and tranquility, as well as *abundance!*

There is little doubt that the child who was born under a predominating Aries influence is the most difficult and yet the easiest of all the signs to manage. They respond readily to *reason*. When one talks to them as equals, giving reasons for commands, they are as a general rule, amazingly responsive. It is, however, almost an impossibility to force an Aries child to obedience when there is a lack of understanding. Children of this solar vibration are almost certain to demand a reason for anything they are required to do. When a command is arbitrary with no explanation, the child will be resentful. These children respond particularly to affection. Indeed, understanding and affection are necessary to both the child and the adult of this sign. *Love should be the guiding factor* in the life of the child.

A great deal of vitality is expended by children of Aries in trying to do too many things. These youngsters are inquisitive, restless, and likely to be constantly active and busy. Parents will find them *out of one thing and immediately into another*. They change interests rapidly and are usually not content to be occupied with one thing for too long a time. The individuality of the Aries child is generally best developed by allowing him to do things in his own way. He likes to feel responsibility for carrying things out by himself, and his tendency is usually to assume a position of leadership and to *give orders* or *dictate* to his playmates.

Youngsters of Aries should never be sharply reprimanded, scolded, abused or physically punished. Physical punishment is probably more harmful to this child than to those of other signs, since it usually requires more punishment to control him than his body can withstand. Severe punishment of a physical nature is likely to have extremely adverse psychological reactions, bringing about strongly negative nervous tendencies in later years. The Aries nature is restless and high-strung, and care should be exercised with children of strong Aries temperament to *shield* them from undue nervous excitement.

They are apt to be stubborn when opposed and particularly are they likely to be *quick-tempered,* seldom turning away from an argument or even a fight. All these things should be taken into consideration in dealing with the child who was born under a strong Aries influence. It is not constructive to rule these children autocratically, and to interfere with their plans. Under such conditions they quickly lose interest in their work or current activity and are likely to throw it aside in order to try something new.

Arbitrary rule will often drive an Aries child away from home, and unquestionably brings about in this sign a great many of the mistakes made by youth the world over. When young people of Aries are restrained too greatly, or are ruled by arbitrary methods, they either give up because of suddenly dampened enthusiasm, or become engaged in some undertaking or course of action to which they will cling stubbornly, even though knowing it is wrong. Violent opposition or too rigid control may bring about the abandonment of a constructive activity for something new, or a continuance in a less constructive activity which is carried out because of pure dogged and perverse determination.

7

MARRIAGES OF ARIES

There is no question about the fact that Aries people in marriage should seek a partner who is on the same cultural or educational level. They are very rarely able to get along permanently with those to whom they can't talk on a basis of mutual understanding. All Aries people tend to have good intellects and basically to *be* intellectual; as a rule, very much more so than physical. A great many men who were born in this sign and as a matter of fact women as well, are engaged in occupations which relate to physical activity, but their own direct contributions are rarely *purely* physical. It is rather unusual for natives of this sign to meet anyone of the opposite sex who *fully* understands their temperamental equipment. As a result, marriage or other close relationships often bring about unhappiness in their lives. This, however, can be greatly obviated by *CULTIVATION of the positive traits*.

It is quite necessary for those who came into the world under this particular solar vibration to learn self-control. As a rule the native of this sign, certainly anyone who came into the world when the Aries influence was strong, will be attractive to the opposite sex and in turn attracted *by* them to a marked degree. This not infrequently brings about difficulty and unhappiness in their lives. People who were born in Aries should, more than those of almost any other sign, be blessed with a marriage partner who understands their particular qualities.

Because of the *impulsive, headstrong nature* of the sign, those qualities are, to a greater or lesser degree, manifested in the native, and many marriages entered into by those who were born under a strong Aries influence are wrecked upon the shoals of misunderstanding. The people of this sign are *intense* in their love natures though this is usually mental rather than purely physical. Affection and sympathy are extremely necessary as the Aries native is more affectionate than truly passionate. The *one particular step,* in which Aries individuals should exercise the most *caution,* is matrimony. They should take into consideration every factor, in the very act of doing so; *restraining* their impetuous natures.

Probably the sign Libra (September 24th — October 23rd) is the most harmonious as far as the pure solar vibration or sign influence is concerned. The highly evolved Libra is kind, tolerant, and sympathetic, alert to the welfare and happiness of his loved ones. The fundamental qualities of Gemini (May 23rd — June 22nd) are also in accord with those of Aries. Children of these marriages are likely to be well equipped both mentally and physically for the struggle of life. Other signs congenial to Aries are Leo (July 22nd — August 22nd), and Sagittarius (November 23rd — December 21st).

Sometimes individuals who were born at a time of day when there was a sign rising which is inharmonious with the birthsign itself, experience a great deal of inner conflict. They are prompted to face the world in such a way as to give expression to things, that their inner instincts and emotions do not prompt them to do naturally. Consequently there is always an inner division, or conflict, which sometimes leads to actual agony of spirit. Not infrequently natives of Aries are misunderstood by other people and particularly by members of the opposite sex. When the rising sign is different than the birthsign, the actual inner outlook upon life bestowed or symbolized by the birthsign is not expressed outwardly.

Aries is the true pioneer of the zodiac. One who came into the world with Aries qualities is happiest and at his best when at the *head of things*. Occupations such as manager, instructor, business executive or director are favorable for natives of the sign, where their ability to make quick decisions, and their natural authority and firmness of purpose can be fully utilized. The Aries native almost always has a great deal of *natural energy* and could be very successful at the head of an enterprise, although it has often been said that those who were born under a strong Aries vibration should associate themselves with another person who is more conservative than they, so that their qualities of *over-enthusiastic zest* will be balanced.

Financial abilities are accentuated for the reason that the native is wide awake and keen. Often people who were born under this influence become completely absorbed in undertakings of financial nature and consequently are quite successful. They sometimes are not able to *keep* money, though they may have great ability to acquire it.

A number of well-known actors were born in the sign Aries. Their quickness of wit, and understanding fit them admirably for a career of that nature. They also make eloquent orators, being popular with the public and having the power to arouse enthusiastic response in their audiences.

The mental adaptability and the aggressiveness by which the sign Aries is particularly marked also fits many men who were born in this sign for the legal profession. The natural qualities of Aries impart an ability to judge fairly and excepting in the case of personal involvement, when his own interests are at stake and his martial nature is aroused, the native is free from personal prejudice. When there is a high state of development in the Aries individual he is, even then, able to remain unprejudiced. However, the tendency of the sign is to be resentful of opposition or restraint and for the native to pursue an objective or course of action even though at heart he realizes he is wrong.

Literary fields are quite favorable and often attractive to the natives of this sign when there was an admixture of influence at birth of air or water signs with the Aries influence. They are then likely to be quite adept at creative work in literary endeavors and even inspired. Some of the greatest writers in history were born in this sign.

There is also a considerable ability along inventive lines and because of the sense of perception, usually there is a talent for architecture. Selling is very favorable for the person who has strongly marked Aries qualities. When his enthusiasm is aroused he is intense in application and determination and his enthusiasm is contagious. Mechanical pursuits as a rule are not particularly favorable excepting that technical occupations such as engineering do have a very definite appeal and the native can be successful in them as long as there is not too much detailed work involved. As a matter of fact purely technical occupations usually afford an outlet for the Aries natives abilities when such occupations are creative, or when they express the *pioneering* spirit.

DISHARMONY OF ARIES

In the terminology of physical science this section would be titled *diseases* of Aries. Disease, however, is always synonymous with lack of harmony in thought processes. The vibrations so produced do not harmonize with the constructive vibrations of the universe. The physical conditions ordinarily referred to as *diseases* are therefore considered in their true light.

Potentially those who received the Aries vibration at birth have *all* the qualities, both positive and negative, which have already been discussed, and the Aries native will note in himself these qualities. *Some* of those qualities, either those which are constructive or those which are destructive, will be most marked. The tendencies toward negative expression when accentuated are most likely to produce in Aries: catarrh, colds, headaches, migraine, troubles with the ears, teeth and eyes, as well as fevers which affect the head. Negatives of the sign which manifest themselves in processes of thought, in turn induce congestion of the brain, paralysis due to ruptures of blood vessels, neuralgia, nervous prostration, and all other conditions resulting directly from restless, nervous traits. These are outward indications of inner negatives.

Restlessness, impatience, nervousness and irritability result, of course, only from apprehensions. There is a direct sympathetic action between the head, the stomach and kidneys which are the parts most liable to disorder as a result of the restlessness which is the mark of the Aries person whose negative vibrations are, at least in part, predominant.

Physically the Aries should have ample fresh air. Walks in the fresh air are extremely desirable for one who received a strong influence from this sign at birth. He should obtain sufficient sleep. Sleeping rooms should be well ventilated, and hours for work and relaxation should be regular. The negatives which produce a desire for luxurious living should be turned deliberately into more constructive channels. Food should be simple, plain and nourishing. The person who came into the world under a strong Aries influence should partake of foods which particularly go toward the building of nerve tissue and which nourish the brain. Cereals, nuts and fish are especially suitable.

Those who were born in this sign should avoid extremes. Alcoholic stimulants in more than quite minor amounts are inadvisable for the Aries native. Such stimulants express, in action, an inner negative. Worry and anxiety are powerful negatives which *can be overcome* by guiding the mind into definitely constructive paths. All of the disharmony resulting in physical disability which has been indicated, is directly due to predominance of the Aries negatives of thought. Intense concentration, combined with nervous anxiety, tends greatly to overstrain the brain. Upsetting conditions during meals should be especially avoided. Meals should be partaken of only when the individual has been able to induce a serene, calm attitude of mind.

It is completely within the reach of any Aries individual to produce *perfect balance of harmony* physically and mentally in his own being and thus to call to his aid the most powerful natural forces.

1977 Your personal life appears to be "taken up" with writings, words that are spoken, or communication in some form. Surprise situations are outstandingly indicated in April (eclipse) with close associates being responsible. I doubt if this year will end without your having many unexpected turn of events in addition to signing several legal papers as well as considerable importance being placed upon correspondence of some kind or telephone messages. Benefit through the efforts of another person are outstandingly indicated with much discussion about a will or an inheritance. I am certain in some unexpected manner your name is apt to receive prominent mention. When you review this period of your life, there is strong indication that you will see it as one of personal accomplishment, and one where you were favored!

1978 Consideration you give your relationships will benefit you, I believe, because as you help those around you to achieve a sense of THEIR worth, you will grow ever closer to a feeling of personal fulfillment. Other people strongly will influence your "income and outgo", in my opinion, or one person in particular. You are apt to feel sometimes that more is asked of you than your returns indicate, but through resourcefulness you surely will have special opportunities for giving more meaningful service in your world. Events touching you during 1978 are likely to lead you into surroundings which are more in keeping with your true desires. I know this will be a cycle of great illumination when you earnestly seek Divine Inspiration.

1979 Steps you take to improve your health will be exceptionally helpful this year, I feel, because you will have a tendency to overdo or overlook practices that will insure your well-being. In my opinion, you will have experiences that encourage you to use your imagination and knowledge even more effectively under this cycle. Reach for the greatest heights your mind can behold in your learning, and 1979 will bring a most gratifying "new beginning" for you, I am sure. You may establish certain associations for more purposeful reasons than some of those you have had in time now gone by because of your changing outlook this year. A younger person's influence or entertaining pursuit will prove exceptionally satisfying for you, I believe.

1980 The urge to "go ahead at any cost" can be very powerful within you at times now, but this year there are planetary influences which strongly caution against hasty steps; therefore, the wisdom of acting with greater forethought and restraint is clearly indicated as of great importance throughout this cycle. Otherwise you may experience deceptive matters involving partnerships or important affairs which will have to be retraced or done over again. Legal or technical entanglements may be discussed as to their validity related to another person. This will be a period when a need to uncover hidden secrets or information touching the possessions of others, possibly even insurance matters, could have a bearing upon attachments that are closely tied to you. Freedom of choice in these areas seems somewhat limited by conditions over which you have little control temporarily, but a breakthrough stemming from the support of another individual is likely to encourage promising plans involving new cooperative efforts. Patience during this cycle is apt to prove highly rewarding later, since other people will be likely to veer between extremes which will lead to dead ends.

1981 New interests are shown this year, forcing sudden plans concerned with the managing of your day-to-day affairs and finances, particularly matters which are of "joint" interest. I strongly feel you will later look back upon this period as one when you increased your efforts in order to organize your life in *one* direction. You are likely to develop an instinctive "sixth sense" for working out unusual ways to resolve dilemmas or impasses which temporarily disrupt particular mutual endeavors that are underway. There is a likelihood others might consider that some of your ideas will prove too inconvenient or impractical. Nevertheless, by consolidating your affairs as well as striving toward balanced, well thought-out plans, this year should be remembered for improving the results of important mutual undertakings.

1982 Startling changes related to "home" and your "position among others" will highlight this yearly cycle, in my opinion. An "uprooting" or turning point will be long remembered, because of a new direction emerging. Business interests are likely to be under a "protective hand" which will lead to benefits . . . but overconfidence or misplaced trust could "cancel out" gains that would otherwise be made. Unusual experiences, possibly through new friendships, are apt to broaden your outlook and encourage you to deepen your commitment to a "new way of life." I feel increased consideration due to the needs and wishes of close ties will be demanded of you at this time; a "drawing apart" or lack of cooperation could hamper your mutual interests.

1983 A "group" which symbolizes what you feel is your "mission in life" is likely to strongly attract your ardent participation during this dynamic cycle. A new educational program is indicated as having an elevating effect upon your spiritual awareness this year. Problems related to shared assets will undoubtedly prove temporarily frustrating, and a burdensome condition with respect to insurance, credit, inheritance, or another "life or death" matter is apt to surface around the middle of this year. However, an unexpected opportunity to travel or meet people from faraway places may lead to highly enlightening experiences that overshadow disappointments or uncertainties in other areas. To some extent, you will be thrown upon your "inner resources" this year.

1984 Entanglements involving relatives or neighbors may arise unexpectedly around the middle of this forecast period. It will probably seem as though you are "in the middle" of problems that originate among other people, for a short time. During the first seven or eight months of this year, "separations" could bring unusual changes that are unplanned. However, your name is apt to appear in the "limelight" to some degree, so that "new directions" may offer a way to throw yourself into an inspiring endeavor — one which you can wholeheartedly embrace! A considerable degree of reliance upon your own powers and abilities is indicated, and I believe you will "start over" in a way which later years will show is the beginning of deep emotional satisfaction.

SUMMATION (Aries)

In many ways, looking back from 1984, I believe you will hardly recognize the person you were in the middle of the '70's! This is another way of saying that the coming few years will be fraught with great change and momentous strides forward toward the "peak" of your abilities! I have always found that people born under the birth sign of Aries can be the leaders others look up to and follow willingly, and you are likely to share in this admirable birth trait. In the years to come, some formidable obstacles will temporarily stand in your way, I am sure. These will largely be of a delaying or restrictive nature and will probably arise through the agency of other people. However, your strong planetary indications for the early 1980's powerfully show that exercising patience during the times that seem to hold you back from your goals will later enable you to take advantage of fortuitous circumstances becoming an aid in your efforts to "win out!"

This will be a period of growing emotional maturity, so that you will begin to understand the true value attached to those who stir your deepest feelings. Aries has often been termed an "inspirational" sign. During this forecast period, I believe "inspiring flashes" will frequently give rise to new and unusual ideas that will lead you to gratifying experiences of an emotional nature as well as enlightening spiritual awareness.

A changing pattern is likely to sweep you into a different kind of "home life," setting your footsteps on a path that gives a new insight as to your responsibilities. Like a thread which is interwoven into each of your experiences, a search for companionship and the loving joys of caring and being cared for will mark this span of your life.

From mid 1978 and during the following two years, a cycle emphasizes the need for greater attention to sensible health "rules." This will be a period when digestive upsets could be somewhat frequent unless an effort is made to avert this disturbance by observing proper dietary habits.

I strongly feel that a culmination will be reached during this forecast period — a turning point from which you will emerge as a more vital and dynamic person! There is every indication that you are upon the threshold of one of the most important periods of your life, when the knowledge gained from past experiences will be the "key" to a bright new future and the "opening door" that will lead you into a happier and more successful life!

The planet Mars is said to *rule* the sign Aries, and Venus the sign Taurus. The qualities attributed to both these planets are most likely to be apparent in those who come into the world during the period of this cusp. The attributes of all the periods of the year are most completely and aptly illustrated in "The Ancient Gods and Goddesses of Greece".

Those who were born in this cusp, are possessed, to an unusual degree, of *brilliant intuition.* This quality which is quite observable in natives of Aries seems to blend with the Taurus vibrations in such a way as to add to them. The intuition is, however, often combined with the unyielding nature, the "stubbornness" of the latter sign. The native of this cusp loves association with others. He is fond of entertaining and from the Taurus vibration he receives that which gives him a particular liking for company during meal time. He is especially fond of surprising others with his lavish hospitality, and delights in entertaining royally, particularly in matters which are related to food. Those who were born under this combination of vibrations are independent to a quite marked degree. Often the native will go considerably out of his way to display kindnesses to others but is quite reluctant to ask favors for himself; seeming to resent the possibility that he may be under obligation to another.

While those who come into the world under the combined vibrations which result in this cusp are not easily influenced, they are likely to be quite broad in their views. As a rule they are extremely practical, although the intuitional and aggressive qualities of Aries not infrequently causes them to be more venturesome than most people. The native of this cusp seems particularly to like to give advice to his associates. Sometimes his fondness for doing so prompts him to offer suggestions or criticisms which have not been requested and which may, perhaps, be unwelcome, yet to a far greater degree than is true of most people the advice is likely to be valuable.

The true native of this cusp period is inclined to be impatient of obstacles. That is true, of course, of those who come into the world under the full vibration of Aries. The native of this cusp, however, has strong tendencies to become violently angry with those who oppose him. His disposition is to override obstacles and not infrequently he has greater tenacity than does the pure Aries. When launched on a course of action, particularly if his fighting instincts have been challenged, he can pursue his course regardless of any opposition or obstacles. Sometimes he is regarded as unreasonable by his associates. Despite this fact, however, he is often extremely successful in carrying through his ideas, even when he finds it necessary to override the opposition of many others.

The native of this cusp likes ease and comfort. He desires that his surroundings be *as he chooses them,* and is very likely to achieve his wishes in that connection. He has natural gifts which are very powerful in nature. He has the ability to develop the *intuition* and aggressiveness of Aries. These qualities combined with the *tenacity* of Taurus enable him to *follow an objective* once conceived.

The birthsign TAURUS
April 21st to May 22nd

If you were born between April 21st and May 22nd, your birthsign is Taurus. In describing it we shall endeavor to encompass all the qualities and characteristics which are part of this basic harmonic or birth vibration. In common with all the other signs, there are positive and negative factors in the sign itself. Sometimes these appear to be contradictory. The birth chart, however, indicates the state of development which the individual has reached, and consequently shows the extent to which either the positives or negatives will predominate.

In referring to positives and negatives, *virtues* and *faults* are meant. All *real* virtues are constructive in nature; they harmonize with the constructive vibrations of the universe. All faults are negatives; harmonizing with the negative vibrations.

Among the Egyptians the sacred Apis bull was considered to be representative of the psychological factors EMBODIED in this vibration. The ancient Chinese called the symbol of the sign *The Golden Ox*. Taurus is representative of the Bible tribe of Simeon, which is one of the original tribes of Israel or one of the fundamental types of human beings. This sign was the original *bull* or Baal of the Assyrians. In the case of these peoples it was sometimes referred to as the *Golden Calf,* or the *Sacred Bull.*

The Persians of a day long past designated the signs of the zodiac by letters of the alphabet. "A" stood for Taurus. That was when this sign, instead of Aries, marked the vernal equinox. Taurus is called the *House of Venus* which means that in the hidden world of vibration the qualities of Venus are basic in the sign. Taurus is feminine. The stone which has similar vibrations is the emerald; the flower which most expresses the vibrations of the sign is the jonquil.

The sign is referred to as earthy, fixed, moist, cold, feminine, melancholy, bestial, semi-fruitful, of short ascension. These words express the qualities of Taurus — in a measure, both positive and negative. Represented by its symbol, the sign conveys reserve force, stability, endurance and perseverance. These qualities, transmuted into constructive effort, provide the most powerful of foundations for happiness in life. The *pure* essence of Taurus in physical characteristics produces

15

one who is rather full of face with rounded features, short flat, rather full lips and a very healthy appearance. The birthsign alone is not sufficient to produce the pure Taurus appearance physically but when Taurus rises at birth, in other words, when one is born at daybreak, the physical characteristics of the sign are likely to be obvious. The symbol of Taurus is graphically illustrative of the unyielding disposition which is a fundamental part of this birth influence.

As is the case with all signs of the zodiac, individuals who were born under the sign Taurus may express different qualities outwardly than those of the birthsign itself. One should always remember that the subject of planetary influence is extremely complex, as are human beings. Innumerable factors in human life are involved. There seems very little doubt that a preponderance of people were born at a time when their own sign was rising and consequently, their personalities tend strongly to express their own birthsign. It *is* entirely possible, however, for one who was born in the sign to be less companionable, congenial and easy-going than are most of those who were born under the same sign.

This sign, of course, is of the earth trinity — the first; the second being Virgo and the last Capricorn, which is the extreme north cardinal point. It should be remembered that the early sages and wise men in referring to the various signs as being of fire, earth, air and water were not alluding to the physical elements at all. They did not mean the seemingly fixed, substantial and solid earth upon which we walk. As to the earth itself, it has no real permanent meaning. It is made up of *vibration* — motion — of the atoms and the energies *within* the atoms which are in fact not *substance* at all. However, the earth signs all tend to be as one might imagine the earth — substantial or *"down-to-earth"*, so to speak. Natives of the sign themselves are *"earthy"*, solid, and steady. They are not likely to be emotionally unstable except in rare cases — as a result of *"earthy"* drives.

In a larger sense the sign rules the throat. In particular this means that the negatives, or the *faults* of the sign, when strongly given expression to, have a direct adverse effect upon the physical mechanisms which are associated with that part of the body. The positive qualities, on the other hand, affect these parts beneficently, giving good vocal cords and often the ability to sing well. Specifically, it is considered that those parts of the physical body most affected by this basic harmonic are the upper part of the esophagus, palate, vocal cords, uvula, thyroid gland (this is particularly significant as the thyroid gland is a very important part of the Taurus influence), the parotids and the tonsils.

It should be readily understood that *all* of the qualities mentioned will not be marked with an *equal* degree of prominence in any one person. The Taurus native, however, will usually recognize the presence of all the traits, though some may be submerged and of minor import, while others are more prominent.

You are quite inclined to be self-possessed. Ordinarily you are easy to get along with, but when aroused you can become extremely angry and are likely to be unyielding. It is not natural for you to seek the advice of other people to any great extent and, perhaps as a result of this, others may think you are at times *difficult* to understand. You have qualities which would make you dependable, practical, and worthy of the highest trust in carrying out undertakings which are entrusted to you.

The native of Taurus, when once started toward an objective in life rarely ever comes to doubt this goal, and consequently is extremely likely to achieve it. Those of your sign are especially fitted for practical occupations. They are not inclined to be creative or to originate new ideas. Their inclination rather is to be imitative, and they have the ability to *carry out* ideas which are conceived by others, and which may be entirely theory until they come into the hands of a Taurus native. There is no doubt that those who were born under a predominant Taurus influence have extremely *active* senses. Their physical appetites are potentially strong and they enjoy things of wholly material nature. While Taurus is a sign which imparts very powerful qualities of execution (the ability to carry things through), there is no doubt that the paths of Taurus people are, in many cases, extremely thorny. The negatives of the sign often cause them to allow passion to interfere with their judgment.

To a considerable degree you are light-hearted and fond of the humorous side of life. By nature you have a warm personality and are inclined to be witty, bright, and fond of things which relate to gayety, being on the whole a very companionable sort of person. You can be quite winning in manner and are likely to be possessed of *unusual magnetism.* People who came into the world in the sign Taurus are apt to be extremely popular. You undoubtedly enjoy many friendships and take a great deal of pleasure in the companionship of others. You love to entertain and are fond of all the *good things* of life. You enjoy good food but much prefer company at meal time than to be alone. Your tendency is to be quite definite in your opinions and ideas. Once your mind is finally made up it is difficult for anyone else to change it. Before you have come to a complete conclusion and formulated definite ideas upon a subject, however, it is rather easy to influence you, particularly when appeals are made to your emotions. Impulses in that connection have ever been pit-falls for the Taurus native. However, this is true only when thought processes have developed along negative lines.

You frequently form judgments of people quickly. You have strong likes and dislikes but occasionally you find that your first judgment has been made too rapidly. You undoubtedly have an active, strong brain and the ability to learn about matters in which you are interested, although you are not, by instinct, inclined to be fond of study for its own sake. You have a good memory. In practical affairs your memory probably is quite active. You can remember to do things of detailed nature which would escape the attention of many other people. When you are once aroused to true constructive effort you have *unusual persistency* in your mental application. Your tendency is to be, in a measure, secretive about your own affairs. In other words, you are inclined to be close-mouthed. In that connection you are seldom inclined to talk at length. There is a strong tendency for those who were born under your particular solar vibration to be guided by *intuition*. This intuition is accurate and dependable when the thought vibrations are of constructive nature.

You are by nature an extremely loyal friend but in association with others you

17

are usually desirous of having your own way. However, though you have this capacity for very warm and loyal friendship, you can also be a *bitter enemy* and do not easily forgive or forget an injury. You have a strong power of will and it is possible for you to overcome obstacles or to adapt yourself to almost any condition of life. You are inclined to be fearful of physical pain but when your determination is aroused you can face the greatest threat or difficulty without flinching.

Your inclination is to be quite fond of physical things. This tends to enjoyment of life but it should be balanced by the spiritual, which will bring about the proper degree of control. You like things of an artistic and dramatic nature and you delight in activities which embody an element of drama. It is probably not extremely difficult for you to obtain money or to make it, and you are not at all inclined to be miserly. In practical ways you are generous and it is not unlikely that at times you have taken on responsibilities which are not properly yours. However, this is an expression of a powerful positive vibration which would be extremely helpful in aiding *you* toward achievement! Your natural tendency is to be extremely self-reliant, and you have a tremendous amount of patience which will carry you through to success in almost anything you undertake, providing the negatives which are part of your sign do not become too pronounced.

Words which express the constructive vibrations of this sign are: persistent, self-reliant, steady, persevering, kindly, magnetic, fearless, careful, practical, trustworthy, composed, constructive, helpful, unswerving. Words which express the negatives are: stolid, exacting, stubborn, dogmatic, selfish, lazy, amorous, earthy, covetous, unyielding. All people who were born in the sign Taurus are on the way toward development of the constructive factors of the sign. The negative tendencies which are present are the result of the animal nature which is strongly a part of the sign. Taurus is, in essence, vigorous, determined and enduring. For that reason the physical equipment is more in need of control.

This sign is lovable and kindly in its higher attributes and the definite turning of the mind to the constructives, which the words previously given express, will enable the native to manifest the most desirable conditions of life. People who came into the world under this solar influence have potentialities which can lead to the greatest good. On the other hand there are equally strong instincts which sometimes lead to extreme evil. It should be borne in mind, however, that evil is referred to here, not in its orthodox sense but as *negatives which tend toward the destructive*.

The consequences of the Taurus negatives are great. The full power of the Taurus influence produces powerful animalistic tendencies. These tendencies are often marked from birth. Though the highly evolved native has learned to direct and control these instincts there are, in every one who was born in this sign, powerful forces which are material and physical in nature. These forces when allowed to develop without restraint, tend to produce a material selfishness to the exclusion of the spiritual. They produce results in the physical body, and upon the affairs of life as well, in harmony with their destructive nature. Above every sign of the zodiac the aim of the person who received a strong Taurus influence at birth, should be toward *self-control* in its fullest sense.

The undeveloped Taurus individual is susceptible to powerful fits of passion and in anger he is almost completely irresponsible and unreasonable. Resistance and opposition arouse him to almost demoniacal manifestations of violent anger. Angry passions upset the chemistry of the body to such an extent as to produce sickness and shorten the life greatly. The lower type of Taurus native is domineering and demanding to the extent that he is dangerous to cross. Among this type of Taurus individuals are those who like their own comfort and ease *above everything else.* Those who are closely associated with such a person, will find life quite difficult. Such people are very exacting, demanding on the part of others, every concession to their own wishes. The man of the sign Taurus who is unevolved will be immovably stubborn, set in his ways, and will insist upon being complete master in his own home. The one real way to development of the higher nature of those who received the Taurus influence at birth is in the acquirement of gentleness, mildness and tolerance. These are the particular qualities which should be striven for in those who realize the lessons which man must learn.

To a considerable degree the majority of people who came into the world under this influence desire to act constructively but the weakness of the sign lies in the strong love nature and the tendency toward uncontrolled passion. They are also likely to be quite easily led by members of the opposite sex. The sign is *ruled* by the planet Venus as previously mentioned, which, combined with the *earthy* qualities of Taurus, leads to extremely strong desires for luxury and the gratification of the senses. It is extremely important for people who receive a strong Taurus influence at birth to strive to understand their own natures and to cultivate the higher attributes of spirit. The basic influence has within itself the strength of determination to overcome these negatives and those who came into the world under this vibration can, if they choose to do so, learn to exercise complete control, *first* of the processes of thought and in natural sequence, the physical. It is not for a moment suggested that one should renounce earthly joys but merely that they should be directed into constructive channels.

The native of this sign has excellent judgment when his mind is turned to constructive activities and when he depends upon his own inner inspiration. For that reason it is usually better for him to make decisions when he arises in the morning. This is more true of the sign Taurus than it is of many, if not most of the others. When once the native has mastered the materialistic tendencies in his nature and has gained *control* over his passions and appetites he may well be likened to a powerful locomotive, possessed of tremendous *reserves of strength and energy* and *capable of overcoming all obstacles!*

WOMEN OF TAURUS

The qualities of the planet Venus are accentuated in the women of this sign. This means that the traits which have been attributed to Venus are likely to predominate. Women who were born in this sign have marked qualities of personality which give them charm and fascination. They are usually quite attractive to men. As a rule they are well-formed and being symmetrically proportioned are likely to be graceful.

They become unusually faithful wives and mothers. The woman of Taurus, it has often been said by students of cosmic vibration, will hold her home together when every circumstance of life appears to be trying to destroy it. Qualities of sympathy and emotional kindliness dwell in this sign, and women who were born while the influence was operating strongly, have amiable natures, and are markedly feminine, clinging and warm-hearted. They are almost invariably extremely fond of children and have a noticeable ability to handle them. They are sympathetic and understanding. It is a trait of women who come into the world under a strong Taurus influence to be able to cajole and caress children until a remarkable control is exercised. They win the confidence of youngsters in this manner and seem to have a natural understanding of the juvenile mind.

Very often in a superficial judgment of women who were born in this sign, without knowledge of their inner nature, there fails to be an understanding of the deeply rooted *tenacity* and stubbornness of the sign which can be unyielding. This is not intended to indicate that the quality of stubbornness is by any means necessarily a negative quality. People who have definite convictions along certain lines and believe in something quite strongly will, if they are in any way to *express* their convictions in action, *be* stubborn. No one who has achieved outstandingly fails to be obstinate to some degree. The stubbornness of Taurus women, however, sometimes comes as a surprise to associates. It may not be manifest at all, when they are not directly opposed. However, individuals of some of the other birthsigns who are themselves inherently inflexible in pursuing their own objectives, sometimes are amazed to find that they have encountered a person who is as unyielding as they themselves. For this reason, of course, many marriages of the sign tend to become filled with strife. It is well for anyone who is associated with a Taurus woman to know when to *give ground* rather than to try to *force* issues.

Venus, of course, is the planet of beauty and of love. It imparts to the women of this sign a fondness for the luxurious circumstances of life. They have marked ability to perform laborious tasks and to continue tenaciously in anything they have undertaken, but their *instinct* is to prefer the good things of life, such as food, comfort and dress, combined with pleasant companionship — rather than hard work. Women of Taurus are dexterous and capable in the use of brush or pen in decorative endeavors. They are successful in business occupations as cashiers, clerks, and bookkeepers, and have an aptitude for the practical affairs of life, such as the efficient handling of money. When there is a strong influence at birth from air or water signs, they have an aptitude for literary endeavors. They are also capable milliners and dressmakers. Anything having to do with food products is a favorable outlet for their abilities. As a rule, the Taurus woman is better satisfied in her own home than in business.

In common with adults of the sign, youngsters who came into the world under a strong Taurus vibration are often quick-tempered, and the quality of stubbornness is accentuated. A child of this sign is likely to be so constituted that he may show strong tendencies toward violent anger when opposed or restrained. He is then apt to fly into a rage and it may be extremely difficult to control him. The youngster of Taurus is almost invariably a passionate, vital child, full of life and likely to be very active in getting into difficulties. Not infrequently the boys of this sign are filled with the *lust of combat* in association with playmates. The parents of the Taurus boy, as a result, sometimes find themselves confronted by the accusing mothers of his playmates, even though these playmates may be older and larger.

The Taurus child is almost always susceptible to kindness and sympathy. Should physical punishment be administered while the youngster of this sign is in a state of anger, it arouses his opposition still more, and usually completely fails in its purpose. Parents of the Taurus youngster should wait until the child has reached a state of calm before attempting to deal with him. Reasoning is always more effective then, but it should be combined with kindness and sympathy.

Sometimes children who came into the world under a strong influence from this sign are not morally courageous, and so may turn to prevarication in the attempt to conceal actions which they are sure will meet with parental disapproval. They can be *very evasive* in escaping the consequences of their acts, but even when they admittedly do things which have been forbidden, they will persist in doing them openly. When they are directly opposed or coerced to refrain from doing certain things (or to do certain things), their stubbornness can become so manifest that they get to a point of being almost impossible to deal with, or to change. Handling them requires a great deal of understanding and sympathy for their personal concepts and their own desires in life. The Taurus native invariably has these qualities to some degree within himself, and for one who was born at a time when another sign was rising there can be extreme conflict between the two, and the male of the sign (even where there is direct opposition) will sometimes be extremely devious while his inherent stubbornness is not altered in any degree. He may not express his tenacity outwardly but whatever has been said to him has not changed him at all. He may *skirt the issue* and take devious means to conceal his inner convictions but in the Taurus native they are invariably *still there*. Harsh treatment and absence of affectionate understanding on the part of parents will naturally add to that trait.

The tendency of the child of Taurus to feel he must have all he wants of everything to gratify his physical desires is likely to be marked. One cannot, however, change this tendency by force. Forbidding the child arbitrarily in such cases has little effect. His mind must be turned into actively constructive channels. The Taurus youngster is possessed of an extremely happy and carefree disposition, and often he does not appear to be fond of responsibility. Frequently these youngsters do not display much aptitude or liking for study. If their interests are really aroused, however, they can be persevering students, yet they should be allowed to choose their own fields of learning as long as their activities are constructive.

MARRIAGES OF TAURUS

Neither the men or the women who were born in the sign of Taurus should ever worry about being *passed by* when it comes to love. The ruling planet, of course, is Venus which symbolizes or actually bestows a very affectionate nature as well as a fondness for luxurious conditions and surroundings. A large number of people who received a strong influence from this sign at birth have quite early love affairs which in many cases result in marriage. The young woman of Taurus is perhaps more likely to plunge hastily into matrimony than one born in any other sign of the zodiac. The love nature, of course, is *strongly marked* and because of her sympathetic, emotional nature, she frequently ventures greatly. One finds a great many natives of Taurus who have entered into two marriages. This is most likely to be the case when a very early marriage takes place under conditions of impulsive haste and adventurous seeking. When there are two marriages in the life of a Taurus native, the second is likely to prove happy and lasting. Unlike those who were born in some of the other signs of the zodiac, the native of Taurus learns by such an experience.

Undoubtedly the girls of this solar vibration should be carefully instructed by their parents in matters pertaining to sex. There should be sympathetic understanding and kindliness, rather than arbitrary rule. Under conditions of too strict supervision, they are likely to resort to deception. It is, of course, equally true that the boys and young men of Taurus are likely to injure their careers or lives by contracting unsuitable, impulsive marriages. Natives of this sign should marry one who is congenial, companionable, and who has an understanding of their inner nature. However, when there is a combination of influences at birth with one of the adjoining signs, either Aries or Gemini, there may be considerable deviation from the general point of view of the birthsign itself. The individual may be extremely intellectual as is Aries, or quick mentally and readily suspicious and devious as is Gemini. One who seeks to understand a Taurus native needs to recall the inner *unyielding* quality of the sign and the dedication of natives to things which they believe to be right or true. Of course, anyone who has the idea that the individual of Taurus is likely to be very easily dealt with, changed, directed or controlled is likely to find himself mistaken.

To a considerable degree, the sign Scorpio (October 24th – November 22nd) is harmonious with Taurus from a matrimonial standpoint. Still, there is some likelihood of temperamental differences between these two signs, in people who are undeveloped. The nature of both Taurus and Scorpio is strong, often stubborn, so that when there is an opposing point of view, neither will give way. However, Scorpio is probably the most harmonious in a general way, of all the signs. Virgo (August 23rd – September 23rd), which is an earth sign, is also harmonious, probably at least to a nearly equal degree. The sign Libra (September 24th – October 23rd) has much in common with Taurus due to the fact primarily, that both are ruled by the planet Venus. Most of the others lack the fundamental qualities productive of harmony which these possess.

The Venus influence is likely to cause some unrest in domestic life. When natives of Taurus, men or women, feel that they are being imposed upon or that someone else is trying to influence them unduly, the contentiousness of the sign is aroused – and the frail bark of matrimony is sometimes wrecked on the shores of discord!

The true Taurus native has the noteworthy ability to judge public opinion, and for this reason there is a strong aptitude, in very practical ways, along political lines. Many outstanding men in public life received a strong Taurus vibration at birth. There is a singular fitness in this sign for all practical occupations, particularly those which have to do with supplying the daily necessities of life to other people, such as shelter, food, and clothing.

The Taurus influence, itself, does not impart strong creative abilities, but gives those who were born in it the *tenacity* necessary to carry things through. Occupations having to do with construction are especially favorable for them. Many men of this sign have been outstandingly successful as building contractors. They have the ability to execute with perfection the detailed plans of others. Those who were born in this sign have become engaged quite successfully in mechanical pursuits that are related to engineering. The Taurus native should be in an occupation which requires mingling with others, which gives expression to the special qualities of the sign, except when the birth chart clearly and definitely shows a powerful inspirational source. He should, in short, be engaged in a *practical* occupation, one which requires qualities of execution, rather than originality of concept.

Due to the influence of the planet Venus however, there may be a fondness for endeavors of artistic nature. In association with practical occupations, there is frequently evidence of creative talent. This sometimes is greatly increased at birth by a strong planet in another sign. Therefore, some natives of Taurus are quite successful as designers of landscapes, of wearing apparel, and in other similar creative fields. They can be very successful in semi-artistic occupations, although the practical part of their natures generally leads them into fields which, though partially artistic, supply a practical necessity. Photography (especially commercial phases), and designing utilitarian objects (furniture and decorations) are favorable fields for Taurus people.

They are often extremely good in the rendition of music but under the surface one finds they usually have the same practical, conservative qualities as those who are engaged in completely prosaic occupations. The people of Taurus are often very successful in occupations that require salesmanship, but usually they are better fitted for positions which require others to come to them, rather than to call upon customers. When they are engaged in such work, it is much better for them to call on the same people repeatedly. Finance is extremely favorable for the Taurus native. He is often an outstanding success in banking, or in the handling of other funds. Many have been extremely successful in working out large corporate ideas and pushing the plans embodied to successful completion. This is a field in which their powerful reserves of energy come into play.

One of the principal qualities of Taurus natives is the trait of being *slow but sure*. They have the patience to await opportunity, and it is extremely difficult to hurry or force them into a false position. They carefully consider every aspect and will refuse to take any step about which they are uncertain.

DISHARMONY OF TAURUS

The condition ordinarily referred to as disease, is always preceded by or associated with negatives in thought processes. For that reason, disease is dealt with here, in that manner. The negatives most often accentuated in this sign have previously been referred to. The *earthiness* of Taurus frequently causes a fondness for rich food. The native of this sign often overeats, and if the thought processes are uncontrolled he makes little attempt to restrain the tendency toward indulgence in all things of physical nature. Food which is too spicy and stimulating, as well as alcoholic beverages, are usually quite inadvisable for a native of this sign. The negatives which produce a desire for alcohol in Taurus people are not the same negatives which produce similar desires in those who were born in many of the other signs. They are, in Taurus, purely a desire for physical sensation. There is a tendency in the sign to obesity; and as a result of overindulgence in stimulating and heating foods, all the other carnal desires are stimulated. It is not meant to infer that tendencies along these lines should be completely eliminated, but guidance of the thought processes so as to bring them completely under control, is a definite necessity.

As previously expressed, the formation of negative thought vibrations will inevitably produce their like in the physical world. Overeating, passion and other stimulating things of earthly nature are often quite injurious to the native of this sign, as they react upon the heart. This sign rules the throat; and Taurus, inherently, has great vitality, but the negatives are likely to produce in the native, disorders of the throat, and in turn the heart, the kidneys, liver and spleen. Because of physical action tending toward excess, rheumatism is likely to occur. The negatives produce trouble with the glands of the neck, mumps, quinsy, goitre, and apoplexy. Natives of the sign, while they are normally of happy disposition are susceptible to extreme moods of depression; accompanied quite frequently by headaches and general physical inharmony. The Taurus native is also susceptible to dropsical conditions.

The basically unyielding quality of the sign sometimes manifests itself in personal relationships. If these are inharmonious, the native sometimes carries his concepts to extremes in his thought processes. He may become very bitter toward another person with whom he is associated and, as a result, he may go to great extremes. This sometimes comes about in matrimony. Almost invariably the resentment and bitterness which is involved results in greater physical disharmony for the native. It renders him much more susceptible to the physical disharmonies which have been referred to, and again it must be stressed that whenever he dwells upon conditions of bitterness or resentment at great length — no matter how justified he may be, the results in his physical organism can be averted only by altering his habitual thought patterns of a negative nature.

On the other hand, when the natives of this sign turn their minds to constructive thinking and activity (which inevitably results in *control* of the physical), they develop a balance of harmony which produces the most vital energy. While physical media are helpful in the cure of what is ordinarily called disease, they can only be helpful temporarily, unless the native of the sign induces himself to produce constructive vibrations of thought, which the nature of his birthsign *enables him to do!*

24

1977 Small, hidden problems possibly in the nature of physical "well-being" are indicated as "cropping up" under this passing cycle, and irritations in "carrying on" certain duties (eclipse). For a time you may be "knocked off your stride" because of "one" careless word — or act — so I would caution you to be wary of speaking without careful consideration of the possible end results. A "turnover" in your relationships will lead to a more solid foundation through "a conclusion" reached in this cyclic period — leaving "a nightmare" behind and the finding of far greater security with more satisfaction out of life than you dreamed possible!

1978 New people are apt to be around you soon, prompting you to use more of your own resources and initiative in situations where you might have depended, at times, on others in the past. You may take a "new lease" in an area of your life as the result of your concern over "problems" you feel you know something about and feel you can help to correct in 1978. I believe you will have opportunities for improving your sense of material security this year, frequently through your associations with "neighboring" places, close ties, and "communications." You are apt to take a rather serious view of pursuits you ordinarily participate in for the sake of pleasure. Someone who needs your understanding will strengthen your pride in your deeds, I am sure.

1979 A growing sense of responsibility toward some of your creative talents may alter a few of your previous goals during this planetary period. You are likely to achieve a greater sense of satisfaction from endeavors you undertake independently than many of those involving other people, because a number of your associations probably will drift away or appear diverse now toward something important to you. There are apt to be sets of circumstances you think are misleading in 1979, and for this reason you might be wise to temporarily treat security matters less trustingly. You will make your "home environment" more pleasing as a result of unexpected changes, in my opinion.

1980 Younger people may seem to pose some rather stubborn problems for a time during the early part of this year; in all likelihood there will be a "turning point" that reverses an attitude, or demands that appear difficult to satisfy. Electrical changes involving partnerships or other close ties may be the rule rather than the exception under these strong planetary influences, creating new arrangements in connection with your daily routines. Possibly never again will you have such an impelling urge to change and to find an outlet from monotonous day-to-day tasks . . . and change may come through some plan you have held in your mind for a long time. A desire to expand a creative idea is apt to mark this year as a time when one of your skills or talents will lead to particular advantages later.

1981 You will be more inclined to view health and physical well-being concerns soberly, I believe, under this new planetary trend, with a strong interest in seeking out methods you feel will be helpful in this area (Saturn's transit). Past practices which favored

TAURUS

healthful conditions are likely to be recalled, and these are indicated as being advantageous for others close to you as well as for yourself. Opportunity through work as well as in connection with other people promises great benefits and security under this powerful trend. Although there will be times when a lack of cooperation seems to "drag" your daily activities down, this is a temporary cycle, and patience with restricting or delaying circumstances will "win the day" for you as time moves on, in my opinion.

1982 January, June, and July of this year are indicated as important "turning points" involving relations with friends, neighbors, or relatives. In all likelihood, there will be significant "beginnings and endings" in these areas that will have repercussions in your "home" surroundings. Problems connected with transportation may temporarily force adjustments not completely to your liking. An unexpected "twist" is apt to influence spending or other money interests, something in the nature of an "accounting" to someone who shares financial interests. During much of this year, your "mood" is likely to be one of greater friendliness, cooperation, and "outgoing" . . . this in turn will tend to evoke similar responses from your close associates. Something of a legal nature may be brought to a satisfying conclusion near this time in your life.

1983 Money interests are likely to undergo changes which demand quick adjustment during this year. "Get rich quick" schemes may be proposed to you, but they are likely to collapse with suddenness . . . although there could be an element of "timing" enabling you to profit from speculative ventures. However, I feel this is a rather "tricky" influence, and a considerable degree of care and investigation should be devoted before you commit funds to "chancy" propositions. Insurance, taxes, credit, or possibly inheritances will be highlighted at this time, and someone close could be the "saving factor" enabling you to emerge with benefits. Close personal relationships are apt to bring additional responsibilities that will need to be met with practical and perservering efforts, although you will come out all right.

1984 Until around August of this year, you are apt to be "surrounded" by quite dynamic influences — as well as people who display an energetic interest in your personal affairs and the progress you are making. I feel associates will "put more pressures" upon you, in connection with mutual endeavors, and some sharp conflicts could arise involving your desire not to be "pushed." Your "sense of justice" will probably be quite strong at this time, but it may be difficult at times to extend this instinctive feeling in matters related to the interests of other people. Obligations with respect to associates will likely seem unusually burdensome but only for a short time.

SUMMATION (Taurus)

Your sense of responsibility — both to yourself and to those who share close ties — is likely to blossom forth during this forecast period . . . encouraging you to seek the "lessons" that experience can teach. I don't mean this interpretation to sound as though you will be over-burdened by "obligations," but rather that you will be put in a better position to understand how to benefit from the responsibilities that come your way.

Throughout much of this forecast cycle, I believe there will be an unexpected "turnover" in your association with other people; that is, old ties will be "dropped" to be replaced by new relationships . . . especially with persons who have unusual "facets" in their personalities! It seems to me that you will experience sudden attachments during this trend, and in some instances you will not want to be "tied down," so I anticipate that some of your associations will end as quickly as they began.

You are likely to be "shaken out" of old routines or interests, to the extent that your outlook becomes increasingly broader, leading you into "changes" you once would have thought almost impossible. I strongly feel that new associations will play a strong role in turning your path toward a different direction!

During the closing two or three years of this period, major changes related to money or other assets held jointly are indicated. Some of these may be in the nature of "reversals" from previous policies, but I am sure that you will be capable of any adjustments needed at this time, because your natural outlook toward money and possessions will be practical!

As this forecast cycle draws to a close, a greatly increased desire to travel will be manifested. I believe 1983 and 1984 will be marked by exciting prospects of new learning and an uplift in your spirits that will help carry you to new heights!

Those who were born in this cusp are strongly under the combined vibrations of the planets Venus and Mercury. All of those who derive from the gracious Venus those qualities associated with the name, are possessed of winning mannerisms and easy, graceful appearances. Venus imparts a love of beautiful things, combined with an inherent desire for artistic expression. Mercury's influence increases the talent in art as well as music. It imparts, in particular, an ability to understand languages and to speak well. The *manners* of those who were born in this cusp are likely to be quite refined and their personalities pleasant. It is desirable for them to be active. They are by nature energetic and should have an outlet for their nervous energies. The sign Taurus, from which the native receives considerable influence, imparts strong tendencies toward companionability, but often an unshakable determination. The individual who was born within this cusp is quite likely to be "hot-headed". He has a great fondness for the good things of life due to the influence of Taurus. It is not unusual for him to become rather stout as a result.

He is likely to possess a basic talent in artistic matters though he may not become engaged in such endeavors. The native is frequently inventive, a thinker, and an orator. When he is not actively employed and does not have something to which he can devote his energies he has a tendency to become pessimistic and even morbid. He has a great deal of pride and he hates to ask others for favors. He would much rather entertain someone else or give to another, than to feel that he is under obligation to anyone. At times he can be very secretive about his own affairs — or "close-mouthed". At such times his powers of concentration are remarkable and he can plan deeply and clearly. There are other times, however, when he feels an inclination to talk more extensively and to take other people into his confidence. At such times his mental processes appear to be somewhat confused and he has difficulty deciding definitely and clearly what he desires to do. There are natural forces which he can use if he will. These forces are potentially capable of aiding him immeasurably to accomplish his aims and desires. They are called into play by the clearness of his constructive imagining, which can be guided scientifically and combined with certain color forms. They then have a tremendous effect upon his life.

The native has much ability along practical lines. Anything which has to do with selling or which combines the practical, such as building construction, with a certain amount of artistic expression, is a good outlet for his abilities. He is usually fond of his home and quite demonstrative and affectionate in his domestic surroundings. He has inherent ability to be quite faithful and loyal to those whom he loves, but when his associations are too material they have a powerful effect, leading him toward a completely materialistic outlook. The Gemini influences are diametrically opposed. The individual of this cusp is likely to be extremely quick mentally, and he combines the plodding, persistent Taurus nature with the changeability of Gemini. As a result he may be very difficult to understand.

The birthsign GEMINI
May 23rd to June 22nd

Your birthsign is Gemini if you were born between May 23rd and June 22nd. As with the other signs of the zodiac, we shall, as fully as possible, describe all the qualities which are inherent in this solar vibration, both positive and negative. The extent to which these qualities are present in you is indicated in your birth chart, but you will recognize them, though some may be almost entirely over-shadowed by other traits of your sign. Gemini has a direct connection with, and therefore effect upon, the shoulders and arms.

You are of the Bible tribe of Benjamin, which means that your characteristics are of the nature which is (mythologically, it is generally assumed) associated with that original tribe of Israel. The symbol of the sign is the Twins, which is strikingly illustrative of the quality which marks the character of Gemini people. Of all the signs of the zodiac they can probably come nearest to holding two thoughts in their minds at the same time. Castor and Pollux of Greek mythology were representative of this sign. They were constantly at war with each other, that fact being symbolical of the dual Gemini nature.

The planet which bestows the characteristics attributed to it upon this sign is Mercury. In the mythology of the ancients, the *"Messenger of the Gods"* of that name was extremely quick, alert, and versatile. Those are marked characteristics of most people who came into the world under a strong influence from Gemini. They are alert and vivacious in temperament, and above everything else, they are versatile, Primarily, the essence of this sign is intellectual. Gemini is referred to as airy, dual, common, flexed, masculine, positive, barren, sanguine, double-bodied, and of short ascension. These words in a measure express the positive and negative factors which are basically a part of this vibration. The gem which has vibrations harmoni-ous with the pure Gemini vibrations is the agate; the flower is the trailing arbutus.

There seems very little doubt that people invariably have the qualities of their birthsign, although these qualities may in some cases be quite deeply hidden. Often, people who are closely associated with them are not aware that they do possess these qualities as they sometimes are not very clearly manifested. An individual who was born in this sign, but who was born at a time of day which indicates qualities that are quite different than those of the birthsign, is different in *personality* and there is almost invariably inner conflict. Other personality traits are more strongly marked than those of the birthsign in such case.

Gemini is of the air trinity, the quality of air meaning particular inner qualities of spiritual, emotional and mental nature. This reference is not to air as a physical element. Gemini, however, is the first among the air trinity. It is not a cardinal sign as it does not occupy one of the cardinal points; east, south, west or north. The fact that it is a dual sign, often reflects itself in the attitude of the native. It perhaps requires greater understanding on the part of other people to really comprehend the Gemini nature than it does any of the other signs of the zodiac, the sign being among the most devious. Although the time of birth may cause the individual who was born in this sign to appear quite direct in action and therefore easily understood, invariably the qualities of deviousness, which are natural to Gemini, are present though they may actually be expressed in an extremely constructive fashion.

The native of this sign who receives *predominating* Gemini influences at birth is fair of complexion and rather small featured. As a rule he is of fine appearance, his eyes being rather light brown or hazel. It is usually noted that the arms are long in proportion to the rest of the body, and that the feet and hands are rather short and well flexed. It is not at all unusual for the native of this sign to discuss a matter with someone along a particular line, *and at the same time* to think of taking some action related to it which is completely opposite in character. Sometimes the Gemini native is extremely affectionate and demonstrative, even though at the very moment he is expressing his regard, he may be conscious in the back of his mind of á critical attitude toward that very person.

The true Gemini loves to gain knowledge of all kinds. He almost invariably reads extensively, covering a wide field of subjects. He has a brilliant and active imagination. Many people who were born in Gemini are extremely original in the construction of ideas for stories and plays. As a result, quite naturally, not a few have been very successful in literary careers. Some of the most gifted orators of all times were born under a strong Gemini influence; also many famous humorists. The Gemini native is constantly getting ideas for things that are new and different. It has often been said that he conceives more new ideas in the course of a day than the average person does in a year. A marked characteristic of the native is that he must be *constantly busy*. If he hasn't something to look forward to which will keep him fully occupied, he is at a complete loss and must *originate something* to engage his time.

It is probable that you are adaptable and could adjust yourself to almost any condition of life or surroundings, with the possible exception of monotony and routine. You are quick to grasp a situation and can immediately adjust yourself mentally to deal with it. For that reason you are capable of being quite tactful, and are unlikely to commit social blunders such as are sometimes committed by those who think less quickly. You can come rapidly to an understanding of the conversations of others and are likely to anticipate them, almost *reading their minds*. You have a remarkable ability to make friends when you choose, and can call this ability to your aid in obtaining what you desire. You have, however, some tendency toward sarcasm and expressions of wit at someone else's expense. Associates who seek to understand your temperament and character find themselves bewildered by the complexities they encounter. They often find you a paradox. Anyone with whom you are closely associated, will find they must move quite rapidly, both mentally and physically, to keep up with your versatile ideas and changeable actions.

You are very fond of beautiful things in art and in nature, yet to a considerable degree you are a realist, observing also the ugly and unattractive in them. This is expressive of the duality of your nature. You are quite inclined to choose attractive surroundings and to become friendly with others wholly because of externals, for the reason that you like things which are pleasing to the eye. Sometimes this may lead you to make alliances with others who lack real worth. You probably admire those who are highly educated in art and science, and you yourself are undoubtedly capable of great attainments along that line, but great success in such a field could be interfered with by the fact that you might not carry through completely.

The positive factors of this sign are such as to lead to the highest degree of achievement in creative fields as well as in business or professional pursuits. The native of Gemini has the most powerful of natural forces to call upon. These forces he can summon to his assistance in the fullest degree by development of the positive qualities which his sign possesses. He is seldom as successful in routine occupations as are those who were born under some of the other signs. When the native of Gemini receives a regular wage he is quite likely to give it away or spend it recklessly so that he does not accumulate. Often it is necessary for the true Gemini to learn, above everything else, the lessons of moderation and at least reasonable conservatism in financial matters.

The highly evolved Gemini is extremely desirous of helping others. He has a deep interest in the problems of humanity and while he is not, as a general rule, as completely humanitarian as are those who came into the world under the sign Aquarius, he will often display marked traits of that nature. Frequently he is deeply religious and interested in spiritual matters, although he is seldom narrow in his views or completely bound by the creeds of one religion. He is, on the contrary, much more inclined to be broadly tolerant, and to feel respect for the religious beliefs of others, no matter what they may be.

Generally, you are sympathetic and kindly at heart, although you have the tendency at times to be critical of others as well as suspicious of their motives. Your natural inclination, however, is to be courteous and refined, as well as genial. You can be very diplomatic, and should be an entertaining conversationalist. You have an extremely active imagination, and there is a certain noticeable brilliance in your mental equipment. You are undoubtedly a splendid companion when you are in the mood to be. It is quite likely, however, that other people, who are more conservative and who accept new ideas slowly, may find your sudden changes of opinion and decisions bewildering. The probabilities are that you have an unusual understanding of human nature, and that you can use that knowledge to considerable advantage. You estimate people with whom you come in contact quickly, and your alert mind enables you to fathom them sometimes with remarkable accuracy.

You have a great natural intuition, and are shrewd in the schemes you are able to work out for the attainment of your objectives, concerning money or otherwise. While it is probable that you are not *careful* in handling money, either giving it away or spending it freely, you love to drive a sharp bargain. It is not unusual for men who came into the world under a strong Gemini influence to use *sharp* methods in doing business. Not infrequently, they are quite shrewd in their dealings and are properly referred to as *schemers*. Often they are extremely original in working out new ideas, not only in connection with *schemes* for making money (often giving a great deal of attention to devising short cuts), but in original design and other creative fields.

Words which express the positive qualities of the sign are: resourceful, liberal, versatile, intellectual, idealistic, understanding, eloquent, sympathetic, studious, observing, tolerant, expressive, inquiring, dexterous, temperate, active. Words which express the negative qualities of the sign are: improvident, restless, scattered, diffusive, evasive, shifty, wayward, tricky, diffident, theoretical, changeable, unsteady, impractical, deceitful, effusive, fanciful.

The Gemini nature quite frequently manifests itself in desires and inclinations of extremely contradictory nature. The enthusiasm of Gemini is often very quick, but in undeveloped natives of the sign it never lasts long. This manifests itself in general dissatisfaction with the conditions of life. Sometimes the native will become dissatisfied with a purchase almost immediately after he has made it. He is often satisfied and dissatisfied, happy and unhappy, almost at the same instant. His inclination is to plunge into things, to be enthusiastic about each one as a great discovery (until he has taken out of it that which attracted his attention) and then to drop it. Those who came into the world under this solar vibration, are also either extremely unselfish or quite the reverse.

Probably to a greater extent than those of any other sign, the Gemini native dislikes feeling that he has been imposed upon, taken advantage of, or over-charged. To a considerable extent, he is inclined to take speculative chances. A great many feel that they are fitted to occupy a position above the average and are sure that their mental equipment is much superior, but they find it difficult to capitalize on their abilities. That is due mainly to the fact that they find it hard to carry anything through to a conclusion; which in turn is attributable to the tendency to conceive new ideas readily, and the fact that their enthusiasms are quickly aroused. In such cases they are quite adept at finding reasons for taking up the new and dropping the old. The native of this sign who allows his negative qualities to develop will take up fads with the greatest intensity, and then shortly lose interest in them entirely, only to take up something new with the same intensity.

As previously mentioned the duality of the Gemini nature causes a great deal of conflict in the native of the sign who is unevolved. He will strive for riches and pray for experiences in life, and at the same time declare he is not interested in them. He is, in truth, not sure where his interest lies at any given time. When he allows the negatives of his nature to grow he will often do certain things (of his own volition and not as a result of being forced), which at the same time within himself he is certain he doesn't want to do at all. Yet, he does them! This results in the bringing of much unhappiness and often, downright misery into his own life and into the lives of others. The undeveloped native is quite inclined to seek advice from friends, and then to plunge recklessly or heedlessly ahead without regard for the advice he has sought. He becomes confused and completely at a loss when important decisions are to be made, the duality of his thought processes pulling him in completely opposite directions. He has no real conclusions about the meaning of life, and no definite standards of conduct.

The Gemini individual who is unevolved is always certain that what he has, he doesn't want, but he finds it quite difficult to decide what he does want. He is frequently desirous of social achievement and wishes to be well thought of, yet he regards his associations with restless discontent, and feels the admiration which he may be able to elicit, empty of satisfaction. Any condition in which he finds himself, regardless of how great his enthusiasm may have been in the beginning, loses its zest for him the moment the novelty has worn off.

These people are possessed of such duality in their tastes and desires that it manifests itself in great extremes. The positive qualities of the sign, when developed, produce among the highest types of human beings; equally the negatives are capable of producing those who are among the lowest. Even in the cases of those who are highly evolved a degree of variety is necessary, since the versatility of their natures requires that they obtain the stimulation of diversified interests. When the native of this sign is successfully engaged in business he should have an avocation, or a hobby.

Worry is a powerful negative in the lives of most people, but it is possibly more so in Gemini natives than of those born in any other sign of the zodiac. For that reason they need abundant sleep. Often they sleep very lightly when their minds are overly active upon retiring. Great responsibility or a tragedy often will turn the native of this sign from a changeable, restless and undependable person into an entirely different individual. He is then seemingly awakened fully to the folly of his course and settles into his responsibilities firmly.

The lives of these people are likely to be either extremely successful or quite the reverse. When they choose to call upon the powerful forces which are theirs to turn to, they can achieve greatly in a wide variety of fields. This sign is extremely lavish in the gifts it bestows upon those who receive the influence strongly at birth, and the possibilities of success are virtually unlimited. Natives of this sign who are evolved have a heritage of understanding enabling them to control and submerge the negative qualities of their birthsign, but those who are unevolved have yet to learn the lesson of persistance, application and dependability.

WOMEN OF GEMINI

Women who come into the world under a strong Gemini influence are more often than not *real homemakers*. They love to surround themselves with all the luxurious conditions of life which they can manage. They love beautiful things, and are likely to be extremely artistic. The true Gemini woman is extremely affectionate, and in return requires love and affection from members of her family. Lacking understanding and affection from others in her life she may become quite reserved. The mental qualities of the sign which are markedly cold become predominant in this event.

A woman of this sign is often not content with things which a short time previously she was *sure she desired intensely*. Consequently she is likely to try constantly to bring about alterations. This urge frequently extends itself to the arrangement of the furniture in her home. The true Gemini native of the female sex is likely to make a *complete change* in the arrangement of her home without having really considered the matter previously, and acting solely upon the *spur of the moment!* As a matter of fact, the negative qualities of the sign when they have been allowed to develop, produce in the women of Gemini a lack of patience and a desire to be constantly busy. As a result they often make changes without due consideration, and may even act in many of the more important affairs of life without stability — *taking steps without taking time to think!*

The nearly pure type of Gemini woman is constantly seeking new sources of interest into which she can pour her energy. Unless there is a definite effort to turn the mind into constructive channels and to cultivate serenity of mind she is, not infrequently, extremely nervous, even to the point of hysteria. She is usually very generous and sympathetic, but the tendency of the sign to observe the negative qualities of others may lead her to be inwardly critical, which sometimes finds expression outwardly in negative comments. In common with the man of the sign, often the woman is never satisfied with her attainments. Once she has reached an intensely desired goal she immediately becomes dissatisfied with it and desires to produce another condition.

A great many women of this sign have been outstanding creators in artistic fields. Not a few have been writers, others have been sculptors, and workers in handicrafts. The women of Gemini are extremely versatile and have it within them to become successful in almost any occupation they take up seriously. They become very capable secretaries; being quick, tactful and efficient but of course not caring much for monotonous routine. The woman of Gemini may scatter her energies in too many interests and, as a result of taking on such a wide variety of undertakings, she sometimes finds she hasn't time to give her attention properly to any of them. She can be an extremely loyal and devoted wife and mother but she requires a great deal of understanding. In trying conditions she can be a "rock of Gibraltar" in her steadfastness to those whom she loves, and is often intensely desirous of seeing to their comfort and well-being. When her creative instincts are aroused however, she is apt to devote her time entirely to the cultivation of intellectual or artistic interests, and could be extremely successful along those lines.

Youngsters of this sign are never content to be idle, but are constantly busy and intensely restless. The true child of Gemini is bright, quite inquisitive, and likely to be difficult to *keep up with,* due to his propensity for suddenly abandoning one activity for another which appears more interesting. Children of this sign require careful guidance and should be taught from early years the desirability of thought processes which produce consistent action. Youngsters of this solar vibration are extremely responsive to affection. They require understanding and a sympathetic point of view on the part of parents and other adult associates. Often older people find it difficult to understand the versatility and the many-sided quality of the Gemini nature. Due to their quick minds and fertile imaginations, when they are ruled arbitrarily or constantly opposed, they quickly learn to be evasive and clever in extricating themselves from positions of blame. Their imaginations frequently develop to the extent that they exaggerate considerably. The child of this sign responds quite readily to calm reason, and he has a strong tendency to heed the advice of his elders when it is given *as to an equal.*

Being possessed of an extremely active imagination the child who received a strong Gemini influence at birth will be likely to imagine all sorts of things, and guidance should be exercised in this connection lest the youngster learn to cultivate and dwell upon weird and terrifying situations. If the tendency is noted in a child of this sign to listen to, or tell, stories about ghosts and other things which tend to terrify, and *to dwell on them,* there should be an effort to guide his mind into more constructive channels. An atmosphere of peace and harmony is necessary to the development of the Gemini child. A foundation for future nervous excitability is laid when the youngster who came into the world under a strong Gemini influence is exposed to continually exciting conditions, or to emotional disturbances.

The true Gemini child is greatly bored by excessive routine and the necessity for carrying through uncongenial tasks. Adults should endeavor to understand this quality in the child of this sign, allowing him as much latitude as possible in his activities. It is of course advisable to strive to teach the child of Gemini not to leave tasks uncompleted, but it must be remembered that often any child learns a great deal from a task which he has started but left unfinished. The next time he may know how to do it, so the relative importance of the task involved should be taken into consideration.

The child who came into the world under a strong Gemini influence should have a great deal of exercise. Physical activity is quite necessary. Unless there is an outlet for physical energies it will be found that the mental restlessness of the sign will transmit itself to nervous movements of the hands and feet so that the child is, literally, never still. A great deal of responsibility rests upon the parents of Gemini children. Much depends upon the way they are dealt with in early youth, as to whether they will reach adulthood as dependable and lovable men and women, or the opposite. Children of Gemini have extremely good minds, capable of the greatest accomplishments when the constructive side of their natures is awakened.

MARRIAGES OF GEMINI

People who are born in Gemini marry early in life less often than do those born in many of the other signs, although the impulsive nature of Gemini will sometimes bring about an early matrimonial alliance. The Gemini nature, of course, is variable and unless there is a strong admixture from another sign at birth, this sign is mental rather than physical. It is certainly necessary for the Gemini native to marry one who is relatively on the same plane intellectually and culturally. While an individual who is associated with a Gemini native might be on a higher level, educationally and, in fact, culturally, it is not likely he will remain so permanently. The Gemini individual may not acquire the same degree of education, but he is likely to be able to give the impression of knowing a great deal more than he actually does. He may be able to discuss complex subjects at considerable length with those who are far ahead of him as far as education is concerned and not reveal the fact that such is the case.

Matrimonially, it is quite necessary that the Gemini marry one who can understand the natural deviousness as well as the suspicious quality of the sign. One who is closely associated with a native of this sign should not be readily disillusioned at finding that the Gemini has said something entirely different than he actually means about a given situation. One needs to understand that the Gemini is likely to take increasing care about what he actually says if there is anything implicit in his statements which might be injurious to another. On the other hand, once the suspicion of the Gemini native is aroused, he may be quite devious in what he says and very often is likely to express something he doesn't really believe at all, and to say he intends to do something which he doesn't intend to do. This very often takes the form of a statement that the Gemini native is going to do something which might be harmful to another person, although he doesn't intend to really do it. This is something that a matrimonial partner of a native of Gemini should endeavor to understand. The *natural qualities* of the birthsign are always present to a greater or lesser extent no matter how little they may come to be expressed in the traits of personality.

The fundamental qualities of the signs Aries (March 20th – April 20th), Leo (July 22nd – August 22nd), Libra (September 24th – October 23rd), and Sagittarius (November 23rd – December 21st) are the most harmonious matrimonially with the sign Gemini. The Gemini native is capable of the highest development and he may be extremely brilliant, creatively, in business. The woman born in Gemini is usually very capable in managing her own home, but she will not feel satisfied if she believes that she is getting the worst of the bargain. The natural quality of suspicion which is based upon her concepts of the motives of other people may come strongly to the fore. Women of this birthsign have the inherent ability to be good wives and extremely good mothers, and they also may be extremely helpful to their partners either in business or in other ways which require application of intellectual qualities.

Among undeveloped natives in whom the negative qualities have become strong, inconstancy in marriage is not unusual. Truth to tell, the native of Gemini often finds himself involved in complicated situations with regard to the opposite sex; and more than one marriage is not at all unusual as the nature of the sign, which we have previously discussed, would indicate.

Above everything else the sign Gemini tends to impart versatility; consequently the native is capable of success in a wide variety of occupations. One finds individuals of this sign in every field of endeavor which requires a great deal of manual dexterity and an active mind. Most often, however, natives of Gemini will be found in creative fields. They are particularly successful as sculptors, artists and in the handicrafts. The sign is also well represented in the professions. Many are successful dentists, physicians and surgeons. They often become excellent electricians, engineers, draughtsmen, printers and engravers. Sometimes, however, the nervous tendencies of the sign are quite apparent in those who are engaged in the last three occupations, as the work entailed frequently proves rather confining and monotonous to the true native of Gemini.

As we have mentioned herein, human beings are complex. Some individuals, of course, are more complex than others, but *all* have complexities which make them difficult to really understand. This is more true of Gemini than any other sign. The tendency of Gemini as we have mentioned, is to be versatile. The earth sign Taurus, which immediately precedes Gemini, and the water sign Cancer which follows it, are quite different. A mixture of either one of these signs in the native will alter the quality of the birthsign to some degree, and, in fact, if the sign rising on the eastern horizon at birth is quite different from the natural qualities of Gemini the personality may be altered considerably.

Among those who are highly evolved will be found extremely successful financiers and those who make business deals which involve considerable money. They appear to be able to engineer such transactions with a sureness which is, and ever has been, the mark of genius. It is usually found, however, that among those who were born in Gemini who have become outstandingly successful in finance, all received some influence from one of the signs having a particular financial quality. This is often an influence from Taurus.

It is rather unusual for the native of this sign to amass any considerable amount of money until past middle life, due to his sudden changes of opinion, and the recklessness he often displays in the handling of his personal finances. When the positive qualities of the sign are developed he is extremely capable of devising financial plans, however. The individual who comes into the world under a strong Gemini influence quite often pursues two careers with success. Not infrequently the native has wide interests in greatly diversified fields. Due to the extreme flexibility of the Gemini mind he is able to transfer his attention almost instantly from one activity to something entirely foreign and different.

To a considerable degree the legal profession is favorable. It is obvious that the quick and clever mind bestowed by a strong Gemini influence would be of great advantage in that profession. The native of this sign is fully capable of understanding blueprints or patterns and, unless there are distractions, will carry out to completion the ideas embodied quite effectively. As mentioned, handicrafts are a very favorable medium of expression for the true Gemini. His hands are often *expressive* of the restless, alert, searching and dexterous quality of his mind.

DISHARMONY OF GEMINI

As with all other signs of the zodiac, conditions ordinarily referred to as disease in the human body are always synonymous and coexistent with their like in thought processes. The lack of harmony and the relationship between physical disability and thought processes is always to be noted in glandular imbalance. Balanced thought and unbalanced glandular activity never exist simultaneously in the same human organism. If there is a balance in glandular activity there is balanced thought. If there is balanced thought there is always balanced glandular activity. Gemini has a more direct effect upon the shoulders, arms, hands, and lungs than any other parts of the body. The negatives of the sign most often produce resultant disharmony in these parts. The sign has a direct connection with the nervous system. The negatives which have been previously expressed will produce very marked nervous disorders.

Any strong Gemini influence shown in the birth chart which indicates negative tendencies, particularly those associated with worry and anxiety, produces susceptibility to tubercular conditions, as well as other disorders and diseases of the respiratory organs. The fundamental quality of the sign Gemini in its negative phases is associated with bronchitis, pneumonia, and asthma. The particular negatives of the sign often result in accidents to the shoulders, hands, arms, and lungs. As a physical means of maintaining a state of well-being, breathing exercises are fine for the native of this sign. However, the most effective course of procedure is the *cultivation of the positive mental qualities*. The determination to dwell upon calming subjects will so balance the glandular activity as to eliminate nervous tendencies and over-excitability. Moderate exercise, especially walking is very beneficial, providing the *mental attitude* is kept in harmony.

Often, as a result of the nervous tendencies imparted by negatives of this sign, there is a tendency for natives to suffer from stomach and kidney disorders, neuritis, particularly in the arms and shoulders, and impurities in the blood. When a native of Gemini suffers from any of these conditions, one may immediately suspect its origin as being in the nervous system and directly traceable to processes of thought and consequent lack of glandular balance.

As previously stated, worry and anxiety, and the impatience and restlessness inherent in this solar vibration are the most important negatives to be overcome by the person who came into the world under a strong influence from this sign. It is true for the Gemini native as for those of all other signs, that *cultivation* of the positive qualities of his sign, as specifically conveyed in the words which have been previously given, will produce perfect harmony and bodily well-being. A conscious effort on the part of the native to remain calm and patient, and to actively cultivate these positive qualities, will enable him to achieve almost any goal upon which he definitely and consistently sets his heart and mind. The native of Gemini is urged to open his heart and his mind to an *inner seeing* and *knowing* of truth as conveyed in all the religions of the world, and to develop the splendid qualities which his sign bestows.

1977 In mid-spring and late fall, friendly ties are apt to be "the center" of all your hopes and wishes. An individual born between late October to late November will probably occupy your interest. Communication in some form, letters written, telephone messages, "hasty words" are apt to prove upsetting. Your "day-to-day" duties appear during this particular year, to contain surprising situations demanding that "you" personally overcome problems or "carry on" matters related to relatives. I have no doubt but that you will feel that you are trying to find your way through a dense forest — all because of other people. The opportunity for you to become "caught up" in "quicksands" that could involve you in an expensive entanglement is more than a possibility. By-pass flirtations and a trap that others might set now during this short cyclic interval by "patiently living one day" at a time, for "wonderful days" lie ahead when this time has passed on!

1978 You may feel that it is necessary for you to take a more retiring position in your world for an interval during 1978, but through the constructive use of your emotions you will develop a growing sense of personal and material security, in my estimation. I think you will go through phases when certain associations will appeal to you because they represent an avenue for eluding conditions which are less pleasing to you than you would prefer, but later on I feel you will be glad you refused to encourage them further. You will be able to use your talents in newer directions, I am sure. Let your highest judgment guide you through every situation in your daily efforts, and even changes in your living arrangements will lead to betterment, I feel.

1979 "Flaring events" will change your whole outlook toward many of your daily activities, I feel certain. In 1979 you should have opportunities for reorganizing your interests in areas which will enable you to use to the fullest some of your most unusual, versatile and intuitive abilities. I think your undertakings will seem even more far-reaching at this time, frequently turning your attention to distant places, newer types of learning, and closer ties. Something you have may appear to hold you away from a few of the things you would really like to do, temporarily, but there are strong indications that your conscientiousness toward both "responsibilities" and details WILL earn beneficial returns for you now.

1980 Unique forms of entertainment and imaginative ideas are likely to "pull" you away from monotonous or "set" routines, during this year of new planetary influences. Situations of a romantic nature are indicated as welcome outlets, making it possible for you to express your emotions in a warm, spontaneous manner. Family matters that have seemed to "drag" recently are apt to change later this year which will lead you to branch out in a new creative direction. Briefly, someone younger may need special attention. Guidance based upon your own experience is indicated as having great significance, due to that person's confusion or uncertainty. Affection and matters of deep love, during this cycle, will be likely to bring an unusual experience — one you will long remember and cherish in your thoughts. Saturn occupies a strong position during this period, as does Uranus, so I anticipate that restless inner urges will spur thoughts of striving for greater freedom, as well as new plans touching occupational independence.

1981 Personal plans or interests "close to home" are likely to conflict with responsibilities that seem to originate from commitments you have made involving other people, children, or a pet, during the latter half of the period. "Speculative" possibilities, both of a financial and romantic nature, will have a strong appeal, in my opinion, while this powerful planetary influence continues. However, there are indications that your good judgment in these areas will be a real help in evaluating "chancy" ventures, enabling you to gain the advantage that is of surprising value later.

1982 It is likely that younger people, especially children, will have a more important role to play in your affairs this year. It may be necessary to assume a temporary burden with respect to a younger person. I think that doing so will impose certain brief restrictions upon your own movements or desires, but the eventual outcome will be gratifying from the standpoint of a "duty well done." Money interests may undergo noticeable changes from the middle of the year, probably in connection with expenses having to do with your "home" arrangements. Both a "limiting" and a "strengthening" of romantic attachments are indicated this year, but disappointments in this area are apt to be compensated for by an unexpected opportunity to benefit by an improvement or enlargement of your "daily duty" interests.

1983 The advisability of closer attention to health matters, particularly to teeth/chest areas and a sensible diet, is powerfully indicated by Saturn's new position this year. I believe this will be a time when you will be asked to take on greater responsibilities with regard to your "home" or occupational concerns. Additional thoroughness and attention to "details" are likely to be required as this cycle moves forward. Sudden changes involving close relationships are shown, possibly in connection with your efforts to seek out unusual or talented associates as a replacement of relationships that have been severed. I am sure you will be inclined to look at the positive side of your close relationships, especially through a willingness to meet others "half way," and through this attitude you will be able to advance your position.

1984 Until around August of this year more strenuous physical activity is likely to be demanded from you. Conditions having to do with "work" may be less agreeable than usual during this period, and it will be to your advantage to "sidestep" conflicts or disagreements with "co-workers" or close ties as much as you can. Benefits of a business nature, probably related to insurance, credit, taxes, or an inheritance, may be a center of interest at this time, but misplaced confidence or the unexpected negligence of an associate could be costly later on. Fluctuations involving personal associations are likely to bring highly unusual or unique people into your circle of acquaintances, from whom you might gain new and valuable experiences in the years to come!

SUMMATION (Gemini)

Almost any long-term cycle, such as the one interpreted for this forecast period, can bring certain opportunities for advancement in personal ambitions or achievement of cherished goals. However, the next seven or eight years are strongly indicated as "sparkling" with unusual changes which may dramatically rearrange your present style of living and overturn some of the values to which you have long been clinging!

This is a dynamic cycle creating a great number of new ideas that will be "born," particularly some of an ingenious nature which can lead to a "turning point" in your attitude toward "work" and the use of your unique abilities. In all likelihood, old associations will be swept away, sometimes with startling rapidigy . . . only to be replaced by a fascinating variety of "new people" who appear on the scene.

As a Gemini, I believe you usually consider life as a "learning process." That is, you are often impelled by natural instinct to study, observe, and inquire into sources of knowledge that attract you. During this years-long cycle, I am certain you will have ample opportunities to satisfy your "thirst for knowledge," because there will be a continuation of planetary influences which tend to encourage a "reaching outward and upward" of your mind in order for you to reap a harvest of learning that can apply in your search for a happier and successful life. There are strong indications that both the beginning portion of this period as well as the closing year to year and a half will be marked by an expansion of your financial position. It is well to bear in mind that "expansion" also implies growth that can "get out of hand" unless properly controlled. In other words, your enthusiasm and desire for gains or improvements "money-wise" during these times I mentioned above could be carried to extremes which might tend to jeopardize previous gains or limit anticipated gains.

I am certain the years ahead will be filled by a variety of stimulating experiences that will help shape your outlook toward a brighter life.

Those who were born in this cusp period are *under* the combined vibrations of the planet Mercury and the Moon. Natives of this cusp have keen minds, but being complex, they sometimes fail to receive full benefit from their mental equipment. They do not like laborious work very well, yet are quite anxious to gain the favor of those with whom they are associated. The individual who was born under predominating influences from this cusp often has a desire to gain public credit for things he does and not infrequently he succeeds in doing so. The natural shrewdness with which he is equipped very readily permits him to gain a considerable share of prosperity and the goods of the world without extraordinarily hard work. He has a natural ability to obtain money and much persuasiveness. Natives of this cusp are often successful in causing money to *gravitate* in their direction and frequently they are able to use their persuasive powers in such a way as to obtain a great deal of financial assistance or benefit from associates.

When their talents are developed they have marked ability to convince others and consequently they are often able to *sell anything* to which they turn their attention. They are not affected by losses or by failure to the extent that those who were born under other planetary influences may be. If they meet with defeat and loss in one direction, they are quick to turn in another – using the reverses they have experienced as a step upward rather than a real defeat. Those who were born *strongly* under this cusp and who become engaged in activities which require a following or support are able to gain it to an amazing degree. They have a natural quality which enables them to develop their vocal cords so as to produce speech which is full of expression and quite mellow. That is, of course, an extremely valuable gift. They are not fond of deep study, but knowledge of history and that which has occurred to people as a result of certain actions is quite valuable to them.

The native quite often has artistic and mechanical ability. He is, in such case, inclined to devote a great deal of energy to working out and perfecting new ideas along those lines. Many highly talented musicians, artists, and others in various forms of artistically professional work, came into the world under these particular solar influences. The combination permits them to acquire a comprehensive knowledge of legal matters and they become good public speakers. Some form of entertainment or amusement is likely to be quite favorable for them. The native of this cusp has a considerable fondness for his home and he may well be devoted to those he loves. Particularly natives of both sexes are devoted to their young. It is a notable fact that women who were born in this cusp will give up everything in order to maintain and protect their offspring and to retain the company of their children. Natives can be very gay, talkative and happy at times, but there are other times when they are subject to moods of great depression. If, however, they learn to use the vibratory forces which surround them and which they can call upon, their powers of persuasiveness stand them in very good stead.

The birthsign CANCER
June 23rd to July 21st

If you were born between June 23rd and July 21st your birthsign is Cancer. The positive and the negative qualities of this sign are of a quite definite and distinct order, and they are distinctly recognizable. Cancer has its definite functions and qualities. Many of the ancient legends, in civilizations widely scattered over the Earth, both in point of time and distance, were concerned with Cancer. The symbol of this sign is the Crab. As with other signs of the zodiac it has been considered by some observers that the symbol was derived from the seeming likeness of the constellation Cancer to the Crab. That, however, is far from being the case. In common with the other signs it is intended to graphically convey the psychological factors which are a part of the sign's vibrations.

Cancer is a water sign and, in common with all the other water signs, it is inspirational and consequently impressionable. The action of Cancer in its pure essence is much less direct, than is the case with many of the other signs; in fact, with most others. Mentally, the native of this sign has a fundamental psychological quality which causes him to sidle away from direct action, in much the same fashion as that which is expressed by the Crab physically.

The constellation Cancer is the least noticeable of any of the constellations. It is very faint in appearance, and has often been referred to as the dark sign. It is considered that the sign is ruled by the Moon, which means that the hidden vibrations from the lunar orb have a direct effect upon the native of Cancer to a greater degree than is the case for any other sign. As we all know, the Moon has a powerful effect over the waters of the Earth. It is a proven fact that the passage of the Moon through the heavens brings about the rise and fall of the tides. That this satellite of the Earth is referred to as watery in nature is not a chance connection. The effect it has upon water is directly connected with the psychologically impressionable qualities of the water sign Cancer.

The gem which vibrates harmoniously with this sign is the moonstone; the flower is the water lily. Cancer is representative of the Bible tribe of Issachar, one of the original tribes of Israel, or one of the fundamental types of human beings. The philosophers of Chaldea referred to Cancer as the "gate of men", through which the soul entered the human body. Occultly this is a significant fact. The sign is considered to be the most feminine of any. It is extremely maternal, the qualities of parenthood being strongly marked in Cancer natives of both sexes. Significantly the birth of a Cancer native occurs at a time when there is a brooding tenderness in the wilderness. The season of mating is past and the young are growing. Nursing mothers among the wild creatures of the Earth abound. All this is significantly expressive of the strong positive traits of Cancer. As with the other signs, we will try to give a complete description of the positive and negative qualities of the sign and the true native of Cancer will recognize the traits which are described; though some may be considerably overshadowed by others which have developed to a greater extent.

You are undoubtedly diplomatic and tactful. You have the inherent ability to be what is commonly referred to as a "good mixer". You are much inclined to be sympathetic and kind-hearted. It is not unusual for the native of your sign to be extremely generous. You are, however, to a greater degree than most people, affected by the mental conditions of those who surround you, as well as to all the physical manifestations you encounter. You are quite sensitive to vibrations which are not readily apparent but which can bring about, within you, sudden moods of depression.

The birthsign imparts inner qualities or psychological traits. The sign which arises on the eastern horizon at birth, however, has a marked effect upon the outward characteristics. The *pure* Cancer vibration produces people of medium stature and of quite attractive appearance. They are likely to be well developed in the region of the chest. That is the area over which the vibrations of Cancer, both positive and negative, have the greatest effect. The parts directly affected are the chest, the breasts, and upper part of the stomach. The sign is related to the thoracic duct, to the pancreas, the lacteals, and the epigastric area. As far as personal appearance is concerned, having been born in the sign does not necessarily produce the Cancer physical appearance, but it is always produced when the influence is strong in the chart, and when rising on the eastern horizon at birth.

There are, actually, two very distinct and clearly divided types of people who come into the world in this sign of the zodiac. The same may be said, of course, in relation to Cancer as to the other signs of the zodiac. A great deal of variation in physical appearance is possible, yet the two specific types of individuals who are born under this solar vibration are quite recognizable in their outward characteristics. One is of medium height or a little taller. This type is likely to grow heavy in middle life and is particularly marked by his ability to become a good "mixer". He is witty, companionable, fond of humorous situations as well as of luxurious surroundings. The other type is about the same height although he may be shorter, slender, wiry, and silent. This latter type manifests the natural conservatism of the Cancer nature in his outer bearing more than the other type. It is hard sometimes to engage him in conversation. He withdraws within himself, and may for several days speak only in monosyllables.

Both types, however, have the natural conservatism of the sign. Men of Cancer make fewer changes occupationally during their lives than do the men of almost any other sign. It is characteristic of the Cancer nature to love ease and comfort. Men of the sign are not usually hasty in making decisions, being rather inclined to dislike haste. To a considerable degree their dispositions are outwardly quiet. When the influence of Cancer is strong at birth the conservatism of the sign is invariably prominent. This *can* be expressed in a positive way, but sometimes it is an exceedingly negative quality. When it is expressed as a negative the native is fearful of financial loss, apprehensive of poverty to the extent that he fears robbery. This is more true of women who were born in this sign than it is of men. It is, in fact, not unusual for the Cancer woman to conceal her valuables in many out-of-the-way places and to use traditional secret nooks and crannies for the hiding of money. It is the woman with strong Cancer influences at birth who in old age lives a life of outward poverty but who has valuables tucked in old trunks and large sums of money hidden in her clothes.

You are undoubtedly conservative and not at all inclined to plunge recklessly without regard for the consequences. It is possible that you have very definite views and that you may often refuse to consider another side to any question about which you have formed a conclusion. You have a great deal of fondness for travel but you like to have a permanent abode to which you can return. While you have a strong tendency to seek new surroundings and new scenes and there is within you an inner desire to roam, yet you like to feel that your *roots* are firmly attached. Cancer is one of the most strongly domestic of all the signs. The Cancer nature inspires a love for domesticity and the shelter of a permanent home. Despite your fondness for travel and new scenes, you are not inclined to adopt new methods. Sometimes this tendency is strongly marked in the Cancer native, depending upon the other planetary influences at birth. When that is the case progress may be retarded.

As a rule the native of this sign is not by nature a good student, but once his interest is aroused in intellectual pursuits the tendency is to become completely absorbed in them. Cultivation of the intellect is perhaps more important to this sign than any of the others. When there is a lack of cultural intellectual development many of the Cancer abilities and talents lie completely dormant. Due to the fact that Cancer is a water sign and particularly susceptible to psychic vibrations, the native is subject to periods of despondency and sometimes extreme melancholy. At such times it is well for him to seek a secluded and quiet place wherein he can meditate upon the higher values of life and, by guidance of his mental processes, produce a state of serenity and peace in his mind. When he does this he is able to develop mental control to an unusual degree.

You are devoted to those whom you love, and are deeply affected by their suffering and unhappiness. While you may not always give evidence of the fact outwardly, you are extremely good at heart. An effort toward heightening the positive qualities of your sign, which are a part of the sympathy and tenderness you have for those who are in trouble or who suffer adversity, should of course, be made. Development of those particularly positive qualities of Cancer has an immediate and measureable effect upon the affairs of life. It is likely that your views in connection with public affairs and possibly with religion are settled to the extent that you have very positive opinions concerning these matters. You are not likely to care for radical changes in your design for living. While you may have positive ideas in connection with public affairs pertaining to reforms you are not inclined to wish to upset the ordered processes of established customs.

There have been extremely exalted men among those who were born in this sign. Not a few have been of high spiritual development, and as advisors they have exerted a powerful influence over the lives of others. There have been a number whose lives were sanctified, and who reached a state of spotless purity individually. In such cases the instinct for fatherhood has widened to take in all the suffering of human kind. The highly developed native of Cancer is invariably interested in aiding mankind to reach a high state physically and spiritually. Philanthropic endeavors appeal to him and, if in a position to do so, he engages in charitable enterprises.

Influences from the hidden worlds of vibration are extremely beneficial to the highly developed or evolved native of this sign. On the other hand, those influences are an ever present hindrance to those who are in an undeveloped state. It is almost impossible for one who was born under a strong influence from Cancer to achieve practical success if he has allowed the particular negatives of the sign to grow. For that reason one most often finds that natives are either quite successful, or completely the opposite. When once the positive factors or qualities are developed, progress, on the road to success, is steady and often rapid. As a rule the latter part of the Cancer individual's life is happier and generally more prosperous than the early part.

Words which express the positive qualities of this sign are: conscientious, domestic, kind, persistent, tenacious, sociable, sympathetic, protective, maternal, tactful, reasonable, calm, cooperative. Words expressing the particular negative factors or qualities of the sign are: impressionable, sentimental, unadaptable, indolent, timorous, untruthful, unprogressive, touchy, resentful, slothful, greedy.

The undeveloped native of Cancer is often difficult to understand. His intimates seldom know what to expect. Fickleness is a strongly marked quality manifested by the undeveloped Cancer man or woman. The unevolved native has an excessive fondness for adornment, which is likely to display itself in a love for jewels and fine clothing. It is more marked in the women of Cancer than in the men, but it is often characteristic of both sexes who are unevolved. The undeveloped native is demanding and vain. His affection for others is not strong enough to restrain him from seeking the best for himself. Such an individual will expect and demand flattery, and is unsatisfied when homage is not paid to his personal importance and appearance. He is also quite inclined to speak *boastfully* of his own accomplishments.

All natives of Cancer are to a considerable degree sensitive, not only to hidden vibrations, but to all the affairs of life. The native who has allowed the negatives of his sign to become dominant resents any sort of criticism of himself no matter how kindly its nature. He feels that any criticism is a reflection upon him and he becomes moody, irritable, and melancholy. When this extreme quality of sensitiveness is aroused, the native will often imagine a slight or a criticism from a look or a word. He is frequently discouraged in some endeavor by a completely imagined criticism.

The native who has allowed the negative quality associated with this sensitiveness to go unchecked will often give up an important or even a great undertaking because of such imaginary criticism or slight. This extends itself to love affairs, often bringing about the greatest discouragement or dejection from a wholly fancied slight. In such an undeveloped native one finds a complete absence of open-mindedness. Positive points of view lead to complete unresponsiveness. Reason and logic are strangers to him. He can be almost unbelievably set in his ideas. The native who has allowed these particular negatives to develop often becomes extremely suspicious as well as prudent and cautious to the extent that he will not venture at all.

We are of course, all in a state of growth and development, not having reached a point of evolution wherein complete control of the mental processes has been attained. The native of Cancer has strongly marked and definite negative qualities which have been mentioned. One who was born under a strong influence from this sign should strive particularly to look for and absorb the good and the beauty in all things. He should struggle to teach his mind to ignore the unhappy, the ugly, and the discouraging, lest it penetrate too deeply into his inner consciousness and become fixed. He should refuse to allow himself to look upon and regard the dark side of life, or the melancholy psychic factors of his sign will grow to overwhelming proportions. The Cancer native has a great many extremely fine traits and is lovable to an unusual degree. *Cultivation of the positive qualities of thought* expressed by the words which have been given will not only produce an admirable character, but they are the KEY which will unlock the doors to the fullest degree of prosperity and happiness. The first *requirement* is recognition of the *necessity* for cultivating the positive attributes of your sign. You *are desirous* of acting in a helpful manner toward others and of doing right. It is entirely possible, once you recognize the desirability of doing so, to *dominate* the negative factors entirely. The life of any Cancer native can be made into a glorious record of achievement when he fully comes to realize the *value* of *directing his processes of thought!*

WOMEN OF CANCER

This sign of the zodiac is intensely "psychic". Women of Cancer are affected by all sorts of vibrations which are not perceptible to others. Their moods are sometimes extreme. It is a marked characteristic for them to be happy and vivacious when the sun shines but to become depressed, and often extremely sad when there are obscuring clouds. Gloomy, dismal, rainy days have an extremely adverse effect upon many women of Cancer.

The true Cancer woman has a strong quality of intuition. Her intuitive judgment is quite likely to guide her to the achievement of security. It is rare to find any woman who came into the world under a strong influence from this sign in a position of insecurity during her later years. She usually has a charming personality and is extremely feminine in appearance. Not a few of those who received strong influences from this vibration at birth are "doll-like" in appearance, and very attractive to the opposite sex. Their natures are vivacious and often charming to the ultimate degree. They have a marked ability to exert their charm at will. The woman of Cancer does not make friends readily among members of her own sex, but is greatly admired by men. She usually seeks exciting male companionship, but is more likely to marry a man who is quiet and steady.

The sign Cancer is ruled by the Moon, as we have said. That satellite of the Earth exerts an extremely powerful influence upon both sexes who were born in the sign. The women in particular, however, are affected by the waning moon, being prompted to seek excitement during that time. This period of the moon's phase is often extremely stimulating to them. Frequently their emotional natures are aroused to a *high pitch* in their search for stimulating experiences.

It is not at all unusual for the woman who was born in this sign to marry more than once. Cancer is a fruitful sign (in fact, more so than any other), consequently, the woman who was born under a strong influence from Cancer almost invariably has a number of children. As well as being the most fruitful of all the signs, Cancer is also the most maternal. Women of this sign are tenderly devoted to their offspring. They are not infrequently inclined, however, to be somewhat fickle in love affairs, yet when their marriages are harmonious the maternal instincts are so strong that they often become extremely devoted wives as well as mothers. They are fond of their homes and are extremely neat, orderly, and systematic in managing them. The true Cancer woman is essentially feminine in her instincts and is a good homemaker.

Literature is often a favorable outlet for the talents and abilities of women who were born in this sign. They can, and often do, succeed in business undertakings. They become capable secretaries and office-workers, but, as a rule, the true woman of Cancer is better satisfied in her own home than permanently in the business world. She will frequently, however, have great ability in creative artistic fields. Interior decorating is likely to be a favorable outlet for the talents of these women. Anything which has to do with homes proves fascinating, and success is often achieved. Business occupations having to do with the serving and preparation of food are also favorable for women who were born under a strong influence from this sign.

Children who receive a strong influence from this sign at birth are extremely high-strung, sensitive, and, in general, highly organized. It is an unmistakable truth that the child of Cancer is intensely affected by vibrations with which he comes in contact. Emanations from individuals are very strong in their effect upon his sensibilities. It is not at all unusual for a very young child of this sign to cry out when taken up by someone whose vibrations are inharmonious. Certainly the child of this sign should never be placed in the care of anyone for whom he shows a dislike, and from whom he seems to recoil. The effect in such case may be extremely detrimental to him, as the nervous system of a Cancer child is greatly affected by inharmonious associations. It will readily be seen that guidance of these youngsters is difficult and that proper rearing requires unusual judgment and tact.

Young girls of this sign love bright colors, particularly of pastel shades, and they are extremely fond of apparel. The true daughter of Cancer will unfailingly display a feminine taste for personal adornment. *She loves clothes!* Youngsters of this sign regardless of sex should be carefully instructed in the mysteries of life, so that the emotional Cancer nature will be prepared, at least in a measure, for the experiences of life. This sign is less frankly material than many of the others, but the psychic quality is such that the emotions are very finely organized. These children should be shielded to as great an extent as possible from everything which has to do with the morbid. Being associated with illness, and particularly with death, leaves a mark on the child of this sign which he never completely shakes off. It is highly inadvisable for the true Cancer boy or girl to attend funerals.

Children of Cancer should by all means sleep alone, as the vibrations from others are likely to be disturbing. It is quite necessary for them to have an abundance of sleep, plenty of fresh air, and a well balanced diet. Highly seasoned foods have a damaging effect upon the Cancer child, often leading to over-stimulation of the nervous emotions. Youngsters of this sign are likely to have fine minds and education is quite necessary to them, perhaps more so than to those who were born in almost any other sign. They often do not express very strong *desires for learning* and they may not be good students. It is, however, quite necessary for the individual of this sign to develop his qualities of intellect, which *he has a basic ability to do.* If their education is neglected, youngsters of this sign sometimes have a difficult time adjusting to life.

In common with adults, the children of this sign show a marked fondness for home and the surroundings and security which is or should be represented by a home. Early insecurity can have a very adverse effect upon the children of Cancer. They are often deeply affected by the numerous changes in residence which parents sometimes make. That, of course, is something which often cannot be escaped and comes about in the natural order of circumstances that are encountered, but parents should do everything possible to overcome the implications of insecurity usually involved in such moves. These children have tremendous potential possibilities which are susceptible to the highest development. The spiritual side of Cancer is strong when it is developed, and should not be overlooked by parents of the Cancer child.

49

MARRIAGES OF CANCER

Men of the sign Cancer seem more often to find contentment in marriage than the women. Matrimony is, in fact, rather a hazardous step for the woman who was born in this sign, unless she postpones the venture until she has reached the age at which she knows exactly what she seeks in a marriage partner. Above everything else, women of this sign desire a secure position in life. They are dissatisfied, unhappy, and resentful when forced to live under conditions of insecurity.

The sign Capricorn (December 22nd — January 20th) has many *interlocking* qualities and traits which prove harmonious with Cancer. To a considerable degree the Capricorn man is a desirable husband for the woman who was born in Cancer. He is quite likely to be steady, dependable, and capable of providing at least financial independence. Pisces (February 20th — March 19th) is also harmonious. Natives of Cancer will find those who come into the world under a strong influence from that sign unselfish and harmonious in their outlook upon the affairs of life. It is the opinion of the authors, in fact, that marriages between natives of Pisces and Cancer in the great majority of cases will prove to be lasting and harmonious. There is a basic understanding between these two signs, and though there may be vicissitudes in the course of life, both will *consistently* adhere to the marriage bond. Scorpio (October 24th — November 22nd) in a measure is harmonious with Cancer, but often the native of Cancer is too sensitive to live in a state of full harmony with one who was born in that sign.

Both sexes of the sign Cancer are quite domestic in many respects, and though they like gaiety in their lives — they *especially long for* a life of domestic peace and comfort. They like, and need, to *have a home* — at least to return to! As long as they have a reasonable amount of personal freedom, they remain steadfast in their marriages. This is markedly true of men who came into the world under a strong Cancer influence. Though the native may, and often does, enjoy travel, and though he may stray from his own fireside temporarily, it is strongly a part of his make-up to desire that his *roots be fixed* in a home that awaits his return. This sign of the zodiac also imparts an unusual instinct for parenthood. Women of Cancer are probably the most maternal of all the signs and make very devoted mothers.

It is rather unusual for men who were born predominately under the vibrations of Cancer to seek dissolution of their marriage ties. The man of this sign is quite inclined to put up with conditions in matrimony which are not wholly to his liking without turning to the ultimate of divorce. As a matter of fact, the man who was born in this sign will usually *fight against* such an eventuality. He does not like breaking up his home or home ties. This is even true of men who do not give strong evidence of the Cancer influence at their birth — because of the fact that there were strong influences from other signs at the time they came into the world. Even such men have *the basic inner qualities* of Cancer in relation to matrimonial ties. Cancer men are not infrequently fond of luxurious conditions and of other things which express the *lusts of life* but it is to be found in general that basically they are devoted to their homes and marriage partners and families — even though they may stray from their own firesides temporarily at times.

The Cancer vibrations are, in some respects, strongly creative. They also impart mechanical ability of a high order. Not infrequently the man who was born in this sign has a great deal of inventive creativeness. In common with the other water signs, Cancer is extremely inspirational in nature; perhaps more so than the other two. There is, in the highly evolved native, a love of color and a great deal of ability in artistic expression. There have been extremely talented professional people in creative fields who were born under a strong influence from this sign. It is also not unusual for the native of Cancer to possess literary ability, but one usually finds in such case that the individual received a strong influence from one of the air signs.

Not a few physicians, lawyers, and brilliant public speakers were born in this sign, but many of them received powerful vibrations from Gemini as well, at birth. The true native of Cancer has a strong tendency to shrink from appearances before the public. On the other hand, a great many actresses were born under a strong influence from this sign. Almost without exception they have been highly emotional in type, and possessed the ability to enter into intensely dramatic parts.

A number of very great scholars were born in Cancer, but the desire for studious application is, in many natives, not aroused. The true Cancer takes to direction in his activities more than those who were born in some of the other signs, and is inclined to be steady and faithful in carrying through duties allotted to him. He does not like uncertainty and insecurity. The man of Cancer has fundamental qualities which make him a splendid artisan in those lines of activity which require a high degree of skill. Manufacturing is an especially favorable outlet for the talents and abilities of the Cancer native.

There is a quality in the sign which enables the individual who received a strong influence from it at birth, to gauge public opinion and, more particularly, the desires and requirements of the people generally; consequently retail merchandising is often quite favorable. This ability to gauge public tastes and desires has also proved a valuable quality to many who have been engaged in politics. They are often able to *strike the right note* unerringly. Politics, as a matter of fact, is likely to be an extremely favorable outlet for the talents of men especially who were born in this sign. A mixture of the Leo vibrations, which often happens, may well create a genius in this field. When an individual whose birthsign is Cancer received an admixture of Leo qualities (when Leo was rising or through strong planets in that sign), he is much more likely to be a good *mixer* and to express qualities of extroversion. Those who received a predominating influence from the sign Cancer itself at birth, particularly if they were born at sunrise when their own sign Cancer was rising, are extremely reserved and they may be quite disinclined to talk. The late Calvin Coolidge was an outstanding example of the Cancer vibrations in outer personality. Usually those who were born in Cancer and who become successful politicians received an influence from Leo or from another of the signs with somewhat similar qualities.

Cancer natives should be engaged in occupations which allow for growth and advancement combined with security; as, like those born in Pisces, they often remain in an occupation where they do not advance, rather than chance making a change.

DISHARMONY OF CANCER

The region of the body which is most directly associated with the Cancer vibrations is that which includes the chest, breasts, and stomach. Conditions in the physical organism, ordinarily referred to as disease, are discussed here in relation to the negative processes of thought which always exist when such conditions are present. The negatives of Cancer are, of course, directly productive of disharmony in the area of the chest, the breasts, and lungs as well as the stomach. The one condition of *primary importance* that the Cancer native needs to guard against — is allowing the negatives which are part of the sign to become excessively strong.

Those negatives which are inherent in Cancer reflect themselves in women as female disorders. It is not unusual for them to have trouble with the mammary glands. Anxiety, nervous apprehension, and worry have a deep effect upon natives of this sign. The psychic nature of Cancer is such that there is frequently a great deal of nervous inner agitation. This nervousness is always indicative of a powerful negative. The stomach being closely allied with the Cancer vibration, natives are likely to be affected in that region. They often have extremely sensitive digestive organs, and food tends to ferment and to remain undigested when there are conditions of nervousness present. Fattening and heating foods should be avoided to as great an extent as possible; and natives of the sign should never partake of food when their minds are in an agitated state.

Inharmonious surroundings cause a tremendous amount of dissatisfaction, inner unrest and despondency in the Cancer native. This also is true of uncongenial associates, particularly those who may be repellent to the native. Tumerous growths, as well as cancerous conditions, are quite likely to be brought about in the Cancer native if he is forced to continue in surroundings which are inharmonious to him, or among associates with whom he is not in accord. While the fact is not generally recognized, some people do draw psychic vibrations from others — sometimes detrimental, and at other times beneficial. People who are associated with natives of Cancer often draw upon the vibrations to their own benefit, but much to the detriment of the Cancer native. He seems to be forced into association with such people whom he finds it very difficult to avoid.

Other negatives of the sign manifest themselves in cholic, biliousness, scurvy, hemorrhages, gastric troubles in general, and indirectly, rheumatism. It might be assumed, and indeed it is true, that strong Cancer vibrations at birth seem to be closely connected with ulcers in natives of the sign. Modern day civilization leads to this physical disorder in many cases, and the particular nervousness and sensitivity to surrounding conditions, as well as people, seems extremely likely to lead to this particular type of disharmony.

There are immensely powerful forces, however, upon which the Cancer native can draw. The intuitive and psychic nature of Cancer is strongly marked and under *proper direction of habitual thought processes* — the native seems unquestionably to be led toward proper diets and other actions pertaining to physical matters which balance his bodily functions so that he has tremendous resistance to disease, and possesses great vitality.

1977 The "lifting" of a grim mental outlook you tended toward in the immediate past, is shown. Your attention seems to swerve overwhelmingly in the direction of "income sources" and "unique" sources of entertainment. They appear to blend into a materialization of "loving human contact" that will arouse a new interest necessary to create the homelife of which you have dreamed. The direction of your love life will be toward "the unusual" or unorthodox which may cause you to seek those where there is a difference in age. A "steadfastness" you have not known in the past will be much more in evidence. A wonderful period of endearing recollections will remain forever.

1978 A sense of "inner contentment" will be imperative for you to strive for throughout this year, in my judgment, because you will have an inclination to view your world with stronger intensity, sometimes overlooking the great advantages you enjoy. Through your seeking and associations which are particularly meaningful for you, you can make 1978 into a year of gratifying "self-discovery," I know, that will enable you to **PREPARE** for an even more satisfying and gainful future. This period of time will benefit you most when you make a policy of looking ever *forward,* I believe, in complete faith of your ability to improve even your close ties. Because you have followed your better judgment explicitly, the later months of this year may bring into your life a touch of sweetness.

1979 The urge to participate in unusual pursuits is likely to be one of your strong motivating forces now. Your constructive efforts to find a satisfying "new beginning" will lead you swiftly into one, I am sure. By taking an interest in restoring something, you may realize particularly pleasing results. Some of your major opportunities are likely to grow out of challenges in the environment you consider your usual activities, and your gentle use of the written and spoken word probably will be exceptionally beneficial. When you have questions you would like to have answered, it might be advisable for you to obtain several opinions now. I feel that you will have exceptional opportunities in 1979 to make your life ever so much more gainful.

1980 It may appear at times that people in your immediate surroundings have an entangling effect upon certain plans or arrangements closely tied to your domestic interests. I doubt that you can pass through this period without your daily activity (regardless of what it may be) experiencing a "cleaning out or a clearing away," with a great deal of "pulling and hauling" as well as readjustment. The coming and going of children, younger people, or a pet will possibly touch your life strongly, causing electrical situations to arise, where they are involved. A very romantic happening is likely to enter your life (I know you'll disagree) — and it may reshape your future, since fear of criticism and the possibility that you will be "left out" or alone will no longer be present.

1981   A new phase is beginning this year; pleasures and entertainment which have not been experienced by you before are indicated. Amusements are apt to be unusual and involve unorthodox situations. Other people, both those who are older as well as younger individuals, are apt to be the dominating influence now in affairs of importance, especially around your family "scene." Nevertheless, the "dictates of your heart" seem reliable guides during this planetary cycle, and I feel that you should follow your intuitions rather than depend completely upon the advice or suggestions of others. A changeful year of exciting happenings!

1982   A very unusual eclipse pattern this year focuses sharp attention upon a dramatic change of direction in your personal life. I doubt that you will be able to avoid "sweeping" alterations in your lifestyle or occupational interests which form your present activities. However, as you are carried into the midstream of these vital changes, I am certain you will begin to perceive, dimly at first, an ever-brighter prospect for improving your "home life," because a lifting of burdens in this area is indicated as 1982 draws to a close. Deep stirring of creative faculties is likely to encourage you to "spread your wings" and soar to new heights of achievement! Romantic urges will constantly "seethe" within your emotions, and richly inspiring experiences could arise, although inner feelings of "aloneness" might govern for a time.

1983   A cycle of "exchanging the old for the new" with respect to close associations as well as family and home ties is shown throughout this significant year. Unusual friendships that "appear out of the blue" are apt to excite and stimulate you, while other associations will change with startling abruptness. Setting and following reasonable practices with regard to eating and other health rules are strongly indicated as a requirement in benefiting your physical well-being. A mood of "live today — forget tomorrow" could strengthen a tendency to "drift along" unless definite habits to plan and prepare for the future are inaugurated. Young people may prove temporarily burdensome, but your "sense of responsibility" will "stiffen" your resolve to carry out obligations that are demanding, I feel.

1984   Your pursuits of pleasure, romance, and creative self-expression are likely to be of a more aggressive nature during this new year, particularly until around the month of August. This will be a period when it will be advisable to exercise extreme discrimination and care in romantic associations, because unwise choices in this area could provoke conflicts or repercussions that would be difficult to escape later. Activities requiring physical exertion might be entered into in a spirit of observing safety precautions to avert mishaps. "Hasty" commitment of money is apt to lead to unlooked for problems or drains under this trend. Your friendliness and desire to cooperate can inspire unusually warm and helpful response from others now, so that things will work out well later on.

At the beginning of this forecast period, much attention will probably be directed toward the development of business insight and skills. I interpret this cycle in terms of a passing need to devote more time and energy to money matters, in connection with your source of income and an adjustment related to expenses or impulsive overspending. Although your "home" surroundings and all that this term implies will be seldom far from your thoughts, around the beginning of 1980 and for approximately two years afterward, a greater intensity will mark your handling of affairs in this area. I feel this will be a period when you will work toward building greater security for yourself and those close to you. Someone older is apt to require more time and attention during this phase. For a short interval you may be somewhat restricted in the management of your personal affairs . . . or to put it another way, you will be satisfying a responsibility and will not be averse to sacrificing some of your own interests temporarily.

I am sure a growing sense of your own inner resources and ability to meet challenges with fortitude and calmness will encourage faith in your powers as this cycle moves forward. The passage of time always brings a certain degree of change, but this particular forecast period is indicated as a time of remarkable and far-reaching alterations which will filter into many aspects of your life. I believe you will be introduced to unusual forms of entertainment which will help satisfy your longing for both "the old and the new." Unusual occupational interests may appeal as this trend draws to a close. Sudden attachments as well as abrupt "severances" are likely to be experienced, with a likelihood that your steps will be turned toward an entirely new direction by someone who has a strong hold upon your affections.

The promptings of your heart will often encourage you to seek out the kind of warm companionship which has always been a "bright spot" in your thoughts. There will be occasions when your intuitive powers seem in conflict with "logic," but I have little doubt that the guidance indicated by your "inner voice" will lead you to happier times and help you "side-step" the pitfalls that could later be costly for some individuals.

The two signs of the zodiac through which the Sun's influence is transmitted to those who were born in this cusp are Cancer and Leo. The Moon is considered to be the *ruler* of Cancer, and the Sun of Leo. Natives of this cusp have many of the characteristics of both signs. Particularly they have unusual ambition and are likely to set their *mark* quite high. They are by nature extremely sympathetic, however, especially with those who are in difficulty, and they can be extremely generous and lavish in their aid to those who need it. Sometimes, however, they will go to great lengths to gain their own ends and they are likely to be particularly clever in doing so. It is much easier for them than for the ordinary person to see the weak points of an opponent and to take advantage of such weaknesses in order to gain that which they have set out to do. However, they have unusual loyalty and regardless of what may have happened to a friend, they still have a quality which impels them to remain a loyal supporter.

The native of this cusp has an unusually good memory and a marked ability to plan capably. He needs, however, to take firm hold of the great natural abilities which were given him. As a result of vibrations from the sign Leo – which is to say directly as a result of the strong, sustaining forces of the Sun, there are powerful, natural vibrations which he can call into being to aid him in carrying out his constructive desires. To an unusual degree he can control and direct the mysterious forces of the universe. To do so, of course, requires very constructive thinking. The native of this cusp is unusually capable of controlling his thought processes when he once makes up his mind to the real necessity for doing so. He is usually better fitted for a mental occupation than for physical labor. One who was born during the period of this cusp can be quite successful in political fields or as a minister, public speaker or in some form of theatrical pursuit. Natives have a tendency to be fond of display and are by nature good *"showmen"*. These influences also tend toward the law and the judicial. One who was born under a strong influence from these vibrations usually has a good natural ability to understand financial matters, but his best field of activity is in some occupation which brings him into contact with many others.

Women who were born under this combination of influences are extraordinarily loyal and faithful and they are naturally charming companions. Individually, they require understanding on the part of the man they marry. Under proper conditions of companionship they fairly bloom. Leo is a sign which imparts much more aggressiveness, and many more marked qualities of extroversion than does Cancer. Leo is dramatic and sometimes flambouyant. Contrariwise, Cancer is retiring, modest in demeanor and the women are quite feminine. These qualities are blended in the cusp period. Marked complexities are often evident in the native. There is a tendency for natives of this cusp to be subject to periods of depression and melancholy. There are times in their personal life rhythms when a definite effort to cultivate positive thought-forms enables them to work in *harmony with natural law.*

The birthsign LEO
July 22nd to August 22nd

If you were born between July 22nd and August 22nd the sign Leo is your birthsign. This sign of the zodiac, or basic harmonic which plays its part in the formation of human character in the physical plane has powerful positives, but it also has strong negatives which are of a quite definite type. In describing this birth sign all the positive and negative qualities which are a part of the sign itself are dealt with. Those who were born at this time of the year, when the solar rays were transmitted through Leo, will recognize in themselves the qualities described, though some may be submerged while others are predominant.

In ancient civilizations, this sign was called the mansion of "*Power and Glory*". It occurs at a time when the Sun is considered to *—reign supreme—* and that central orb of the universe has always been *—the ruler—* of Leo. The principal star of the constellation has often been referred to as the *Royal Star,* the *Kingly Star,* the *Fortunate Star,* and the *"ruler of the affairs of heaven"* as well. The birthsign Leo has always been symbolized by the Lion. As with other signs of the zodiac, the symbol is intended to convey graphically the fundamental or psychological qualities inherent in the sign. It represents courage, electric energy, a fiery quality; but also rapaciousness, destructiveness, and sometimes "braggadocio".

Leo is referred to as masculine, choleric, hot, dry, fiery, fixed, barren, positive, bestial, northern, and of long ascension. It is also referred to as kingly, royal, or fortunate. The gem which has similar vibrations is the ruby and the flower is the poppy. Leo is representative of the Bible tribe of Judah, one of the twelve original tribes of Israel, or fundamental types of human beings.

The *pure* Leo type is of medium height and splendid proportions. He gives an impression of sturdiness. He has a pleasant and strong voice; a quick and firm step. His head is finely shaped, his complexion frequently ruddy, and his eyes are often hazel though sometimes blue, and quite keen and friendly. People who were born in this sign, however, are frequently not given the physical characteristics of the sign, as other vibrations are intermingled. The rising sign (the sign rising on the eastern horizon at birth) is quite strong in the formation of physical characteristics — working in harmony with heredity. Hidden vibrations are continually at work upon the people of this sign. When the spiritual qualities are developed, in which case the individual is highly evolved, these forces manifest themselves outwardly to the extent that there is a luminous soul quality, and the native may seem to be possessed of almost supernatural powers. The true Leo is almost invariably courageous; in fact completely fearless and impulsive, as well as generous.

Naturally, the intensity of the fiery qualities inherent in this sign being in their higher attributes powerfully constructive, are for that very reason quite the opposite when the material and animal side of the nature is allowed to become predominant. They may then become extremely potent forces for evil. Excepting when the native is undeveloped, the spiritual side of the Leo nature is strongly accentuated. When it *is* developed, and the native applies himself to constructive endeavors, his power of intellect is great and the spiritual nature manifests itself in an outward radiance. Because the native of Leo is impulsive and possessed of strong desires, he sometimes plunges into widely varied activities without regard for consequences, and often difficulties in life arise as a consequence. It is not intended, however, to indicate that one should be fearful of taking any step to which he is prompted by urges from within, *providing his endeavors are constructive.*

Excepting in unusual cases, and when planetary positions at the time of birth produce a lack of bodily vigor, the native of Leo is possessed of great vitality, vigor and brilliance. He has then a commanding bearing, and an imposing demeanor which makes him a natural leader. The vitality of the native when his evolutionary state is reasonably high, is such that he retains a youthful appearance and his zest for living until he is well advanced in years. It is quite likely that the people of Leo are more affected by the *impulsive qualities* inherent in their sign than are those born in any other. Resulting from strong inner urges and desires, their impetuous natures often lead them to make investments which result in loss, and to change their positions as well as their personal relationships. The native often finds himself involved in controversy or argument. All the fire signs are in a measure impulsive, but Leo is particularly susceptible to flashes of quick anger and an impulsive urge to change. He seldom holds a grudge, however, and soon recovers from angry passion.

You are sympathetic and generous to a marked degree, and you undoubtedly have a pleasing personality. Leo imparts great gifts. You should be talented in dramatics, in poetry, art, or music. The latter medium is a source of great solace and gratification to the native of this sign. When planetary positions in the chart at birth support him, great success is attained in musical fields. Inspiration is great, and there is probability that he will develop splendid technique. In any case, the native of Leo being susceptible to vibrations of all kinds and his nature inspirational, is affected greatly by music and should on every possible occasion listen to the rendition of forceful and uplifting melody. When the chart at birth shows a talent for music or for other artistic endeavors, every effort should be made to develop it. To do less is to neglect a great source of potential good as well as accomplishment.

Those who come into the world under a strong influence from this vibration are fine conversationalists, and possessed of great personality and charm. They have a fundamental ability to make friends easily and quickly and are likely to be very popular. You probably possess a happy disposition, being naturally inclined toward joviality, and you are undoubtedly good company. You are usually able to inspire confidence in others. The pure Leo is so agreeable in manner, so frank and engaging, as to win the support of others to the fullest degree. You undoubtedly are particularly fond of amusement. You are by nature quite affectionate, and also extremely loyal; ready at any moment to fight for those you love. You have marked tendencies toward the creation of *ideals*, and it is possible that you might be *blinded* to shortcomings in others as a result of that tendency.

Your fundamental aspirations are toward the most pure, loyal and abundant love; but the material factors of existence may well lessen the power of the constructives, turning them into grosser and therefore less constructive emotions. Your intentions are good and, for the most part honorable; yet the tendency you have to be impulsive and perhaps overly generous can at times lead you into difficulties. The native of this sign is quite inclined to accept those who come into his life's sphere at their face value. One is never harmed by contact with others when his own processes of thought are wholly and entirely constructive; but all of us are in the process of evolution, and we express many negatives in our thought patterns and consequently in our acts. You have a keen insight into human nature; but sometimes you jump to conclusions about those whom you meet, either forming an immediate liking or, in some cases, a strong dislike for new acquaintances. Often you are right in these intuitive conclusions, but at other times (especially when the outward demeanor and bearing of a new acquaintance does not please you), you may discover later that your *instant reaction* was a bit hasty!

You have an extremely good memory in many ways. Particularly you are not at all inclined to forget kindnesses, and you would be the last to forsake a friend — although you might become tired of very intimate relationships and break off some of them without compunction. Affection, sympathy, and understanding are highly necessary to your well-being. You can no more exist without them than can any of us live without the benign and warming rays of the sun. You are probably not especially fond of great physical exertion, and like your amusements to be of a more sensuous sort. Few people of Leo are as studious as those born in some of the other signs. They do not care for close and painstaking analysis, or for the grinding study necessary for academic achievement. You have remarkable intuition, however, and are able to absorb knowledge without the close application to study necessary to many others. It is unnecessary to teach most Leo people many things, as they have an instinctive capacity for absorbing information without being fully aware themselves of how they came by it. You much prefer human contact to the more or less hermitlike existence necessary to him who would achieve scholastic distinction.

You are greatly affected by weather conditions, the sun having a strong bearing upon your spirits. When there is bright sunshine you are light-hearted and gay, as well as filled with confidence. You have the ability to adapt yourself to almost any condition or circumstance, but essentially you are fond of the comforts of life. You love warm ease and luxurious surroundings, as well as ceremony and pomp. While you are impulsive to a considerable degree you have the ability to be secretive. You can conceal your motives as well as your thought processes from others to a remarkable degree. You are not inclined to be a traditionalist. That is, while you have great respect for custom, and particularly for law, you can brush aside all convention or tradition in a moment and proceed towards your goal, ignoring those things which might interfere and which are customarily done. Almost invariably what you accomplish is as a result of inspiration; consequently, your endeavors are most likely to result from a mood, or some immediate driving urge from within. You are not, therefore, by nature, inclined to be persistently plodding in your efforts.

As previously mentioned your sign has both powerfully constructive and negative qualities of potentially powerful nature. Words which describe the positive qualities of Leo are: inspirational, courageous, intuitive, loyal, kindly, magnanimous, chivalrous, optimistic, inspiring, magnetic, fearless, industrious, sincere, spiritual, affectionate, cooperative, hospitable, comprehending. Words which express the negative qualities inherent in the sign are: overbearing, impetuous, proud, pompous, arrogant, slack, shirking, dictatorial, condescending, domineering, sensuous, fussy, promiscuous, prodigal. Direction of the thought processes is, of course, the only method of developing the positive qualities. Negatives are *eliminated* by dwelling on their opposites. The native of Leo who wishes to make the most of his life will *develop his positive qualities,* which are of a lofty order.

The individual who was born in this sign, and who lives in a lower material plane has many destructive qualities – destructive primarily to himself. The fiery nature of Leo tends to make him impatient, argumentative, often hot-headed and overly impetuous. He is able to conceal his innermost thoughts, and can appear to desire something entirely different. He is deceitful, tricky, and overly fond of sensual pleasures. Uncontrolled physical passion is strongly accentuated in the native of Leo who is undeveloped. The fondness manifested by natives of this sign for the opposite sex has brought into their lives a great deal of suffering and misery. That is only so, of course, when it is unrestrained. While the undeveloped native is inclined to be deceitful and tricky, he is seldom *coldly* so, as are those born in some of the other signs; but his earthly desires lead in that direction. He is the one who goes to extremes in his affairs of life which are wholly material in nature. The unevolved native is extremely positive in his opinion, and skeptical of all things which present a different viewpoint. Therefore, he is hard to convince about anything that opposes his firmly fixed ideas.

Actually there are no more magnetic, lovable and charming people in the world than those who came into the world under a strong influence from the sign Leo; but a definite control of the negative qualities is an absolute *necessity* before the native can realize true happiness. He who was born in Leo, and who lives on a purely material plane, is controlled entirely by his emotions. Instead of directing his powerful urges into constructive channels, by *mental control,* he is like a man who drives many wild horses as a team, but allows them to run at will, exercising no control. He is thus likely to experience disaster at any moment. The love nature, for example, in the undeveloped native sometimes gets completely out of hand, becoming uncontrolled passion. His temper then becomes easily aroused fury. These powerful negatives naturally lead the native to become sensual and coarse, so that his existence is entirely material, and his only desire is for self-gratification. The Leo person who resolves to develop his better qualities will guide his mind into channels which develop the constructive qualities inherent in his sign; thus he is able to cast out lust for continual gratification of self, and he becomes increasingly powerful in his ability to achieve constructive goals.

It should be remembered that the pleasures of life are to be enjoyed; that there is no intention here to convey the impression that one should completely eliminate natural desires. The emotions are the power supply by means of which any individual accomplishes constructive objectives, but control which comes about as the result of the *direction of thought processes* alone is an absolute necessity, and *particularly* is this true of the Leo native. The undeveloped individual who allows the negatives of this basic vibration to predominate, invariably pays the penalty in personal unhappiness, misery, heartache, and pain. A powerful negative inherent in the sign is a tendency to *dwell upon faults in others*. Any native of Leo who finds that tendency growing, would be wise to admonish himself against searching for shortcomings in those around him. To dwell upon the imperfections of others is to tune in upon powerful negative vibrations which are directly allied with discontentment and unhappiness.

As previously stated some of the highest and greatest people of history were natives of Leo; but in every case their accomplishments in the course of a lifetime were the result of overcoming their material negatives through the development of constructive thought processes, which inevitably leads to *constructive action*. The native of this sign can *control* and *command* hidden forces to a remarkable degree. The possibilities of accomplishment are unlimited when once he realizes the necessity for *directing his thought processes* so that the powerful emotional side of his nature can be focused in the direction which will bring him to the realization of his loftiest aspirations.

WOMEN OF LEO

As one would have concluded upon reading what has previously been stated about Leo, women who were born under this solar vibration are extraordinarily sympathetic, affectionate, and impulsive. While the women of Leo are very friendly by nature — being almost without exception extroverts, they need in their associations harmonious companionships. Not infrequently they have friends with whom they really have very little in common and who do not understand them and with whom they cannot really talk with mutual understanding. They do have a tendency to make friends regardless of such actual rapport, however. Not infrequently women of this sign have specific interests. Either in their daily association with other people or in marriage there should be a common ground of interest.

Women of this sign are exceedingly capable in any field pertaining to dress; and they are especially successful, also, in occupations having to do with the preparation and serving of food. They are *natural* cooks. It is rare to find one who comes into the world under this solar vibration who lacks that ability. Among the signs they are perhaps the finest home-makers. The woman who is a native of Leo is usually much better fitted to be in her own home, and prefers a life of domesticity to a career in the business world. Certainly there is no sign of the zodiac which produces women who are basically more devoted to their families than are women of Leo. They have the capacity for becoming extremely loyal and faithful wives and mothers in marriage but women of this sign in general because of their ability to develop friendships so readily may find their interests divided as a result.

The woman of Leo is fierce in defense of those whom she loves; and in particular will spring to the most *furious* defense of her young. Seldom does she heed advice or suggestions from others about the raising of her children, no matter what the source. She follows her own instincts and her own ideas, and is usually very successful in gaining the understanding of her children, as well as in managing them. She often displays great wisdom of an intuitive nature in that connection.

Women of some of the other signs are likely to remain in the background — but not the woman of Leo. She — as is true of the Leo man — seldom meets a stranger! She is always interested in everything other women do, and she may occupy herself with lengthy discussions of little things in others lives. She is not inclined to gossip viciously or meanly, however; — but she does love *lengthy discussions*.

Love and affection are highly necessary to both sexes born in this sign. Particularly, the woman of Leo must receive frequent demonstration of regard upon the part of her marriage partner. She must be *told* that she is loved. Among all the signs this is most true of Leo. She is an extraordinarily devoted, sympathetic, and affectionate wife and mother, but when she is neglected by her marriage partner or when there is lack of affection, and particularly should her spouse ever show signs of interest *in another direction,* she will sever the marriage tie and seemingly thereafter have no regrets. When the woman of Leo has decided that she has come to the parting of the ways, she is usually *fully decided* and she takes the step which is final. There is no finer, sweeter, more attractive and warm-hearted woman, however, than she who is born under a strong Leo influence.

Parents of youngsters who were born in Leo should make the greatest effort to guide their mental processes into constructively imaginative lines. It is of the utmost importance for these children to learn *self-control*; and the best way for anyone to do that — young or old, is to be absorbed mentally and physically in something of constructive nature. These youngsters are self-willed, affectionate, impulsive, imitative, and quite frequently — highly talented. Their hands and their minds should be busy constantly in tasks which arouse their interest; and they should have plenty of wholesome amusement that is sufficiently varied as to meet with the imaginative, impulsive quality inherent in the sign.

Youngsters who are born under a strong influence from this sign learn readily and quickly, but they are not fond of close application to study. It should perhaps be stressed that they are very rarely good students. It might be stated, in fact, that no child who received a *predominating* influence from the sign Leo at birth is by nature a bookworm! However, they do *acquire* a tremendous amount of information, although those who are closely associated with them — parents, teachers, etc., may find it difficult to understand exactly *where* they got the knowledge. They have extremely good *intuitive* sense and they absorb a vast amount of information; though they themselves are not always aware of exactly how it came to them. It is usually a mistake to worry about their seeming lack of application to study; often the information they pick up is more vital and will be more important to them in dealing with life than knowledge obtained from books and ordinary scholastic endeavors. Children of Leo almost invariably prefer to engage in things which relate to social activities — mingling with other people and participating in all sorts of extracurricular activities, rather than in quietly reading or studying.

Certainly there are no more lovable, affectionate and spontaneous children than those who were born in the sign Leo. Their faults are likely to result from — impulsiveness, an overabundance of energy, and a tendency to take other children or adults at face value. As a result of these traits they are sometimes disappointed in their friendships (or in their associations with elders), although they are less likely to give outward expression to such dissatisfaction than are those who were born in other signs. Not infrequently they are disillusioned by adults who tell them one thing and themselves do something else. This applies, of course, to moral values of every kind. All human beings, of course, are in a state of development in evolution, and in our modern day and age even adults can be extremely confused by the conditions of life, and they are often not to be blamed because they find it difficult to deal with children.

Leo youngsters need love and understanding, as well as affection, to a greater degree than do most of those who were born in other signs. Those who are in control of these youngsters should never display impatience and anger in dealing with them. Because of the sensitive Leo nature, they need sympathy. Lacking it, their quality of *self-will* is strongly aroused, and they become much more *combative* than is the case when they receive sympathetic understanding. Proper parental training, guidance, and discipline — without harshness — can bring these children to realization of the highest and greatest good; and help develop them into fine, noble, and upstanding adults.

63

It is, of course, obvious that the native of Leo should marry prudently. Particularly, it is advisable for anyone who came into the world under a strong influence from this sign to have a life mate who is affectionate and understanding. When the Leo person for any reason marries another who is by nature reserved and undemonstrative, the marriage is almost sure to result in unhappiness and misery, with more than a probability that it will end in disaster.

Being impulsive, affectionate, and warm-hearted, both sexes who come into the world under this sign of the zodiac are extremely likely to contract early and ill-advised marriages. One who was born in Leo should not, in fact, enter into matrimony until he has become at least reasonably settled in life; but humanity, of course, profits only by its own mistakes and must follow its bent until needed lessons have been learned. Not infrequently Leo women whose marriages have been disrupted become disillusioned with marriage in general and not a few women of this sign have been known during their lives to more or less *"play the field"*! Sometimes under such considerations they get a reputation for doing things they don't actually do. Illustrative of the qualities sometimes displayed by Leo women, Mae West is an outstanding example of the type we have in mind, she having been born in the sign. Some of you who read this may be too young to remember what Mae West was like. If you don't remember, ask your parents and you will understand the typical characteristics of this sign. Mae West was quite exotic; she liked beautiful clothes, and beautiful diamonds in particular, which is quite characteristic of those who were born in this sign. She was more or less a *symbol* of sex; actually as a matter of fact her approach was more or less a *"kidding" of the subject*. In actual fact, personally she wasn't the immoral person she represented herself to be. This is also quite characteristic of the sign.

Almost all women of Leo are extroverts; extremely good mixers in any kind of society and quite likely to occupy the center of the stage in any company. It is extremely advisable for the native of Leo to marry one who is on an equal plane socially, as well as culturally or intellectually. Wide differences in any of these matters will produce in the Leo considerable dissatisfaction and probably unhappiness. The sign Aquarius (January 21st — February 19th) has many qualities which might be termed of interlocking nature. It is actually the opposition sign of the zodiac, but in many ways has fewer inharmonious traits than any of the other signs. Therefore a marriage contracted by the Leo with one born in that sign is likely to prove happy.

Fundamentally, the sign Aries (March 20th — April 29th) and Libra (September 24th — October 23rd) are also harmonious. Aries is sometimes impetuous and head-strong, however, and for this reason there may prove to be inharmony, especially if there is not a high state of development in both parties to the marriage. Children, when the Leo native is married to a Libra, are likely to be healthy and strong; but fondness for the pleasures of life may grow in such a partnership (on the part of both), to such an extent that total achievement suffers. Leo, as mentioned, has been called the royal sign and this has a very definite meaning. People of this sign are basically of a very *high order* and capable of the broadest development in which their constructive tendencies are used to the great benefit of those around them.

The fundamental vibration of Leo being of the nature of fire imparts qualities of leadership essentially, but does not have within itself the traits which lend themselves readily to plodding. As a result natives of this sign are much better fitted for mental than physical labor. Many of this sign have been very powerful leaders in public affairs. The attractiveness of the Leo personality is such that the native is often especially fitted for occupations which take him before the public. He also is likely to have an instinctive judgment of the reactions of others which he sometimes uses unconsciously. Consequently, he is able to convey his ideas in such a fashion that they are readily accepted.

Oratory has always been a favorable outlet for the talents of Leo. As public speakers their warm, genial personality, combined with their bearing, are such as to inspire response and confidence regardless of what they say. Consequently, it has been possible for them to attain a great deal of prominence without extensive education or knowledge. The love of ceremony and theatricals often makes them highly proficient in the drama. They are successful as public speakers to a remarkable degree, and have been outstanding ministers. The magnetism and personality which are inherent in the sign draw others to them amazingly.

Natives of this sign will be found as successful manufacturers, bankers, and brokers. They have also been highly successful in military careers and as leaders in widely varied fields. They make especially capable chefs and confectioners. As a result they quite frequently succeed as restaurateurs. The highly evolved Leo native is extremely interested in the welfare of people as a whole and will often be found working for the benefit of humanity.

The true Leo native has a strong tendency toward fondness for display. He is a great admirer of power and of grandeur. He, therefore, often aspires to a high position where such symbols of title and authority are to be expected. He makes a splendid lawyer, being especially apt in court appearances. He is possessed of fundamental qualities which often make him a fine judge. The native has also been known to excel as a physician, inspiring greater confidence in his patients than those perhaps of any other sign. Women of Leo are perhaps the most efficient nurses of those born in any of the signs, principally because of their cheerful and inspiring manner. The most obvious quality of the sign is leadership, however. Natives are seldom to be found in positions which require them to follow the direction of others. The ability to lead is too strongly marked for that.

True Leo natives are independent, and more than likely to resent being told what to do. They do not care greatly for details, and would far rather plan an undertaking than carry it out. That is an executive quality which is more or less pronounced in all people who were born in fire signs. They do not take readily to immediate supervision, preferring to work in their own way. Certainly the highly evolved native of this sign is far more fitted to rule than to be ruled. Although his impulses are often hasty, the native is likely to have keen and sound business judgment. Real responsibility will often raise the constructive qualities of the sign to a high level.

65

DISHARMONY OF LEO

While the *vitality* of people born under a strong influence from this sign of the zodiac is great, there should be a determined effort on their part toward moderation and balance in the diet. The negatives which are inherent in the sign, and which have been previously referred to, have a definite rate of vibration productive of disharmony in the physical body; disharmony, which is ordinarily referred to as disease. These negatives express themselves in immoderation in diet as well as excesses otherwise.

Leo rules the heart or, in particular, affects that vital organ; consequently *temperate living* is essential for natives of this sign. Such living always follows constructive thought processes. The heart is indicative of ardency, generation, and vital power. The negatives of the sign expressed often in physical action of various kinds, result in what are known as heart diseases, fevers, meningitis in various forms, angina pectoris, palpitation of the heart, locomotor-ataxia, and pestilential maladies. Indirectly, the native suffers from inflammations. These are all to be overcome and obviated by *cultivation* of the *positive qualities* of the sign. Harmful physical action (resulting from errors of doubt and other negatives which lead to these conditions) ceases when the mental processes are guided into constructive channels of thought.

The Leo native should seek to *order* the processes of his mind. When he does so his physical actions are calm, orderly, and quiet. Over-impetuousness, excitability, and dissatisfaction are all outward indications of the particular negatives inherent in the sign which have been allowed to grow. Excitement and over-exertion, being also expressive of negatives, are dangerous in the long run for the native of this sign. Colds, and other ailments of similar nature, result when the vital forces of the body are depleted.

Some of the negatives which are part of this sign produce responsive vibrations which directly result in skin disorders and diseases of various kinds which are usually traceable to poor circulation. When any condition of disharmony in the physical organism of one who was born under a strong influence from the sign Leo becomes manifest, one should look directly to the negative which is implied in his birth chart. Unless influences are quite bad at birth, however, (indicating a state of evolution requiring the necessary learning of important lessons) the native of this sign has tremendous vitality. He is able to throw off illness and disease quickly as a result of his original bodily resistance, though also greatly because of his natural tendency to be optimistic and courageous.

Despite the fact that the true native of Leo is naturally fearless and courageous to the ultimate degree, he is subject to periods of despondency. Under such conditions his every effort should be to turn his mind from those things which are depressing, and to call into his consciousness scenes and thoughts of an opposite nature. He should seek to meditate in quiet, so that he can be free from nervous stresses and strains for a short time, in order to quickly eliminate the powerful negative quality of deep moods of despondency.

1977 Your world is taking on "a new setting", leaving behind its familiar course. The month of April in 1977 is likely to be especially meaningful as is the month of October. Your mental outlook, I feel, will tend to be more "sober" and not as inclined to "over-confidently take charge" or move forward as in the past. Any change or new plan started at this time will not prove lasting but will have to be redone, I am certain. Because of Neptune's influence, you are apt to hold an unrealistic concept of a particular person. An old, old companion will be by your side bringing surprising good fortune.

1978 Creative pursuits and imaginative entertaining may give you some of your greatest pleasure. I think this is a period in your life when you will have reason to be particularly grateful for past efforts which have developed your resourcefulness, because many of your ties with the past will change now, leading you into meaningful decisions touching your living arrangements. Your friends and acquaintances are likely to display the genuineness of their kind feelings toward you more than once during 1978. Through your experiences, you will transform your mind powers so remarkably, in my opinion, that gradually a "new set" of circumstances and relationships will suit you better. During this turning point in your personal affairs, PREPARATIONS and other "hidden elements" are apt to seem especially helpful to your progress.

1979 Because your "purse strings" may appear ever tighter, you are likely to have a growing desire to create a more solid, fulfilling path in life. "A protective hand" will rest over your more gainful efforts, perpetually aiding, I believe. You may not always recognize "possibilities and probabilities" just yet that are "taking hold," but through your ability to meet conditions constructively, you WILL improve your situation substantially, I feel sure. You have a capacity few people have for using your talents to the fullest, in my estimation, and now you should approach steadily those circles of activity where your true abilities will be most greatly appreciated. Let Divine Understanding be your inspiration, your illumination, "tomorrow's" entranceway.

1980 This should be a dramatically outstanding period in your life because of the eclipse pattern this year which is likely to touch off a chain reaction. One new plan or decision may cause hidden moves that, in the course of development, will demand or necessitate another arrangement. Quarrels and sharp words with electrical situations resulting are indicated strongly, especially involving your close associates. While misunderstandings may start between other people, later you may be drawn in. Changes connected with domestic interests are powerfully shown, and these may encourage the idea of putting aside a "nest egg" or hiding possessions of value, particularly since recent restraints upon spending or other financial matters seem to be of first consideration. The suggested idea of a safe investment could become increasingly attractive, leading to conversations in this area, I feel.

1981 People nearby, relatives, or others outside your close surroundings are apt to play a very prominent role in your affairs during this year. Messages that have gone astray or the written or spoken word which is misunderstood could cause some brief complications now, delaying plans you are considering. Hidden elements which hitherto have been "unknown" will probably come out into the open so that they become general knowledge. There is strong likelihood of your becoming involved in a matter from the past that you would prefer was kept secret. However, at the "last minute," so to speak, something of a protective nature is likely to come to your notice, helping you "untangle" troublesome involvements through a quick grasp of the situation. I believe your place of residence is headed for major changes, and a more settled condition will follow.

1982 Moves that are made from "hidden or unseen conditions" could trigger unusual changes around the middle of this year, probably having a bearing upon your domestic affairs. A "shake-up" that relates to "who is responsible for what" is apt to assume larger proportions during this cycle, leading to a "readjustment" in your relationships. The search for greater satisfaction in "home" surroundings is likely to lead to consideration of moving or "redoing" in this area. I believe you will find that much you have sought "elsewhere" now will seem centered in benefits to be derived from your "home" locale. Transportation "to and from" may briefly pose more problems than usual, and it is likely that "communications" to and from others will be subject to temporary delays or passing complications which will then ease later on.

1983 This is an unusually expansive period when you will be impelled to seek out the "pleasant side of life." Greater desire for a "round of gaiety" will need to be balanced by attention to the more serious responsibilities of your life; otherwise, pleasures could assume undue importance in your affairs, and neglected matters would have to be taken into account later on. Domestic responsibilities may overshadow other interests throughout much of this cycle. Brief "moods" of loneliness may be expected, under this kind of planetary trend, causing you to seek expressions of love from others, but a conscious effort to uplift the spirits of those who are troubled will have a very salutary effect upon your own outlook, I am sure. Unexpected and sometimes exciting romantic encounters could appear with great suddenness at this time!

1984 Your domestic "scene" is likely to be the source of much activity, especially until around your birthdate this year. Stresses may briefly touch this area of your life, sometimes because of mechanical "breakdowns" or sharp divisions of opinion concerning "home life" issues. For a short time there may be restrictions or temporary obligations which force some curtailment of your own desires or personal interests, probably in connection with someone older. Health concerns are indicated as being under a "protective hand" during this cycle, and I believe it will be easier to respond to the friendly overtures of other people, because your own mood will tend to be amiable and reaching out for friendships and loving encounters.

SUMMATION (Leo)

"Topsy-turvy" conditions are likely to characterize your home scene on more than one occasion during this forecast period. Abrupt changes may remove some of the people around you with great suddenness, and similar alterations may bring a return of other individuals into your immediate surroundings. I feel you will have a deep longing for more settled and stable conditions in your "home" locale. In the process of seeking the kind of security you desire, you are apt to try a number of different "approaches," some of which represent startling departures from your previous outlook. Freedom to "come and go" as you please within your "home" environment may be the source of much discussion, some of an acrimonious nature. People who possess unique distinctions or "ahead of the times" ideas will undoubtedly cross your path . . . and many of these "contacts" will be centered around your "home" or living arrangements.

Ideas for better or more responsible handling of money or your source of income are likely to emerge around the middle of this period. I believe a growing awareness that if *you* don't take a "starring role" in practical management of your funds, probably no one else will prompt you to watch expenses with a "careful eye" and, at the same time, to investigate ways to better protect your assets so that opportunities for gain can be taken advantage of.

The closing two or three months of 1979 until approximately one year later are strongly indicated as the most auspicious time to benefit from money moves. This will be a period when opportunities are likely to be abundant, and unexpected support should enable you to seize advantages for improving your money position.

Some rather peculiar circumstances related to affairs of the heart may introduce brief disappointments into your life during this trend. It will be easier to "mislead" yourself as to the prospects for a particular relationship, so that at such times it will be helpful to "count your blessings" rather than dwell upon disappointments. Speculative or risky ventures may seem unusually attractive throughout this period, chiefly owing to a tendency to concentrate upon the advantageous side without considering possible disadvantages.

I believe this will be one of the most changeful periods of your life, but at the same time, from these changes I am certain will come the growth of a new pattern developing from your former "style of living" which happily will satisfy your longing for loving companionship and security.

69

The two signs which play an important part in this cusp are Leo and Virgo; the former being *"ruled"* by the Sun and the latter by Mercury, and both markedly affect the characteristics and the lives of those who were born in this period. They are, in common with those of other cusps, more complex than the average individual. These natives are more cautious than those of Leo, but less so than Virgo natives. Those who were born in a cusp period such as this combine many wonderful qualities. They are likely to have unusually good dispositions and are able to adapt themselves to almost any condition and circumstance of life. They are likely to be *"good mixers"*. If their associations are congenial and they find companionship through those whom they encounter, they can themselves be fine and loyal companions. They are extremely good associates and neighbors being likely to attend to their own affairs and to allow others to do the same.

The native is not at all inclined to be critical, although due to the influence of the sign Virgo, he is likely to be very *observant* and consequently to notice the things that other people do which vary from the conventional and which they perhaps shouldn't do, yet he is quite inclined to feel that it is their *own business,* and that they can do as they choose. He is not at all likely to be sharp in speech and faultfinding. As a matter of fact, he is much more apt to *take things as they come,* and to feel satisfaction in merely living and being surrounded by those for whom he cares. Those who were born under predominant vibrations from this cusp are, to an unusual degree, in sympathy with nature. They can do much to bring out the simplicity of their own fundamental qualities and to harmonize with the beautiful in nature's laws. The tremendous calm and peace of the earth itself is essentially a part of their natures. They are likely to be very much at their best when they are outdoors and therefore not confined within the walls of home or office, and enjoy outdoor pleasures and exercise.

Natives of this combination of vibrations are extremely fond of gardens. They love their own arrangements of design. However, they are likely to have some tendency to be easily swayed by the opinions of others, particularly if those opinions are expressed in a positive and convincing manner. Still, those who might possibly induce them to believe things which would be of disadvantage to them, or perhaps harmful, are rendered powerless by the natural forces which they unconsciously call to their support as a result of their naturally constructive mental processes.

The woman who was born in this cusp loves to give deep thought to the furnishings of her home and the surroundings which she has chosen. Her Virgo instinct makes her fond of neatness in arrangement. She is fond of ornament or at least beauty in clothing, to an unusual degree; consequently her attire is likely to be *different* and is often outstanding. Those who were born in this particular cusp are especially good in literary fields if their ambition is aroused in that direction. The intellect of Virgo combined with the heart and fire of Leo, makes one able to write well. This combination frequently finds outlet in journalistic fields.

The birthsign VIRGO
August 23rd to September 23rd

Your birth occurred in the sign Virgo, if you were born between August 23rd and September 23rd. It is an Earth sign and its qualities are manifested by *"down-to-earth"* practicality and perfectionism. In ancient times symbolism was used extensively to depict meanings in the operation of natural law. Thus it was that the *"Virgin of August"* came to Earth as a goddess to instruct man in the proper cultivation of the soil and the reaping of his harvest. In a measure the Virgin is a symbol of the harvest season. More particularly, however, she is intended to indicate graphically the psychological factors or qualities that are inherent in the birthsign. Mercury is considered to be the ruling planet, which means that the qualities of Mercury are predominant in certain of their phases in the sign, and the planet itself plays an important part in the working of cosmic law relating to the individual involved. Virgo is representative of the Bible tribe of Naphtali, one of the twelve original tribes of Israel, or basic types of humanity. The sapphire is the natal stone of Virgo — the cornflower is the flower. The sign is referred to as earthy, dry, cold, common, feminine, barren, northern, melancholy, human, negative, flexed, maternal, and of long ascension.

It is true of Virgo, as with all other signs of the zodiac, that this is a basic or fundamental vibration which has within itself both positive and negative factors. The positions of the planets at the time of birth will indicate the state of evolution which the individual has reached, and the extent to which he will manifest the positive qualities inherent in his sign. As with the other signs, we shall describe *all* of the characteristics and qualities which are fundamentally a part of this sign, both positive and negative, and those who were born in the sign will recognize these qualities within themselves, although some will be more predominant than others.

The planet Mercury bestows splendid mental capacities. In Virgo it imparts wit and ingeniousness, but particularly the qualities of mind are analytical. Virgo, in itself, is above all else *orderly* and *methodical,* as well as thoughtful. Those who come into the world under strong Virgo vibrations are seldom impulsive in their actions being more inclined to analyze any situation at some length before making an important change. The native of this sign is precise, accurate, neat and discriminating, unless there were extremely strong planetary positions at birth in other signs. He prefers order and harmony in his surroundings, and it is usually difficult for him to apply himself to work unless he can do so under such conditions. The tendency of the Virgo native is to be quite accurate in speech, and to distinguish to a fine point in the selections of words and phrases; and it is not unusual for the native to be greatly admired for his wit.

The *purer type* of Virgo is graceful; has a well-proportioned figure — usually somewhat above average height; possesses clear cut features — a rather aquiline but straight nose, lips rather finely chiseled, and even, perfect teeth. The countenances of pure (or nearly so) Virgo people are intelligent; in fact, frequently intellectual. Their complexions are clear, and their skins quite sensitive. Their eyes are more often blue than brown — and they are extremely expressive. Their manners are poised and gracious. Their dispositions are kindly, and among the women downright sweet. Their voices are well modulated and harmonious; frequently quite musical and soft.

The tendency of this basic vibration, however, is toward a materialistic rather than a spiritual viewpoint. While both sexes often have a soulful expression about the eyes, they are not inclined to accept anything which is not *measurable* and *verifiable* in this physical plane of existence. Their conclusions are almost invariably based upon a physical or material viewpoint. When the *evolved* native, however, does enter the domain of the spiritual he becomes a worthy exponent of the most lofty philosophical teachings, and he has the capacity to comprehend the higher esoteric concepts. The native of Virgo is essentially well-balanced. He is not likely to go to extremes. He can more often study and apply himself to occult matters — and retain his completely normal or well-balanced viewpoint, than can those born in most of the other signs. The *middle ground,* as far as his acts are concerned, more often appeals to the true Virgo than do extremes in any direction.

You are undoubtedly inclined by instinct to be refined, modest, and have a tendency to be retiring and quiet in manner, rather than to be aggressive. This tendency may have been a hindrance at times. You are probably extremely neat and orderly, which is a reflection of your analytical tendencies and the desire for order which is a natural quality. You undoubtedly have very clear ideas about how things should be done and you are not inclined to admire others who are careless or are in any way unkempt. Natives of your sign usually like to see things executed with *meticulous* carefulness. You probably dress quite well, giving considerable thought to the neatness and harmoniousness of your apparel. You are undoubtedly poised, of confident bearing, and are inclined to be particular in your choice — not only of clothes, but of your surroundings and friends. The esthetic appeals to you greatly, in the sense that you tend toward a preference for the highest in art and literature. You prefer harmoniousness of color and sound. Yours is basically a beautiful sign, imparting a fundamental purity and strength which is susceptible to the highest development. There is a chastity in Virgo, a fastidiousness and a quality of discrimination which is unmistakably evident in both sexes who come into the world under a predominant influence from this sign. This fastidious quality may show itself in a distaste for being too close to people — even a dislike for being touched. It is almost an impossibility to bring the true Virgo to a degraded state of life, regardless of how evil or vicious his own early environment might have been. Invariably the individual who receives a strong vibration from this sign at birth will rise above such conditions. The Virgin Mary is symbolic of the Virgo basic harmonic or vibration.

In common with other Virgo natives, you are resilient and probably have a considerable ability to rebound from reverses or disappointments. It may readily be nearly impossible *to hold you down!* Your mind is quite practical in its approach to the problems of life, and you seek a secure position. Very seldom do people who were born under this particular solar vibration remain in conditions of poverty or want for very long. They are almost invariably able to rise above these conditions, and to achieve a position of relative independence at least.

You are logical, quick to learn, and have an adaptability which enables you to fit yourself into widely varying conditions of life — although you would be dissatisfied and seek to change (probably successfully) any condition in which you found yourself that you considered inharmonious or disorderly. You are not at all inclined to be radical, and you prefer a position of substance (rather than achievement) in any field which would brand you or set you apart greatly from the rest of humanity. You like to make a good appearance, and you desire your associates to be normal people — preferably those who have a good (or at least substantial) position in life. You have an ability to judge situations and people with a keenness which is not easily misled. A marked characteristic of the Virgo vibration is the ability the native has to note any condition which departs from the conventional or customary practice.

Despite the fact that you are affected by periods of depression (which may be unknown even to some of your close friends), you are by nature hopeful — and not permanently daunted or discouraged by vicissitudes of fortune. You have a tendency to be selfconscious at times, yet you really recognize deep within yourself your own qualifications which would enable you to excel. As a result, you are not inclined to look upon many people as your superiors. You are conservative in your judgment and in your opinions, particularly when they apply to your own affairs. You are not likely to be an originator, except perhaps along literary lines. It is, in fact, entirely possible that your conservative outlook and point of view may have prevented you from grasping opportunities which came your way in the past.

Being of a practical turn of mind, the Virgo native desires to enjoy life as such. He wishes to get *all he can out of it.* You are a keen observer and the *details* of anything that comes to your notice rarely escape your attention. You can be relied upon to fulfill your obligations to the best of your ability. You are fond of your home and, by instinct, devoted to the members of your family. You do desire *personal* freedom, however; although you could submit to considerable domination by someone else rather than to take a decisive step which might change your entire life. You are not at all inclined to lose your self-possession. It is not easy to work you up to the point where you become so agitated that you do not know what you are doing. That, incidentally, may not be said of those born in some other signs of the zodiac.

73

VIRGO

Very few of those who were born under a strong influence from the sign Virgo show their real age when they begin to get along in years. Almost invariably they retain the appearance of youth until quite late in life. As a matter of fact, they are quite likely to be long lived. The Virgo native is almost invariably successful when he devotes himself to any branch of learning. He is by nature a good student. The true Virgo whose interest is aroused in reading — at any time during his life, becomes a wide and voracious literary addict. It has often been said that the journalists of the world come from this sign. That is particularly true of the women; many have become very successful in the journalistic field. Also, there are no better proof-readers in the world than those who were born in Virgo. It has been noted that such proficiency is acquired by natives of this sign that they are able to pick out the errors in a whole page of copy — almost at a glance.

You wish to be respected by others and, in fact, are quite inclined to demand that you be treated with respect. The evolved native of Virgo has a remarkable quality of seeing into the minds and hearts of others. This is often referred to as a psychic quality, yet the true Virgo is not psychic in the accepted meaning of the term. He is, however, capable of *seeing through the pretenses* of others. He is skillful in the exercise of his mental faculties, and when he really strives toward development of the spiritual side of his nature he becomes powerfully magnetic, though in a quiet and poised fashion. The native of Virgo who is evolved has a calm, unruffled bearing; and while he observes details — and consequently the errors of others — his criticisms are constructive and corrective, rather than destructive. He has a splendid sense of what is right and wrong and he never betrays a trust. If, however, another person once loses the confidence and trust of a Virgo native — he may not regain it!

The fundamental harmonic of Virgo has powerful positives but, in common with all the other signs of the zodiac, it has potentially strong negatives. Both the positives and the negatives are, as is always the case, of a quite definite kind. Words expressing the positive qualities of the sign are: discriminating, serious, thoughtful, discreet, concise, orderly, intellectual, efficient, contemplative, prudent, industrious, provident, methodical, thrifty, perceptive. Words which express the negative qualities are: cold, mercenary, unresponsive, timid, anxious, apprehensive, secretive, fearful, critical, indecisive, skeptical.

The *unevolved* native of Virgo is unduly proud, and becomes quite calculating and mercenary in his desire to occupy a substantial position in life and to attain security for himself. He is proud of his powers of observation, and he will go to great lengths to ferret out information about others. He delights in bringing short-comings or unpleasant facts to their attention. In this connection no detail is too small to escape his notice or to be dragged forth into the light.

The undeveloped Virgo native is often sarcastic and bitter. It is observed that among women who are so unevolved, many are, in early life, extremely attractive in appearance — with soulfully expressive eyes and equable dispositions; but as time progresses and they allow the negative qualities of their natures to develop they become critical and even carping. They become excessively neat and prim, the mouth develops fine lines which completely encircle it and the lips become pursed — and there is a constant tendency to point out the shortcomings of others.

The native of this sign *is* sensitive and — when undeveloped, his pride is easily wounded. The unevolved Virgo is egotistical, particularly where his mental attributes are concerned and is likely to consider himself greatly superior in the quickness of his wit or his ability to outdo others mentally. He lacks patience with others, and is unkind and severe to those who do not measure up to his standards of convention. He is extremely apt at worming information from his friends without their being conscious of the fact that he is doing so. His curiosity is avid, and he has an insatiable thirst for trifles. He pounces upon that which may be scandalous or unfavorable to another. While the evolved native is a model of discretion, virtue and truth, the one who remains unevolved is clever in hiding his inmost thoughts, and sly in making plans.

One of the most powerful negatives of Virgo is a tendency to develop imaginary illnesses. The native who has allowed this negative to develop becomes addicted to the use of drugs and medicines, and will adopt all sorts of fads, in an effort to cure what he imagines is wrong with him. It has been said that the native of Virgo should avoid drugs and medicines to as great an extent as possible.

While the evolved Virgo native loves all things which are beautiful and orderly and harmonious, the unevolved native allows his habits of critical analysis to spoil for him that which might be otherwise beautiful. His mind focuses itself upon his pride of observation, and the beauty of the object is ruined for him by his preoccupation with looking for flaws.

The powerful positives of Virgo are of such a nature to make it possible for the native to reach a very high plane of physical existence if he but takes advantage of them. He is capable and has the inherent ability to become highly intellectual, possessing sound, yet generous judgment; and he is also able to achieve a high degree of material success. Cultivation of his positive traits will enable the Virgo native to come to the realization of his most ambitious dreams and aspirations.

The woman who approaches the pure type of Virgo is above all chaste, pure, and fastidious. In this pure type of Virgo woman there is a particular sweetness about the eyes and the countenance generally which is the indefinable yet unmistakable stamp of this basic vibration. She expresses in her actions, her appearance, and her expression, virtue and chastity as well as great reserve. She is repelled by all that is coarse, gross, and disorderly. She shrinks from the low animalistic tendencies in man, and although for that reason her marriage may not prove altogether happy, she is still capable of the greatest devotion. She is a thrifty housewife. Being extremely neat, she is proud of having her home always in order and everything in its place.

The women of Virgo become extremely loyal and devoted wives and mothers, though they do not always choose matrimony. There are more *"bachelor girls"* who received a predominating influence from the sign Virgo at birth than from any of the other basic vibrations. That is due to the analytical trend of mind and the quality of discrimination imparted by the sign. The woman of Virgo is seldom blinded by emotion or carried away by impulse, as are those who were born in some of the other signs of the zodiac. She has essentially a practical point of view, and seeks a secure, ordered, but independent existence. Despite every obstacle, handicap, or disappointment encountered, she almost invariably raises herself to a position of respectability.

In common with the men of Virgo, she is by nature impelled to an interest in hygiene, and is a natural student of dietetics. She becomes an extremely capable and efficient nurse. She is always calm and soothing, and her temperament is such that she manifests a placidity of outward bearing which is quieting to her patient. In addition she has the understanding and capacity to know her job well; and, particularly, to carry out instructions faithfully. The true Virgo nurse is always meticulous in caring for the patients in her charge.

The woman of this sign has a quick eye, and is able to succeed in almost any occupation which does not require great originality or creative ability, but in which ability to observe and analyze are important factors. In common with the men of the sign, women of Virgo are almost always quick to observe anything which is done *differently* than it is usually done. This is the foundation of the ability they have to be good proofreaders. As previously mentioned, they are perhaps the best proofreaders of any of the twelve signs, being able to observe a misspelled word or other errors in a page of copy almost immediately. This ability to observe and to analyze is extremely valuable in many of the affairs of life. Many Virgo women, as stated before, become remarkably successful as journalists. Not a few have been well known writers in various fields. It should also be mentioned that a disproportionately large number of teachers received at birth a strong influence from the sign Virgo.

Women who are natives of this sign invariably display the most refined taste in their dress. They are fond of beautiful things, but prefer them to be useful rather than purely ornamental. They are successful as milliners and modistes, having a quick and accurate eye for that which is pleasing in form, line and color, and an understanding of fashion — often expressed to the ultimate degree in their own apparel.

The positive and the negative qualities of this sign have been rather fully discussed, and it becomes obvious that the Virgo child has potential character traits of the most constructive and noble kind. The youngster of this sign, however, is likely to be greatly influenced, if during his early years there are those around him who frequently condemn others, or point out faults in a sharply critical fashion. The tendencies imparted by the sign toward *meddlesomeness* and *inquisitive prying* can grow, though the youngster naturally is unaware of this growth, until the habit of looking for things which are not as they should be, becomes fixed. The most important lesson for the Virgo child to learn is the *unkindness* of criticism. By example and precept he should be taught and shown that tolerance and kindliness are admirable virtues. He may need to be reminded that all things have much good in them.

It is unusual for the child of Virgo to have poor mental faculties; quite the contrary is the rule. The true Virgo is a good student and has the ability to apply himself to arduous study. He is capable of persistency and the unexcitable Virgo quality enables him to withstand monotonous application. Children of this sign rarely require encouragement or urging when it comes to study; in fact, they may become *bookworms*, and it may be necessary at times to encourage or urge them into physical activity. While they do not require urging as far as study or reading are concerned, they often are not at all inclined to be aggressive in some other walks of life. Often the Virgo child has a sense of inferiority and he shrinks from active contact with others. This is particularly so if his mental faculties have been aroused early so that he has become more interested in books or study than in active physical sports and games. Children of this sign may find themselves being dominated by or imposed upon by other children. It is found that sometimes in starting to school the child of this sign has almost to be literally driven to go.

Virgo youngsters are likely to form quick and definite likes and dislikes. This is more true of matters concerning their personal possessions and their food than it is of people, however. The child of this sign often acquires ideas about food, refusing to eat a great many things and being hard to please in matters of diet. While Virgo children should be required to eat the kinds of food which are known to be good for them, so as to provide a balanced diet, they should not be forced more than absolutely necessary to eat things which they reject. In the event that the youngster of this sign becomes absorbed primarily in mental pursuits, and shows a disposition to be dainty and *choosy* in his eating he should be carefully supervised so that he does not develop stomach and bowel disorders.

The true Virgo youngster requires very little teaching or urging in connection with neatness and cleanliness. Both are instinctive with these children. There is no question but that the children of this sign have a tremendous potential for intellectual development but parents of a Virgo youngster should watch for any tendency in the child to feel that he is more *clever* than other children. This sometimes leads to certain forms of cheating. The wise parent will make himself aware of the activities of the child and will recognize tendencies along this line if they are present, and will deal with the child with kindness and understanding.

MARRIAGES OF VIRGO

From the foregoing it becomes apparent that natives of Virgo are quite likely to be ultra-conservative, and consequently slow in placing their affections. While those born in many of the other signs often contract early and impulsive matrimonial alliances, that is seldom true of those who came into the world under this solar vibration. Women of Virgo are never blinded to the shortcomings of their would-be suitors. If they do not marry it is not as a rule because they have lacked opportunities. In fact, the charm and beauty which are often possessed by these women make them sought after to an unusual degree. It is seldom, however, that the woman of this sign selects a partner until she has reached the twenties at least. Many do not marry until late in life; and not a few never. Both sexes whose births occurred under this solar vibration are romantic, although their tendencies in that connection are colored by their practical viewpoints. They are basically sentimental, however, and in marriage are devoted and remarkably true to their marital partners. They are affectionate, but when the negatives which are inherent in the sign are allowed to develop they often become quite undemonstrative and reserved — in some cases to the point of coldness.

There is no other sign of the zodiac, however, where the natives are more superior in their fidelity to the marriage vows. Even though they contract an unfortunate union, one which lacks much to make them happy, their tendency is to remain steadfast and true. Sometimes this is not because of tenacious loyalty, but results from lack of inclination to change and of physical passion. However, an unfortunate or inharmonious marriage is usually disastrous for the Virgo native. His critical faculty, his coldness, and his reserve are brought to the surface under such a condition, and though in other ways his unhappy matrimonial situation may not be apparent, he is inwardly bitter and completely disillusioned. Matrimonial mismating almost invariably leads the Virgo native to a nervous state in which he develops neurotic tendencies leading to bowel disturbances. These result from powerful negatives inherent in the sign.

When two Virgo people marry, which is not infrequently the case, their union is likely to be quite happy. It is extremely important, however, that there should not be a wide difference in education or social position. Virgos of both sexes are too fastidious to be able to successfully tie themselves to another who is markedly inferior. Virgo natives often find congenial matrimonial partners among those who came into the world in the sign Pisces (Feb. 20 — March 19). Scorpio (Oct. 24 — Nov. 22) in many ways is fundamentally harmonious, especially the latter part of the sign. The sign Taurus (April 21 — May 22) is also basically harmonious to a considerable degree. In a measure, Capricorn people (Dec. 22 — Jan. 20) have a similar outlook as far as the practical affairs of life are concerned. An alliance between these two signs, however, is almost entirely dependent upon equality in evolutionary development.

People of both sexes who were born in this sign are quite frequently extremely attractive in appearance. The women of the sign are often downright beautiful, but both men and women need to guard against a too great sharpening of their mental faculties and thought processes, lest that same sharpening occur in their features. Virgo natives can usually maintain their happiness in a state of monotony better than most of the other signs, and are not apt to seek variety and change.

The legal profession is a favorable outlet for the talents of Virgo. The native is particularly apt in the preparation of cases. Being a patient analyst, and possessed of the ability to apply himself diligently and painstakingly to details, his cases are models of care and perfection. A great many men of this sign have been successful in mercantile careers. They are especially adapted, however, to accounting, statistical research or similar branches of commerce. The various printing fields are also good outlets for the abilities of Virgo. This includes publishing and certain branches of advertising. The fact is that the sign has a vibratory affinity with paper. A great many natives have been especially successful in businesses which deal exclusively with that commodity.

The Virgo born individual may achieve distinction in musical and artistic fields, but it will usually be found in such case that there were powerful planetary positions at birth in one of the inspirational signs. The pure Virgo vibration does not, in itself, make the native creative, or apt in the rendition of music; but the qualities of patience, perseverance, and analysis make for accomplishment in creative fields when the necessary qualities of inspiration and creative inclination are imparted. It has previously been stated that the journalists of the world come from this sign, and it is indeed amazing to note the number of Virgo natives who are engaged in such a career. Also, of course, a great many writers who have achieved distinction were born in this sign. One finds, however, that in the fields of literary, dramatic, and artistic *criticism,* the sign Virgo is particularly well represented. The ability to analyze, combined with a fondness for harmony, liking for color and form, and observation of detail makes the Virgo native extremely apt in those fields.

While it is true that often those who were born in this sign find it difficult to accumulate any considerable amount of money, a few Virgo natives have done so — several with outstanding success. As a matter of fact, millionaires are far from being unknown among natives of this sign. Of course, the analytical ability, meticulousness and patience of Virgo brings about in many natives, basically good financial sense. When a native of the sign has a real desire to accumulate money he is able to devote his energies extremely effectively in this connection. He is painstaking, patient, and he is certain about every factor of any undertaking of which he is a part. A blend of Leo influences is likely to add venturesomeness to the Virgo native.

There have been extremely forceful and successful politicians and statesmen who were born in Virgo. While Virgo itself is not aggressive or fond of public appearances, the native sometimes receives a strong vibration from another sign which greatly adds to his aggressiveness. It should again be mentioned that occupations associated with hygiene are extremely favorable for the Virgo native. He is a natural student of dietary laws. Chemistry and allied subjects are also good mediums of expression for his talents. The true Virgo who is highly evolved or who, in other words, has been able to still his negatives of apprehension, self-consciousness, fear of criticism and the like, is able to inspire the greatest confidence on the part of his associates. He comes to be known as one who never exaggerates, is sure of his facts, and expresses them concisely and graphically, and he is capable of *more than average* success.

DISHARMONY OF VIRGO

As with all other signs of the zodiac, conditions of ill health, or disharmony do not exist, excepting as they are coexistent with the negatives which are inherent in the sign. Virgo has immediate harmony with the abdomen. The disorders with which negatives of the sign are synonomous are: colic, worms, dysentery, cholera, constipation, obstruction of the bowels, malnutrition, disorders of the intestinal tract, diarrhea, plain stomach ache, and indigestion. These disorders are referred to as disease or as physical malfunctioning, but they are directly traceable to the specific negatives of the sign. There is a tendency on the part of Virgo natives to be overly conscious of their digestive processes, and their stomachs, in a negative fashion.

They often become interested from a mental standpoint in diet, and will readily accept fads in that connection. This is the result of nervousness, apprehension, and the quality of hypochondria which the particular negatives associated with a super-consciousness of the physical functioning of the body will develop. Nervousness is, of course, evidence of apprehension or worry. While the native of this sign does not always show his nervousness outwardly, he still may find inner relaxation difficult. Excitement and nervous agitation almost invariably produce reflex conditions in the stomach, and as previously stated, this sign is directly associated with, and its vibration has a definite harmony with, that part of the body.

The mental qualities being directly affected by the vibration of Virgo have an immediate nervous reaction, and while natives of this sign are benefited by the use of reasonable care in diet, they should specifically cultivate the positive qualities which have been referred to as an aid in the relief of either stomach or bowel troubles. Often the Virgo native resorts to strong cathartics and other medicines and drugs, all of which are more likely to be injurious than beneficial. While Virgo natives often use medication, they probably need it less frequently than do natives of most other signs. The native of this sign must first turn toward the correction of his mental processes by cultivation of the powerful constructives which are part of his sign. Certain it is that when there is harmony in thought forms, it is impossible for *disease* organisms to gain a foothold in the bodies of Virgo people.

The tendency of Virgo to be excessively analytical sometimes leads to pre-occupation with minor details and to an extremely critical attitude. Such an attitude produces vibrations which are in harmony with their like among the cosmic forces of the universe. The conditions allied with the parts of the body mentioned are aggravated by such a mental attitude. Under proper conditions of mental control and direction, natives of this sign, however, are able to quickly throw off physical conditions of disharmony. Anyone who was born in this sign and who finds himself susceptible to the conditions mentioned, should re—evaluate his habitual thought patterns. Having done so, and corrected some of the negative tendencies which he may find present — his physical disharmony should quickly clear up. Situations or conditions which are unpleasant (in personal associations, or work, or inharmonious marital relationships) often result in negatives of thought which the Virgo native finds extremely difficult to control. The development of optimism through thought forms which are free of worry and fear is extremely necessary for the native of this sign.

1977 Strange provisions or odd benefits are likely to prove to be "a windfall". "A concealed" act stemming from "the past" might cause difficulty because of "a false front" or sense of guilt. Jupiter's position ruling financial matters, promises what might best be termed as "a truly lucky break" coming to you. While the benefit may actually be delayed for a short time, the way will be opened during this period for you to receive it later — I am sure. The over-all climate of your life is shown to be of such a nature as to turn your mind toward "wills or the possessions of others" with considerable discussions about "settlements" — and a surprising outcome for you.

1978 When you seek betterment, this year will lead you into more surprising situations than your mind can imagine just now, in all probability, because your close ties, correspondence and associations with neighboring areas seem tremendously influential in your planetary patterns for 1978. Certain people may have aspirations for you which you are not sure you really have for yourself, but you might be wise to think twice before you refuse TANGIBLE offerings now. Temporarily, you will feel subdued by conditions touching your living arrangements, I think, but because I have so much confidence that you will center your efforts on **A PARTICULAR GOAL**, I know you will grow closer, every moment, to realization of the dream you most cherish.

1979 You are apt to "retire" from your world oftentimes during this cycle in order to pave your path into the future with even better "materials" than many of those you feel you have used in the past. Later on, I believe you will be so glad you looked forward with faith and enthusiasm, no matter what circumstances appeared before you for brief intervals — because you will recognize in your efforts the growth for improvement that has arisen throughout your personal affairs. Rely upon your own resources in situations where you ordinarily would depend on another person, and I think someone you "confide in" will prove outstanding for their sincere abilities to guide you correctly toward the happiness you seek, and I believe you will have.

1980 There are strong indications that planetary influences will open up new responsibilities, but this also will lead to unlooked for opportunities, in my opinion. At times brief periods of moodiness may "weigh" you down during this period, as though you were carrying a load on your shoulders without anyone to share your burdens. While you may feel intense nervous pressures because of so much happening at the same time, I am confident that you will later recall this period as one when your efforts to organize your affairs along more orderly lines were the means of bringing benefits to yourself and those you love. You will be apt to idealize a particular relationship with someone close, as well as be aware of an inspirational guidance stemming from friends in influential positions, or an especially intimate companion.

VIRGO

1981 I think you will tend to cast a more "watchful" eye upon expenditures, especially during the latter part of this year. You will probably hesitate to buy or spend until you are assured of "full value" or convinced of the need to make cash outlays. In either case, I feel you will begin to build the structure of a more secure financial future, relying upon practical measures, and using your ability to make sound monetary decisions while analyzing the prospects of matters from which you hope to gain. Toward the close of this period, explosive situations (arising from "hidden" elements connected to the past and which you probably would prefer to remain confidential) may be disclosed. I believe this matter will involve nearby ties, a relative or something having to do with written or spoken messages.

1982 One of your cherished hopes is likely to undergo a decided "turn-about" around the middle of this year. I believe this change will signal a new direction that at first you will be reluctant to follow. It seems that decisions will need to be made relating to trusted relationships, so that for a short time you are apt to be "put in the middle" . . . which could get you mired down or at cross-purposes with a close tie or someone younger who has a problem. I feel you should analyze your situation very carefully before you commit yourself to an undertaking or obligation, owing to the likelihood of someone misleading you. Your financial affairs and other gainful activities may be improved through an association with "nearby places," in my opinion.

1983 Surprising changes might alter the pattern of your "home life" during this cycle, possibly in connection with a "new idea" that grows in your mind. Departures and arrivals will probably characterize your living arrangements with startling suddenness around this time. Improvements or "redoings" with respect to your "home" locale are apt to be more seriously considered during 1983, with cost being a major factor in forming your decisions. Your desire to travel, as well as gather "new experiences" is apt to be stronger, but restraints that keep you from doing so as freely as you would like will need to be taken into consideration. Someone in an "authoritative position" may withhold approval, so that you will be forced to make a sudden adjustment with regard to a plan you hope will advance your prospects.

1984 Until around August of this year, an unusually strong planetary influence indicates the advisability of special care as you "come and go," because of possible mishaps, especially when driving or when other forms of travel are involved, tending to result from negligence or failure to observe safety precautions. Your interests touching on areas of affection and love are likely to be expanded throughout most of this period. Those who are younger may strike an especially responsive "note" in your heart at this time. You might tend to mislead yourself as to someone's intentions toward you . . . leading to your ascribing imaginary qualities to someone because of your own thoughts. I am sure your awareness of religious or spiritual values will deepen during this phase and things will work out so that you will advance your position.

82

SUMMATION (Virgo)

Your tendency to evaluate life by facts and logic will be greatly strengthened by the unusual and significant planetary influences forming and developing during this forecast period. You will probably be labelled a "perfectionist" at times by some of your associates, because you will often be put in a position where the efficiency of your methods and the thoroughness with which you accomplish responsibilities will encourage you to speak out to others who lack your thorough approach to needed undertakings.

More than usual, you will be examining old ideas or beliefs, in an effort to discard what has become outmoded or no longer of practical use. I feel you will be extremely skeptical of "hearsay" throughout this period, preferring to evaluate the ideas which come to you through your own observation and experience. I am certain you will be highly aware of "flashes of inspiration" that strike your mind, sometimes with amazing quickness during this trend. Your thinking is apt to be stimulated to greater keenness, and I believe your intuitive powers will enable you to gain the kind of insight that will help you make instinctive "right" choices when important decisions are at stake.

Studies, especially of technical subjects, will undoubtedly be strongly in the foreground, and as a result of information gained, you are likely to undergo a decided change related to a particular goal. Someone close is indicated as furnishing an idea that will have a powerful impact upon your thinking, which may lead to an unusual "change of direction."

Early in the forecast period, some passing health concerns may be manifested, but during the following years I feel beneficial influences will be "working" in your behalf, so that your physical well-being will respond more favorably to the care you take to get adequate rest and guide your dietary habits toward reasonable practices. It is my opinion that everything will work out well so that later you will find success through the plans you worked out during this period.

The *"ruling"* planet of Virgo being Mercury and of Libra, Venus, these two planets play an important part in the lives of those who were born in this cusp. The natives are likely to be extremely kind, generous and enthusiastic. They almost invariably have fundamental artistic ability, though they do not always develop it. A great many of those who come into the world under this combination of planetary influences have been extremely successful, however, as designers of wearing apparel and of jewelry, stage settings and the like. They are usually interested in a variety of things and their enthusiasms are easily and quickly aroused. It is quite difficult to limit the occupational abilities of the native of this cusp. He can unquestionably succeed in any endeavor having to do with the development of original ideas, publicity, advertising, original artistic design or in a profession — unless he is comparatively quite unevolved.

The native of this cusp shrinks from unpleasant conditions or situations. That which is sordid or unclean affects him mentally, far more than it does the average person. He desires harmony in his surroundings. He prefers to *get along* with people and he is particularly fond of happy and pleasant associations. He is usually unselfish to a far greater extent than most people. His disposition is quite happy and he is deep and sincere, as well as warmhearted. He loves order, yet under certain conditions of unrest he is not very orderly in his methods. One who was born under these particular influences is not usually fitted for anything having to do with the sick. Although he may be scientifically interested in matters of that nature, the surroundings associated therewith are likely to be too unhappy and morbid for him. Above all he needs plenty of exercise in harmonious surroundings. He is usually quite high strung and his nervous sensibilities are great — though he may not show it outwardly. The later period of his life is likely to be happier than the earlier.

The one thing which people who were born under this combination of influences need to overcome is the tendency to take up ideas *too quickly,* resulting from easily aroused enthusiasm and then dropping them for the reason that conditions seem to be hard or the environment into which they get themselves is unsympathetic. The native is not at all inclined to like coldness, harshness or uncongeniality. He is much inclined to be a philosopher and can become quite intelligently interested in studies along these lines. The natural kindliness of his nature expressed in a constructive fashion brings into play many of the powerful forces which are his to command. He is likely to give expression to the analytical qualities of Virgo, yet he does not usually use that which he derives from analysis, commercially. His interest is much more likely to be intellectual. He is rarely a *driver* in his ambitions and is not likely to insist upon having his own way in personal relationships, though he ·can develop a marked stubbornness. He has a remarkable quality of intuition. There are natural forces upon which he can call to an almost unlimited degree, but he needs to control his thinking processes so as to eliminate the morbid, to which he is susceptible.

84

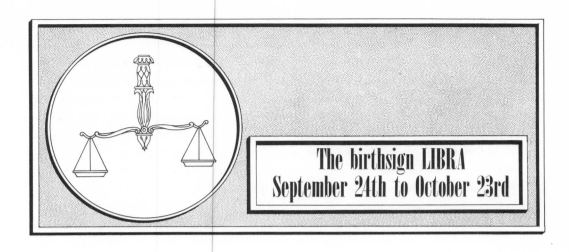

The birthsign LIBRA
September 24th to October 23rd

our birth occurred in the sign Libra if you were born between September 24th and October 23rd. The word *Libra* is the Latin word for *scales* or *balance*. All the domes of the capital buildings in the United States are representative of the symbol of Libra, and of course the human female figure of justice holds the Balance or Scales, which is further representative of the sign. The same being true of this, as of all other signs, the symbol is a graphic illustration of the fundamental qualities inherent in it. Like the others, the character traits are expressed both positively and negatively. The native of Libra will recognize in himself the traits of the sign as they are described. Of course some of the positive traits will be much more prominent than their negatives, while others among the negatives will have been allowed to develop more fully.

The native of Libra is prone to *balance and weigh*. In its higher attributes, the sign is one which expresses justice and tolerance in their loftiest forms. Libra is the seventh sign of the zodiac, the first being Aries. The number seven has an important occult meaning. In nature it is highly significant, recurring repeatedly, there being seven days in the week, seven notes in the musical scale; and in the cycles of life it is a number which repeats itself in the life of every individual. We know that each cycle of seven years is representative of the completion of a definite period in life, and that the human body is renewed completely in that period of time. In the ancient cabalistic works the number seven always meant perfection of quality. Those who receive a strong influence from Libra at birth have potential possibilities of the *greatest* good.

This basic vibration is referred to as a cardinal sign; as semi-fruitful, scientific, hot, airy, moist, movable, western, sanguine, and masculine. The gem of Libra is the diamond; and the flower, the violet. Libra is representative of the Bible tribe of Asher, one of the original tribes of Israel, or one of the basic types of human beings. The planet Venus is strongest in its influence upon natives of Libra. This means that the qualities attributed to the goddess of that name, as well as to the planet, are predominantly a part of the Libra characteristics.

The native of this sign is fond of all in life that represents the beautiful and luxurious. He dislikes unclean surroundings as well as unclean tasks; and is less interested in purely physical or material activities than in those of a philosophical mental sort. He expresses a fondness for dramatic art, poetry, music, languages, and particularly philosophy. The highly evolved native of this sign is above all philosophical in his deeper processes of thought. The particular sign or combinations of signs which affect physical characteristics play a more important part in the inner qualities of Libra than they do upon many of the other signs. For that reason there is a definite line of demarcation between the physical types of this sign, and in their aptitudes and abilities as well.

It has been considered that there are two distinct types of people who are natives of Libra. Of the two physical types, one is tall, slender in youth but with some tendency to add weight in later years. The face and head are narrow or oval, and the eyes are blue or gray. Natives of this type are quick mentally, versatile and inclined to be quite creative; but especially they formulate ideas quickly and their enthusiasms are easily aroused. They are remarkably capable sales-people, and their instinctive judgment of what to say to a prospective customer is unexcelled. The other of the two types is much shorter, fuller of body and the countenance and head are much more rounded, the eyes are brown rather than blue, and are spaced farther apart. These persons have much broader foreheads than the other type. They are sturdily built, usually of well-formed physique. Natives of this latter type are inherently good mathematicians. They have marked mechanical ability, as well as a fundamental ability to understand languages other than their own and to learn to read and speak them with great facility.

You are by nature kind, generous, tolerant, gracious, and affectionate. You have a great deal of instinctive foresight, and you know from intuition what to do in your own affairs better than anyone can possibly tell you, although probably you do not always follow this intuitive guidance. The Libra native is often brought to a state of confusion by his efforts to reconcile his instinctive judgment of what is right with the ideas and opinions of others. The true Libra is generous to extremes, and his courtesy to others extends itself into every walk of life. He seldom feels himself too busy or too superior to be unapproachable to anyone who seeks to reach him.

Your most marked quality is one of tolerance for the shortcomings of others. You can always find a reason for their failure to do what is right, and can excuse their faults, sometimes more leniently than your own. You have a natural faculty, however, for observing imperfections in the endeavors of others, and are apt at devising ways and means of bringing them to a greater point of efficiency. You have marked inventive traits, and while your tendency to note shortcomings or imperfections in the work of others is not a critical faculty, as you are always ready to explain and condone mistakes, still you are quick to suggest ways and means by which imperfect work may be improved. You are not likely to remain long content in a subordinate or menial position, being far too independent and imaginative for that. You are essentially original in your thinking, and you are not satisfied to carry out someone else's ideas, preferring to devise plans and methods of your own.

The native of this basic vibration is interested in progress, and is immediately intrigued by new and intricate or ingenious devices, being impelled to examine such things with the closest attention. While the person who was born in Libra is primarily philosophical, he is almost invariably fond of matters pertaining to all branches of science, and often he reads widely along scientific lines. He acquires knowledge from books very readily, and also is a shrewd observer of life. A strong Libra trait is the love of excitement and activity in places where events move rapidly. The highly evolved native of this sign is greatly stimulated by contact with many other people. His speech is usually quick and his judgment, guided by intuition, is almost instantaneous. In the *major* affairs of life, however, the native of this sign who is highly evolved will usually seek quiet and seclusion in laying out his plans, so that he may not be affected by the opinions and ideas of others. Thus he is guided into the right path. The native of Libra almost invariably makes his greatest mistakes in life when he adapts himself to what other people think is right and fitting for him to do. He rarely goes far astray when he follows his own judgment. The highly evolved native never wants for money, for health, or for any of the good things of life. He is persistent in his efforts, and capable of bringing a most balanced judgment to bear on any problem which confronts him.

You are inclined to be greatly interested in the problems of humanity and have a great desire to help others. You are extremely sympathetic about the suffering of others, and you have great pity for the unfortunate. Your heart is tender toward all things which are distressed, both human and animal, and you are ever ready to extend your sympathy and your active help to those who need it. Any cause which is really worthy immediately brings you to its defense. You will stand by others who are oppressed and who are being treated unjustly, no matter what the result may be in your own affairs. You have a strongly marked faculty of loyalty, and will never abandon a friend because of the pressure of circumstances or the influence of others.

Often the decisions of people who receive the Libra influence strongly at birth *appear* to be impulsive; but, despite that fact, they are quite likely to be correct, and in business or even speculative ventures the quick judgment of the Libra native usually proves to be the proper course. The true Libra tendency is toward balancing, weighing, and comparing. Individuals who were born under a strong influence from the sign look upon both sides of any question which comes to their attention, particularly when a decision on their part will affect the affairs or the lives of others. When they are called upon to render judgment, they are extremely fair and impartial. The highly evolved native of this sign is an exemplification of truth, justice, and charity; and he never misuses the great powers which are bestowed upon him.

Libra people rarely waste their time on small details. They are seldom inclined to haggle over matters of comparatively minor importance. They like to see things accomplished quickly. They want action, and they usually seek conditions of life which make such action possible. While the man of Libra is often an extremely shrewd buyer of merchandise, having an instinctive knowledge of prices and of other factors which are involved, he is seldom inclined to haggle over the *details* of a transaction. He will either act in the matter at once, or completely refuse to do so.

Those who come into the world under this basic vibration are extremely kind, courteous, and loving to the members of their family. They seldom choose friends because of their position in life, but are drawn to others because of the personality traits and the mental standards or development which have been attained. The native of Libra is always, at heart, eager to plan for the welfare and happiness of those he loves, and is constantly on the alert to devise means through which his friends may profit. Often he thinks of the welfare of others to his own detriment or disadvantage. He sometimes assumes too many responsibilities and too many burdens, frequently because of *over-enthusiasm*.

As previously expressed, this sign in common with all others has its strongly negative qualities as well as positive. Words which are expressive of the positive qualities of the sign are: balanced, gracious, refined, just, unprejudiced, understanding, affectionate, forgiving, tactful, creative, idealistic, impartial, peacemaker, foresight, sympathetic, cooperative, controlled, generous, truthful. Words expressing the specific negative qualities of the sign are: vain, temporizing, impressionable, vascillating, indecisive, apprehensive, uncertain, reckless, extreme, hesitating, susceptible, aloof, uncontrolled, unbalanced, illusive.

All people who were born in the sign Libra do not live upon a plane of existence which is an expression of the *higher qualities* of their birth sign, and consequently they fail to receive the *inner guidance* which the more highly evolved individual does. The native of this sign who is unevolved often plunges into things *too quickly*. He is impulsive, and impatient of routine. His ambitious wish is to progress quickly, and his easily aroused enthusiasm sometimes causes him to get completely out of his depth and to become involved in heavy obligations, financial and otherwise. He is likely to jump to conclusions, and his quickness in making decisions is prompted by materialistic and negative impulses rather than by the true inspiration which is a part of this vibration.

Usually, all people who were born under this basic solar vibration find it difficult at times to give a reason for their acts, due simply to the fact that they *are* prompted by intuition. Additionally, they find it boring and trying to explain to others, in detail, the reasons for their acts. The unevolved native, when pressed for a detailed explanation of his every move, becomes irritated to the point of exasperation. His temper then flares, often to the complete bewilderment of his associates. The Libra native who has not yet evolved to the point of using his positive abilities should constantly beware of allowing outside and purely material influences to govern his decisions. When he expresses *through his thought processes* many of the strong negatives of the sign, he finds it almost impossible to make a clean-cut and definite decision in his personal affairs. He constantly seeks the opinions of others. He asks for advice in his problems; wavering and hesitating, and torn between a strong belief in his own inner promptings and the influence and judgment of others. He fears disaster. His apprehension is, in itself, an extremely powerful negative, which often finds expression in the material affairs of his life.

While the Libra tendency is to be courteous, kind, and tolerant, the native in whom negatives of the sign are at work can be extremely cutting, cold, and even cruel in the things he says. The true Libra has a powerful sense of justice which balances and weighs both sides of every question which comes to his attention. When he believes that he has been treated unjustly, or should he feel that another is being treated in such a manner, his wrath for the moment may be great; and, under such conditions, he may utter words which wound others deeply. The native often feels that he is not appreciated by those around him. He comes to believe that his work or his efforts are not valued at their true worth. This leads to much inner distress and confusion of mind, and he then allows affairs of trifling import to cause him the deepest distress. Libra being an air sign, his thought processes are often very rapid, and he can quickly build a chain of negatives leading to the blackest despair.

Despite the absolute balance of which natives of Libra are capable, the unevolved individual becomes easily confused. He is impatient to a degree which causes him to lose much of his effectiveness, and to accomplish only a small part of what he *can* accomplish. The unevolved native is usually anxious to meet with the approval of those with whom he comes in contact, to the extent that he is easily induced to ignore his own judgment in order to try to do what others seem to expect of him. Frequently this leads to a certain coarseness and vulgarity which is, actually, assumed for the purpose of pleasing his associates. The native who has still to make much progress in his evolution is unduly proud, egotistical, and is likely to be a thorough exhibitionist. He is vain of his appearance, excessively fond of adornment, and is inclined to be somewhat unscrupulous where the opposite sex is concerned.

Cultivation of the *higher attributes* of this sign, a definite *building* of the positives which have been expressed, will open the channel of communication for the native so that his intuitional guidance will carry him through every trial and difficulty which he may encounter in this physical plane of existence. Surely there is no more courteous, kindly, lovable, and trustworthy individual than the Libra native who has *developed the powerful forces* which are constantly at his command. The highly evolved Libra has an ability to acquire knowledge of occult matters to an extraordinary degree. Spiritualization of the Libra vibration will bring almost any accomplishment within the scope of both men and women who were born under a strong influence from this sign. The native must learn to use his sense of inner balance. He must gain a a mental poise and equilibrium which *he can do* if he once comes to realize the desirability and, indeed, the *necessity* for doing so.

WOMEN OF LIBRA

Among the women who were born in the sign Libra will be found the most beautiful, kindly, courteous, and charming represenratives of their sex. The woman of Libra is essentially kind-hearted, refined, a gay and responsive companion, quite amiable and undemanding, fond of refined and enlivening entertainment, and understanding to a remarkable degree. She is artistic, has extremely good taste, a fine sense of color harmony, and a natural love for all that is beautiful. Women of this sign are very devoted to their families. They become affectionate as well as self-sacrificing wives and mothers. They are cheerful under difficulties or hardships, and are always primarily interested in the welfare and happiness of those whom they love.

In common with the men of Libra they are fitted for artistic endeavors. They, too, often succeed in literary undertakings, and are creative as designers in various fields. The theatrical profession is a splendid outlet for their talents and abilities, as it is for the men. As designers of costumes, millinery, and wearing apparel they excel. They are also capable of exercising the best of good taste in interior decoration. Their fine sense of color values, and of what is harmonious in design, makes them quite capable in such endeavors. In common with the men, they are instinctive judges of merchandise and have the basic qualities which enable them to become extremely successful as buyers in such fields. Combined with their knowledge of color and style this can be an extremely beneficial attribute. They are competent secretaries and efficient office-workers; although, as a rule, they are not particularly fond of arduous routine. This sign has fine scientific aptitudes and is particularly inclined to be philosophic. Women of Libra have not been left out as far as these qualities are concerned. They are extremely likely to have a broad understanding of science and may be especially fitted for endeavors which relate to some sort of research or affiliation otherwise with scientific endeavors.

Due to the delicate balance of Libra and the strong inner sense of justice women of this sign are very likely at times to be quite undecided, sometimes in matters of negligible importance. They do have a tendency to allow themselves to be influenced by the judgment of other people and are almost invariably far better off if they follow their own intuitive judgment and when they learn to trust their own inner promptings. The negatives which have been discussed, and which are inherent in this sign, sometimes make the women of Libra extremely apprehensive where their loved ones are concerned. In such case, they waste much of their energy in foolish fretfulness, which was in the beginning completely without reason. When they allow themselves to give way to such apprehensions, they become quite melancholy and fretful. These conditions lead to a chain of negatives, and the woman of this sign who gives way to them often becomes impatient and careless with her personal possessions.

In common with the men, women of Libra are extremely courteous and warm in their friendliness under ordinary conditions, but they can develop a great deal of stubbornness when their sense of justice is violated. Many women of this sign have become noted for their breadth of human understanding and tolerance. The potential of these women is great when they come to a realization of their *own inner powers,* particularly of intuition, which actually means guidance from the One First Cause.

Youngsters who were born in the sign Libra are enthusiastic, positive, and thrive on praise and encouragement. The adult native of this sign loves conditions of harmony and order, and this is equally true of the children of Libra. They are made unhappy by dissension or harsh criticism, and the ugly things of life make a deep impression upon their sensitive natures. They respond quickly to reason, but they do not yield readily to *strict* discipline. Under such conditions of discipline they are inclined to learn evasiveness and deceit, in order to escape punishment for their misdeeds.

These children are likely to be impulsive, extremely affectionate and lovable, and frequently quite demonstrative. When there is understanding on the part of parents or guardians, they are quick to admit their faults and will anxiously strive to overcome them. They are not like the children of many of the other signs in the sense of being determined to have their own way. As a matter of fact it is not unusual for Libra children to have relatively few intense desires. The Libra child may want something in the nature of a plaything or otherwise but he is likely to be less insistant about getting it than most others would be. If he does not get what he has really wished for, he quickly dismisses it as of no importance.

This very quality is sometimes a hindrance in his accomplishments. He is likely not to want anything badly enough or intensely enough to strive for it desperately. In our modern day and age of the world this is not infrequently a handicap when it comes to the achievement of material success. Parents of these children sometimes find it difficult to inculcate such deep desires for achievement. For reasons having to do with evolutionary development it is impossible to impart such intense desires to many children or in fact to people who were born in this sign.

Youngsters who were born in Libra are inclined to be rather easily led. They have a strong tendency to wish to do whatever their immediate associates expect of them. For that reason it will be immediately apparent that wise guidance is very necessary. These children are benefited by being taught the truths of nature in very early life. They should receive early guidance in matters related to sex. A great deal of care and patience and understanding are particularly necessary for youngsters of this sign. They frequently have outstanding inventive ability and originality of ideas, but their interest along these lines needs to be stimulated. It usually requires tactful handling and understanding to interest them *constructively* in such activities, otherwise they are likely to spend their time in just *dreaming* about them.

There is a tendency among youngsters of this solar vibration to *exaggerate,* but rarely is this of a vicious nature. Every effort should be made on the part of those in charge of them to understand that it is merely an outward expression of their *vivid imaginations,* and they should be listened to with love and kindliness, yet gently guided toward truth in their statements. They have potential possibilities which can lead to the greatest good and the most worthy accomplishment, but tendencies they have toward self-gratification, over-indulgence, and fondness for the material things of life in general, can grow to dominant proportions, unless they are carefully guided toward *development* of the positive and constructive traits inherent in Libra.

The basic harmonic of Libra imparts a great deal of attractiveness to the native of this sign, and the Libra person, whether man or woman, is usually attracted *by* the opposite sex to an extensive degree. Being fond of gaiety, luxury, and entertainment, both are inclined to forget the more serious affairs of life in their pursuit of those pleasures and relaxations which their natures crave. The native of Libra, when he allows the negatives of the sign to become predominant, greatly dislikes being bound by marital ties. His desire for the lighter, gayer things of life, makes him rebel at being compelled to endure the often humdrum, unexciting, demanding conditions of matrimony, as well as the responsibility.

A great many inharmonious and unhappy marriages are often contracted by the natives of this sign. That is perhaps true of Libra to a greater degree than any of the other signs. This is not by any means always the fault of the Libra individual, excepting to the extent that he seems (more than those born in other signs), to make mistakes in choosing a life partner, and is frequently attracted to those whose natures are not harmonious. He often gets one who is practical and who believes in proceeding in the affairs of life according to a well-devised plan based upon step-by-step reasoning. This might seem to be a favorable state of affairs for the Libra individual, as it would appear that such a mate would be helpful. The Libra native, however, is too *independent* and too often follows his own *intuition* — without careful and detailed planning, particularly such planning as he might wish to discuss with another person. He definitely does not like to explain his actions well enough to find that type of companionship wholly congenial.

The sign Aries (March 20th — April 20th) is fundamentally harmonious as are the signs Leo (July 22nd — August 22nd) and Sagittarius (November 23rd — December 21st). The sign Aquarius (January 21st — February 19th) is also quite harmonious, but the combined airy quality of the two signs often produces an ill-balanced life wherein there is some lack of stability. The qualities, however, of Aries and Libra perhaps blend better than that of Libra with any of the other signs, particularly when the individuals have reached the same level of development.

Sometimes the people who were born in this sign for various reasons (frequently associated with their own physical appearance which is likely to be expressive of beauty) come to the point of feeling that they are due admiration, which extends even to their mates. In extreme cases women of this sign come to imagine themselves almost as goddesses on a pedestal. Though this is relatively rare, it does occur and the women of this sign should take particular pains to avoid such feelings. They are likely to bring about rifts in domestic harmony and they never lead to ultimate happiness. Remarriage is rarely a solution and consequently the individual of Libra who tends to feel that he or she should be the subject of intense admiration, suffers a great deal of unhappiness, particularly in later years of life.

Both the men and women of this sign are particularly susceptible to inharmonious relationships in their personal surroundings, and are likely to be made extremely unhappy by dissension. When they do find mates who understand their desire for harmony, however, their marriages are unusually happy ones.

The pure Libra basic vibration is inspirational, philosophical, imaginative, and artistic. The stronger the Libra influence at birth, the less fitted the native is for any coarse, gross, or contentious pursuits. His aptitudes are much more in the direction wherein tact, diplomacy and kindliness of expression are the rule rather than the exception. A great many natives of this sign will be found in professional occupations. Both the men and women of Libra are creative along artistic lines, often achieving outstanding success as designers of wearing apparel, jewelry, or stage settings, and as interior decorators. The infusion of earth qualities at birth (which is shown in the natal chart of the individual), will, however, produce a greater aptitude for practical affairs. The native of Libra often becomes an extremely capable buyer of merchandise; his *intuition* helping him under those conditions.

The true Libra who has developed his positives to a reasonable degree is, however, able to fit himself to almost any condition of service in the world. He is able to act with precision and a great deal of insight into the vagaries of his fellow men. It has often been said that natives of this sign are more capable of conducting a business or managing their own affairs more completely than those born in any other sign of the zodiac. The evolved native is able to lay his plans with great efficiency and carefulness and to execute those plans with precision, without letting the opinions of others sway him in carrying them through. He seldom shirks responsibility, and the highly evolved native is ready and willing to shoulder any blame which may come about as a result of his acts. Even those who have allowed the negatives inherent in this vibration to become strong are rarely reluctant to assume responsibilities.

It has often been noted that the Libra native is extremely skillful in all things which pertain to the handling of metals. Many of those who both design and execute patterns in jewelry, and various other metal crafts, will be found to have received strong Libra influences at birth. The native of this sign should in his spare time, if he is not already engaged in such an occupation, devote his energies to the cultivation of his artistic inclinations. Wide reading in matters relative to the occult sciences is usually very beneficial in its result on true natives of Libra.

The native whose thinking processes tend toward the positive often becomes a stockbroker or speculator. He may speculate in the stocks of other concerns, or he may be a speculative buyer of merchandise. His intuitional faculty guides him in remarkable fashion to the achievement of independence. His success is frequently a mystery to his friends, since they are unable to understand how he can decide so quickly — how he can feel such sureness within himself. The legal profession is also favorable for the Libra native, as are science and invention. One who receives a powerful influence from this sign at birth may well obtain distinction in the fields of science. Judicial vocations are an especially favorable outlet for the abilities and talents of the Libra native. He is often able to achieve success in literary endeavors and in various branches of the theatrical profession. Philosophy in all its branches is extremely interesting to the highly evolved native of this sign; and when his interest is aroused his philosophical reasoning is of the highest order.

93

DISHARMONY OF LIBRA

The same being true of Libra as of other signs of the zodiac, conditions which are referred to in the physical world as diseases, never exist excepting as they are accompanied by negatives in thought processes. The particular negatives to which this sign is susceptible have been referred to and described. The zone of Libra influence in the physical body consists of the reins (the kidneys), and the region of the ovaries. The negatives of the sign manifest themselves in physical conditions of disharmony such as nephritis, Bright's disease, weakness of the lower back, and all of the physical ailments which are associated with these conditions. There also is susceptibility in this sign to diabetes and lumbago.

All people who were born in Libra are, to some degree, susceptible to sudden changes of mood. They are affected by all kinds of hidden vibrations. The thought forms of others impress them deeply, although they are often unconscious of this fact. Natives of this sign are so sensitive to the thought vibrations produced by others, that they *unconsciously* adopt the opinions and mannerisms of those around them. Often the Libra native will change abruptly from hopeful optimism to extreme melancholy. These changes of mood come suddenly, usually are unpredictable by any ordinary means, and consequently are unexpected. Sometimes a slight condition, or even a suggestion, will bring about in the native a train of thought which very quickly leads to such a mood of despondency. Inharmonious environment will produce such moods to an extreme degree, and shifting planetary influences are an extremely strong factor. Not infrequently the Libra person is completely unaware of the reason for his despondency. That is almost always true when cosmic vibration is directly responsible.

There is a tendency for natives of Libra to over-indulge in the pleasures of life which, combined with occasional excessive impatience and nervous apprehension, brings about inharmonious states in the physical body. In the case of such unevolved natives there is often a neglect of the ordinary affairs of life, and a desire for that which is sensational and exciting, to the extent that matters of minor nature which are necessary to any degree of orderly living are completely ignored. In such case, the native is overly fond of material pleasures and reckless in the pursuit of them. Perhaps to a greater degree than of any other sign of the zodiac the native of Libra tends to be a sybarite. He is likely to be particularly addicted to sensual pleasures, to luxurious surroundings, and seeks to be constantly amused. Even in such a case, however, the true Libra native is not often coarse or gross in his outward expression or mannerism; but is still likely to be refined in manner, elegant in bearing, and more *artistically* degenerate than is true of some of the other signs. The Libra person, however, who allows the negatives which are a part of his sign to develop, sometimes becomes extremely careless in his dress, and indifferent to the refinement which he would otherwise desire.

The native of Libra should have plenty of fresh air and *mild* physical exercise, the latter not being carried to extremes. The most important factor, as with other signs of the zodiac, is a well-balanced mind. The Libra person has a particular ability to attain such a balance. Cultivation of the positive factors will assure Libra natives the best of health and great vitality.

1977 "Significant alterations" are more than a likelihood in this period surrounding your close ties or someone who might be best categorized as having been "a partner". A large margin of your personal world will be formulated by "other people" creating thought and effort according to what someone who has "the last word" does. This is a transition period where "old ties" are being put aside or severed for new arrivals. You will incline toward dwelling mentally upon a distant place so that the mailing of letters or messages in this connection will create nostalgic memories as well as prove fruitful. A lively year filled with action and benefit!

1978 Your associations may seem so important to you now, and yet I feel it will be beneficial for you to trust **YOUR OWN** judgment this year, seeking **YOUR** direction from the Source of ALL Knowledge. The more far-reaching you allow your circumstances to be, the greater you are likely to appreciate the returns you receive from them during 1978. You will have extraordinary opportunities for touching those circles of interest which can guide you swiftly toward the position in your world you most desire to reach, I am sure, as long as you do not mind sharing "your secrets" with everyone you know. You are apt to change something about your appearance this year, and I believe your source of income will change, too.

1979 "True friendship" will appear in your relationships under your new planetary trends, I feel. Your mental impressions are likely to be so keen that you will have to make a special effort to touch reality, but on the other hand, you are apt to appreciate the finer things with an uncommon sense of inspiration. I think it wise for you to sidestep risks to your emotional or physical health during 1979. You probably will have greater privacy for designing those gratifying "steps" you intend to take later on, because in all probability, you will seek newer doors which may open into an avenue of expression unlike the one you have often followed in time now gone by. I think you will approach the summit of a satisfying success when you try.

1980 Near your birthdate this year (and most of the year following), you are apt to feel very expansive due to Jupiter's position, and for this reason you are likely to get yourself involved in something as a result of spending impulsively on the spur of the moment. Relatives or other visitors are apt to figure in misunderstandings now, sometimes because of unrealistic attitudes based on surface impressions rather than a consideration of the "facts." Correspondence or messages could easily be misinterpreted under this planetary cycle, unless special care is taken to "get to the root of the matter." Inspirational ideas may literally "force" themselves into your thinking, particularly those which would enable you to influence others through mental suggestion. Fluctuations are likely to touch your financial interests strongly throughout this forecast period.

1981 One of your greatest successes will probably be plotted now, through an inspirational idea which could reshape the entire pattern of your life for many years to come. I doubt that you can go through this year without separating yourself from some person, association, possession or old ties, as elements related to the past as well as older people will figure more prominently in your activities. You are apt to own something, then be away from it for a time during this planetary trend. "Moody" periods may temporarily be more noticeable now, with alternating periods when your spirits are unexpectedly low, then suddenly shifting to "high." Careful attention to diet and promoting a harmonious "climate" around you is especially indicated this year, enabling you to "by-pass" feelings that could depress others, and will enable you to surmount the passing challenges and emerge victorious.

1982 The "world" of ideas will have special meaning for you during this year, in my opinion, because important changes related to old ideas will now undergo startling reversals! Around the middle of this period, an unusual eclipse pattern will influence a great "turning point" which will bear upon your relationships with those who are important to you, according to my interpretations. In all likelihood, you will begin active plans which might not otherwise have left the realm of your imagination. Poetic thoughts are apt to sweep you more and more toward artistic pursuits (music, design, art, putting your ideas into words, or actual useful projects). Your attitude toward money is indicated as becoming more hopeful in outlook, leading you to look for benefits in areas that have escaped notice before.

1983 For a brief time financial responsibilities may be more burdensome than usual, but a "lesson from the past" will encourage you to work your way around seeming obstacles that apparently stand in the way of maneuvers money-wise. You are likely to feel that you are forced into rather definite decisions concerning your close relationships. Instead of trying to get someone else to choose for you (so that you will be free from blame in the event it is not the "right path" to follow), I am sure you will make a real effort to calm your thoughts and take a step at a time toward a practical solution. The idea of short trips or making postponed visits will occur to you frequently, and the reaping of an unexpected benefit may follow! Something you desire will be within your reach this year, I feel certain.

1984 From January until near August of this year, it may be advisable to safeguard money and valued possessions as carefully as you can. Others may question the handling of money at this time, and it would be wise to respond in a helpful manner; otherwise heated arguments could disrupt certain relationships. A flurry of sparks that emanate from a situation involving an important "goal" is likely to play a dominant role in your affairs this year. Commuting back and forth is apt to shape many of your daily routines, although unexpected problems related to transportation could be temporarily frustrating. I believe you will find unanticipated benefits sifting down from another person's efforts — into your hands. A stranger from a distant place will possibly be one of the highlights of this period. An exciting year!

At the beginning of this cycle, "far places" may shift your interest to people or matters at a distance, but later many of your thoughts are likely to be centered upon the "nearby." The grip of new ideas that are ahead of their time which may lead to a changing of your "lifestyle" is indicated as particularly strong and tenacious throughout this forecast period. I doubt that you will be able to resist (and later you will be glad that you did not!) an upsurge of altering circumstances which leads to an unexpected "turnabout" that will shape the form of your personal affairs for several years.

Private thoughts about changes you either are considering or feel are being forced upon you are apt to pull you back and forth between opposing viewpoints for a time. However, I am certain your ability to make judgments upon the basis of "looking at all sides" will enable you to emerge as a stronger and more "success-oriented" person, because of the challenges that will bring out your "fighting efforts."

Toward the close of this forecast period, a growing absorption in spiritual values is likely to deepen your sense of attachment to "home and family," so that this will be a time of working to improve and bring more comfort to your immediate surroundings. A "helping hand" that seems almost providential in its appearance could brighten your prospects and open the way to a more gainful path. Relatives are apt to dominate much of your planning and efforts.

Although *extremes* may sometimes seem the rule rather than the exception, especially with regard to sudden money fluctuation occasioned by "changes" brought about by other people, I believe the events of this years long cycle will begin to assume an advantageous pattern which will encourage you to put in use an *ingenious* idea that might otherwise not see the "light of day."

Subjects which are mysterious or seem "far out" to others because of their being out of the ordinary or unorthodox will exercise a strong mental fascination for you during much of this trend. It will be to your advantage to communicate your ideas as clearly and cogently as possible, because this is the kind of cycle which often promotes a sense of euphoria or "day dreaming" which sometimes reflects in your expressions as an "up in the air" quality so that others find it difficult to follow your reasoning or the meaning of your words.

The coming years are likely to see you more firmly settled in your efforts to win security, and I have absolutely no doubt that the changeful circumstances which are indicated will lead you toward a splendid and harmonious future!

The two signs which play a paramount part in the formation of characteristics and which continue to play a part in the working out of the destinies of those who were born in this cusp are Libra and Scorpio. The *"ruling"* planet of the former is Venus, and of the latter Mars. These two planets are strong in their effect upon the native. He is quite reasonable in his ideas but not at all inclined to accept the standards ordinarily accepted, either for rules of conduct or in a business way. He may be considered a dreamer, although he has a very practical sense when it comes to the application of original ideas and plans. He sometimes has difficulty in adjusting himself to the conditions of life, but he is likely to have unusual vitality and due to the influence of Scorpio a magnetism which enables him to make friends more readily than is true of most people.

Men who come into the world under this particular combination of influences, when properly educated and when they learn the rules of self government, become very successful in medicine or surgery. Scorpio, being intense and controlled, imparts coolness, ability to observe and a detached skill. Libra imparts a keen intuitional faculty, often enabling the native to advance greatly. His qualifications allow him to maintain any position he may achieve. Those who were born under the predominating vibrations of this cusp have, however, some tendency to be retiring. Due to the influence of Libra, this sometimes over-shadows the Scorpio aggressiveness and in the blending causes the native to hesitate in facing issues. He has a strong tendency to be tactful and not liking to hurt other people's feelings, he may at times evade an issue which should be faced.

In many cases, natives require *bolstering* of their self-confidence, which is sometimes greatly shaken by events which occur suddenly and seem to threaten their well-being. As a result of the influence of Libra, the native often becomes successful in original design. Combined with the ideas of color this sign imparts, the keen eye for discerning shades which is bestowed by Scorpio, makes any kind of decorative work quite a favorable outlet. Women who came into the world under this combination of solar influences, it is noted, are artistic in their homes as well as good managers. They also have naturally creative talents. They have qualities which cause them to be quite faithful and loyal, but they need understanding on the part of their mates.

The tendency of the native to be friendly is quite likely to make him popular. His tactfulness, however, very readily tends to make him do a great many things in order to be a good companion and to fall in with ideas of others, which he would not do if left to his own ideas. The fact of the matter is that vulgarity is likely to be quite repulsive to him, but under conditions where he is forced into association with those who are vulgar, it is quite possible for him to adopt the line of least resistance and to express many of their ideas and expressions outwardly. This is something which he should really fight against. There are few who have greater *natural good qualities* than do *true* natives of this cusp.

The birthsign SCORPIO
October 24th to November 22nd

f you were born between October 24th and November 22nd your birthsign is Scorpio. This solar vibration imparts quite distinct and definite qualities. In describing the sign we shall endeavor to encompass all of the qualities inherent in this vibration — both positive and negative. A great many of the legends, particularly those of ancient Greece, dealt with this sign of the zodiac. This, among the original tribes of Israel, is the tribe of Dan, or one of the twelve fundamental types of humanity. Weather prophets of an ancient day considered the sign Scorpio as being significant of, or indicating, stormy weather. The Scorpion is the symbol of the sign and is intended to represent the recognizable psychological qualities inherent in the sign itself. Scorpio is referred to as watery, fixed, cold, nocturnal, feminine, southern, violent, negative, phlegmatic, and of long ascension. The topaz is the gem which vibrates most in harmony with the quality of Scorpio and the red carnation is the flower. Mars is the ruling planet and, as one would naturally conclude, the qualities which were attributed to that god are a fundamental part of the psychological factors inherent in the Scorpio nature.

Except when there are extremely adverse planetary positions at birth, the native of Scorpio is of robust physique and possessed of tremendous wells of vitality. Of course, other planetary positions indicate the state of evolution which has been reached by the individual and, working in harmony with heredity, the equipment he is given for life in this physical plane of existence. Electro-magnetic currents and the hidden forces of vibration play about true natives of this sign to a greater extent than may be said of those born in any other sign. In their positive phases, the people of Scorpio have tremendous natural forces to call to their aid. Among the magnetic healers of the world are many who received strong Scorpio influences at birth.

In describing the characteristics of the sign, it should be remembered that both the positive and the negative qualities are discussed. The individual who is highly evolved will express *through his processes of thought,* and consequently *his actions,* the positive traits of the sign. There are many degrees of thought vibration

99

from the positive to the extreme negative. All human beings are in a state some-where between the two. All are developing, and thus evolving, to the point of being able to express the most complete positives. Natives of Scorpio will recognize the qualities described, though some may be almost entirely submerged, while others are more predominant. Words which express the positive qualities of this sign are: intrepid, dauntless, tenacious, optimistic, energetic, positive, fearless, devoted, ambitious, eloquent, unswerving, faithful. Words expressing the negative qualities are: sarcastic, vindictive, quarrelsome, passionate, dictatorial, scheming, severe, suspicious, jealous, tyrannical, willful, intolerant.

The positive qualities of this sign are extremely powerful, and the negatives also reach to extremes. The native of Scorpio, however, who realizes the desira-bility (in fact the necessity) for cultivating higher attributes of character, has within himself the *power to direct his thought processes* into the most positive and therefore the most constructive channels. He is able to surmount obstacles in the material physical world due to his tremendous power of will, and so is able to completely dominate his destructive instincts, turning his mind from thoughts of vengeance, violence, and the predatory traits expressive of the Scorpio nature.

The true Scorpio native has great ability to exercise self-control. He has a coolness and bearing which manifest themselves in a positive demeanor and decisive actions. He generally has strong powers of observation, keen perception, is quite inclined to be aggressive, and possesses a great deal of determination to gain his objectives. He is almost invariably positive in his ideas, and equally *determined* to *carry through* in whatever he does. Once he becomes interested in a particular goal, and *actively* engages in attempting to achieve it, he is *tenacious* to an extra-ordinary degree. The nearer he is to the pure Scorpio type (the less his Scorpio vibrations at birth were blended with others), the more tenacious and indomitable he is. In early youth, natives of this sign are usually slender. The pure type of Scorpio has aquiline features; the countenance is broad and open. The pure vibration from this sign will invariably impart sharp features and a penetrating glance.

The Scorpio native has the capacity to be both courteous and affable; but, when aroused, he can be extremely sharp, cutting, and sarcastic. The Scorpio vibration in itself imparts a great deal of shrewdness, and the native is equipped by nature to achieve almost any goal. His language is concise and to the point; his mind is pro-gressive; and he has a tremendous natural ability to sway the opinions of others. One who was born under a strong influence from this sign is likely to be an extremely brilliant talker; and his sharp wit and keen analysis of situations often enable him to put to route any opposition, in conversation as well as in practical affairs. He is an extremely good and daring debater, never being at a loss for the most effective words and ideas. The native of Scorpio has a pleasing manner and quite frequently has a powerful influence over members of the opposite sex. He is likely, in fact, to have a great deal of influence over all those with whom he comes in contact, and because of his intense inner powers he frequently *dominates* them.

Individuals who come into the world under a strong Scorpio vibration are usually extremely clever in gaining information or in making investigations. Highly evolved natives are prone to champion those who are oppressed, and they are militant in their defense of those who are meek or who are being treated unjustly. In that connection perhaps, Scorpio natives are more warlike, determined, and aggressive than are those born in any other sign of the zodiac.

Often those born under a strong Scorpio influence love combat. They welcome obstacles of all kinds, and seem to delight in the stress and struggle of accomplishment to a far greater extent than the rewards. Quite frequently they are active in the cause of social and educational reform; usually having many ideas and suggestions for improvement along those lines. Some of the greatest reformers and champions of *"lost causes"* were Scorpio natives. When individuals who were born under this sign become interested in a reform, particularly one of a religious nature, they are determined, persistent, recklessly courageous, and extremely impatient of restraint or opposition. The true Scorpio *is* bold and courageous in carrying out his ideas. Also the calm bearing, dignified mannerisms, combined with the sensible speech of the evolved Scorpio, inevitably gain for him the esteem of all those with whom he comes in contact; and, though he may encounter obstacles, he overcomes them.

Rarely is the true Scorpio easily frightened by any condition of life or by any threat. He is fond of adventure, and is irresistibly attracted by any dangerous undertaking which requires daring and is uncertain in nature. He will extend himself when he encounters such conditions, showing extraordinary vitality and a vaulting ambition which often enable him to accomplish the seemingly impossible. He is fascinated by difficult projects. Quite frequently the native is able to achieve success, perhaps to establish a business, despite every obstacle or hindrance and he seldom overlooks the advantages in any business transaction. He has an inherent ability to effectively and efficiently guard his own interests. The true Scorpio native is an executive *par-excellence*. He soon learns how to handle others, and he can usually succeed in getting people to carry out his desires as he is able to use the most effective methods in each individual case.

The Scorpio native is inclined in many ways to live *within himself*. He is secretive about his own affairs, although he may give the appearance of being completely frank and outspoken. The shrewdness of Scorpio is such that the affairs of life soon cause him to learn how best to protect his own interests. He has a high respect for those who have accomplished a great deal, and he desires to emulate such an example. He is often accused of being cold and unsympathetic. Actually, however, he often takes a more practical method of helping others than the mere use of words and encouragement. Sometimes he seems to be completely unfeeling about the troubles of others, but he may then take decisive steps to relieve those same troubles.

Usually conservative in dress, he has extremely good taste. This is, of course, especially true of the evolved native. One born in this sign is usually fond of dark, rich shades; seldom does he like weak and insipid colors. The woman of this sign likes dark, rich, wine colored draperies, oriental rugs, and in general those things which express the roundness, fullness, and intensity of the Scorpio nature. The tastes of people born in this sign are similar in music. They prefer colorful compositions, martial music, and dramatic opera. They are seldom intrigued by less intense melodies. Large bodies of water rouse a deep response in them. They love travel by sea and, particularly, enjoy sitting beside the restless waters at the shore.

The native of Scorpio who is relatively unevolved has many faults which are not so much to be termed weaknesses, as definite expressions of negative forces. The choice of such expression is always deliberate. The individual who is thus unevolved expects to rule his own business, and usually does so. He is resentful of all opposition, and is extremely severe when aroused to outbursts of wrath. Under such conditions, he does not hesitate to choose the most abusive language. The native who is in a low state of evolution is greedy and lustful, and has strongly marked tendencies toward cruelty. His imagination and tenacity, in combination with the intensity of his nature, impells him to great extremes in his determination to rule others.

This sign particularly affects, and actually represents, the generative organs, in the innermost meaning of its vibration. For that reason, the negative expressions of the sign tend strongly toward animal passion which, *if not controlled*, becomes gross and violent. In this connection, the unrestrained physical emotions of the Scorpio native may well include jealousy; sometimes this becomes the predominating force in the unevolved native. This is true of both the men and women of the sign. In such cases, their jealous rages approach frenzy. Unevolved natives are fault-finding to an excessive degree. They are extremely critical of the actions of others and seem to regard themselves as the "accusing angels" of the human race. To the Scorpio, who has not greatly developed, there seems to be an ever-pressing necessity to supervise the actions of others, in order to hold them strictly to account for a complete observance to duty. This is so, even though the native himself may not be completely fulfilling his own obligations.

The unevolved Scorpio is satisfied with himself to an obvious degree. He has the greatest self-assurance, and does not hesitate to push himself forward no matter what the circumstances. A rebuke, or disdain, on the part of others will either arouse his violent antagonism, or have no affect whatever upon him. The native who is evolved in some respects, but remains strongly negative in others, often develops his intellect greatly. In such case he is a dangerous opponent either in argument, or in other and more material ways. In debate, or in the company of others, the Scorpio native who has so developed his intellect often delights in ridiculing and prodding those whom he decides to oppose. He will often take great pleasure in goading his victim of the moment into uncontrolled rage, while he himself remains coldly efficient. In doing so he may make the most illogical statements, but his ability to reason logically, and express himself concisely, prevents him from making himself ridiculous.

The true Scorpio who is in a low state of evolution does not hesitate to make every possible use of those whom he calls friends. He has a particular way of calling on them to assist him, and of using an ingratiating manner and a persistency which does not permit refusal. When they cease to be useful to him, however, he tosses them aside. He never hesitates to call upon others, no matter how shoddily he may have treated them in the past. He can be extremely *tricky* in business, and will use every means which his fertile imagination can devise to gain his own ends, whether in making money or in the gratification of personal desires. The lower and unevolved Scorpio native *prys* into the affairs of associates, and he does not hesitate under any condition to use the information he is able to obtain to further his own interests. He is a merciless critic, and he is sure to remind others, in the most cutting way, of obligations which *they* have neglected or ways in which *they* have failed to live up to their full duty. It is difficult for the unevolved native of this sign to admit his faults. Though within himself he may fully realize them, his choice in perpetuating them is deliberate. He has formed a definite conception of life, and he feels that he is justified in seeking his own ends to the ultimate degree.

While the individual who was born in this sign is often an extraordinarily powerful force for good, being the staunchest imaginable defender of those who are exploited by others, the undeveloped native becomes, on the other hand, quite clever at influencing groups of people for his own purposes. He is often a convincing and capable public figure, though there is a wide difference between one who is unawakened and one who is the opposite. The inclination of the unevolved Scorpio native is to dominate all those with whom he comes in contact. Often, when it is possible to do so, he accomplishes his own desires by means of the fear he is able to inspire. When certain of the negatives in this sign have developed strongly, particularly those which cause the native to look for the shortcomings of others, he becomes a reformer of the most aggressively vindictive type. He delights in probing into every matter concerning the moral lapses of others, and every violation of law; dragging them into the light of day and being determined that the law-breakers shall be punished.

The intensity of the Scorpio nature is such that the native throws tremendous reserves of energy into whatever course of endeavor his inner impulses may urge him toward. Due to the fact that the negatives of this sign are extremely powerful, a great many natives suffer wholly unexpected difficulties. They encounter ups and downs during life, but development of the *positive* phases of their natures enables them to lessen the reverses. When they have developed their higher attributes, they become the staunchest defenders of fairness and justice. Always the individual who receives a strong influence from this sign and therefore approaches the pure Scorpio type, has within himself the *capacity* for the most *lofty* achievements.

WOMEN OF SCORPIO

Women who come into the world under a predominant Scorpio influence are invariably highly magnetic. They have splendid powers of intellect, and are adaptable to the extent that they can apply themselves with a considerable degree of success to almost any line of endeavor. They often accomplish a great deal, are extremely good managers in their own homes, and are efficient in whatever occupies their attention, but they are not always easy to get along with. There is a tendency for them to dominate those who surround them and to be somewhat willful. They are demanding at times, and often as a result of their ambition and determination to achieve success or security, they exert a constant pressure which, in undeveloped women, becomes fault-finding. Occasionally the feminine nature of this sign is difficult to understand because of the propensity to speak harshly. She may be prone to outbursts of temper. An admixture of other signs at birth lessens the pure Scorpio vibrations in this connection. When one finds a native of the sign Scorpio who is of rather placid nature, invariably it will be found that other basic harmonics which carry within themselves this particular quality were strong at the time of birth.

The Scorpio woman is intense but often controlled, determined, and extremely tenacious. A great many famous actresses were born under this solar vibration. They invariably have a great inner force; their powerful personalities being strongly felt among audiences. The woman who comes into the world under a strong influence from Scorpio is frequently original in her ideas, but primarily she is *persistent* in her application to anything in which she wishes to succeed. She is capable of being an extraordinarily devoted wife and mother. Often she will sacrifice herself completely, and is inexhaustible in her efforts to bring security into the lives of those she loves. Unfortunately, if the negatives which are natural to the sign are allowed to develop, the Scorpio woman becomes harsh and fault-finding. The *demon of jealousy* always lies at the bottom of the Scorpio nature. In the developed or evolved native, it is subdued and supplanted by more positive traits; but in the undeveloped man or woman of this sign, this tendency is something to reckon with! The unevolved Scorpio woman needs to be constantly praised, flattered, and conceded to by her husband, and when he fails to do so, she is quick to let him know about it. She sharply criticizes minor faults, and is inclined to regiment her family to the strictest performance of duty.

In financial fields, Scorpio women are extremely successful merchandisers. They are fitted for occupations connected with advertising, and often become highly successful interior decorators and designers. They are likely to be very talented in their instinct for color combinations. In common with the men, they are extremely good superintendents, and the evolved woman who was born in this sign has the capacity to become an extraordinarily capable executive. These women have a magnetism which is particularly felt by members of the opposite sex. Frequently, they are extremely fascinating and able to bring men to do their bidding completely. There is no sign of the zodiac where the women have greater potentialities for the highest degree of constructive good. There is no more kindly and helpful woman in the world than the evolved native of this sign. Her helpfulness takes a particularly constructive form. She can be a very symbol of strength, courage, and goodness.

Children who come into the world under a Scorpio influence which is sufficiently strong to be predominant, should, at a very early age, receive the most careful guidance and instruction relative to the facts of life. Particularly, knowledge of the sex functions should be imparted in a constructive fashion. Youngsters who were born in this sign are likely to become hard to manage. They have an intense desire to finish what they have once made up their minds to do, and are likely to be extremely hard to divert from an undertaking, no matter what its nature. Quite frequently, they are obstinate and willful, though they are often lovable to an extraordinary degree. It is probable that in order to bring out the extremely powerful constructive factors of this sign, the Scorpio child needs more careful and understanding guidance than do those born in any other sign of the zodiac.

True Scorpio children quite frequently give evidence early in life of a desire to dominate those with whom they come in contact. These children are almost certain to notice the faults and shortcomings of their playmates, and are likely to play upon those shortcomings or faults for their own benefit. Parental example in the use of constructive speech, which naturally is an outward expression of constructive thought forms, is extremely advisable. Youngsters of this sign should be impressed by the correct precepts and teachings from the very beginning. When they *understand* that they should, from a practical standpoint, formulate constructive thoughts, they have formed habit patterns which will last them throughout life. They come to look for good in others, and to know that true accomplishment comes only as a result of co-operation with others and of kindliness. They have the power of determination to follow such teachings, and to control their thought processes more fully than is possible for most of those who were born in other signs.

There are no children with greater natural powers for lofty accomplishment than those who received a strong influence from this sign at birth. There is no doubt that some of the greatest and most inspiring leaders of the world were born in Scorpio. A particularly important lesson for the child of Scorpio to learn is that harsh criticism of others may often be quite unjust and that it may cause deep distress. Guiding these youngsters into paths of kindliness, tolerance, and helpfulness will invariably pay dividends of the most valuable kind. Unless planetary influences are quite adverse at birth, cosmic forces working in harmony with heredity, impart to these children tremendous reserves of vitality. Illness is improbable, excepting in the cases of epidemics. Providing there is proper bodily harmony, which is synonymous with constructive thought forms, the youngster of this sign should be extremely vital and well. Children of this sign are greatly benefited by an environment wherein culture is expressed. Educational advantages are quite important. The child of Scorpio has a tremendous capacity for self-control and driving, constructive energy. As a result, he can become a powerful factor for good. No effort should be spared in guiding these little ones, as their possibilities are as nearly limitless as human powers can make them. Many of the highly constructive steps that have been taken by human beings in the past were inspired by the urgings and the example of some intrepid native of the sign Scorpio.

It is most important for those who were born in this sign to find matrimonial partners who can understand the *deep loyalty* which often underlies their intense application to everything in life; an intensity which frequently leads them to give expression to temper resulting in quarrels. Their tendency to react strongly, when something to which they have applied themselves intensely fails to develop as they wish, also needs understanding.

Two marriages often occur in the lives of Scorpio natives, and sometimes more. Love rarely passes them by, and it is not unusual for them to have a number of *affairs* of the heart, many of which may be secret. It is invariably a mistake for a person who was born under a strongly predominating Scorpio vibration to marry one who is argumentative or quarrelsome. In many ways, the sign Pisces (February 20th – March 19th) is not only harmonious with Scorpio, but especially desirable, as natives of that sign are good foils for the aggressiveness and ambition which are a strong part of the Scorpio nature. In a measure Virgo (August 23rd – September 23rd) is harmonious, as also is Cancer (June 23rd – July 21st). Among natives of Scorpio who are highly evolved, many successful marriages are contracted with one who was born in the sign Taurus (April 21st – May 22nd), but it is quite necessary that they be on an equal plane of understanding and evolution. Two people of a low state of evolution who were, respectively, born in these signs, will invariably engage in violent expressions of opposing points of view. They have, however, many interests in common. Their outlook upon life is frequently similar, and they have qualities which to a considerable extent *complement* each other.

Rarely is anyone who was born in this sign, either man or woman, dominated by his or her marriage partner. Any woman who marries a Scorpio man with the idea of possibly reforming him or changing him in any way should be prepared for a difficult time, to say the least. As a matter of fact this is equally true of women who were born in this sign. The man who marries a Scorpio woman and who tends to be neglectful, or who deviates from his marriage vows, is likely to find himself dealing with a veritable *tartar*. It is well for one who marries a native of this sign to be prepared to *submerge* his ideas to the positive opinions of Scorpio!

Basically, people of this sign are strong characters for the most part. In marriage as in executive supervisory capacities they are likely to be quite demanding in their insistence that other people live up to their duty. They are not only likely to ask other people to do this, but they themselves are more than likely to be extremely meticulous in discharging their own obligations. While in speech they may sometimes be biting, sarcastic or harsh, they are, in doing that which they consider to be their duty, likely to be extraordinarily faithful and undeviating. The marriage partner of a Scorpio is likely to find them extremely well able to manage and faithful in most of the practical affairs of life.

The man who was born in this sign is an extremely good provider for his family. He is able to fight the battles of existence and to obtain for himself and for those near him the best that life affords in a material way. The Scorpio native almost invariably desires *all that life affords* in the way of comfortable and attractive surroundings.

Natives of this sign are especially fitted for governmental occupations of a supervisory nature. They are over-seers and superintendents of the first order. They are extremely capable in political occupations, being able to develop the ability to talk well and convincingly, as well as to plan a course of action most efficiently. They are extremely capable when it comes to getting the best out of those under them, and highly successful in getting others to carry on work under their personal supervision and direction. All branches of trade are favorable for natives of this sign. They are most capable in merchandising fields, being extremely shrewd.

The true Scorpio has an extremely good eye for form and color, and in consequence has qualifications for success as a decorator and designer. In the creation of styles Scorpio people often excel. A great many natives of this sign are musical. When they receive influences at birth which impel them toward musical expression, they are extremely forceful in rendition. Some of the foremost composers, orchestra directors, and band leaders were born under a strong Scorpio influence. Advertising in its various branches is a favorable outlet for the fundamental Scorpio talents and abilities. Being shrewd judges of the likes and dislikes of other people, they are able to put this knowledge to good account. Often, they are highly capable salespeople, being energetic, persistent, and able to talk well.

The Scorpio native is invariably a magnetic and compelling public speaker when he turns his energies in that direction. He is often able to exert almost a hypnotic influence over his listeners. He can be very forceful, and his intensity (which is natural to all natives of this sign) is reflected in his oratory. Many Scorpio natives have been great leaders — often reformers. One finds perhaps, a greater number of Scorpio natives who have been leaders of forlorn causes than those of any other sign. The natives of this sign rarely give up, they must be beaten to the final ounce of their strength before they can actually be defeated.

All natives of the sign have some affinity with insurance as well as with wills and legacies. Also they seem to have a strong talent for dealing with or handling estates. As a result, many have been successful lawyers, specializing in these particular fields, or as far as insurance is concerned, *in* the insurance business. The men of this sign also become remarkably successful and efficient surgeons. They have complete self-control, a coolness and poise which makes them capable of performing surgical operations with the greatest skill and daring.

The native of this sign is almost invariably interested in mysteries of all kinds. Not a few have been highly successful writers of mystery plays and stories. They have fertile imaginations in the construction of plots and great force and fire in their language. Scorpio is also extremely well represented among investigators of all classes; many will be found as highly efficient and successful detectives or secret service operatives. Sometimes natives of this sign defeat themselves as a result of their *intensity* when it is prompted by negatives which are weaknesses, to a greater or lesser extent, of all human beings but which may be intensely destructive in the Scorpio. The natural forcefulness and magnetism of the native, however, is alone often responsible for his outstanding success in whatever field he chooses.

It becomes immediately apparent when one has read the foregoing that the powerful negatives of Scorpio will in time be productive of extreme physical malfunctioning and conditions which are termed disease — if those negatives are allowed to develop. The true Scorpio is invariably able to endure a tremendous amount of mental and physical stress. Expression of negatives in thought forms, however, almost always lead the Scorpio native to *excesses of material nature.* He is quite inclined to over-indulge at the table and to be intemperate in the use of stimulating liquors or of foods that are also overstimulating, which frequently leads to other excesses. To a large extent, conditions of disharmony in the physical body result from these indulgences. It cannot be stressed too strongly that these expressions on the physical plane of existence always are synonymous with negatives of thought vibrations. Every individual lives in a world all his own. The vibrations he produces in mind are reproduced in his physical surroundings. Neither does, nor can, exist without the other.

Those parts of the body which are particularly affected by the vibrations of Scorpio are the bladder, the urethra, the ureters, the groin, the prostate gland, the rectum, the colon, the gall-bladder, and a portion of the kidney function. Negatives of the sign manifest themselves in the conditions referred to as gall-stones, kidney-stones, ruptures, piles, fistulas, venereal diseases, and other affections of the generative organs. These conditions, of course, may have a far-reaching effect on the body. Symptoms of such states may manifest themselves almost anywhere in the physical organism. A powerful Scorpio influence at birth, however, would lead one to look first for the manifestation of specific negatives inherent in the sign (previously described), in that part of the physical body which is most directly affected.

A great many forms of skin disorders as well as heart troubles are traceable to the negatives of Scorpio which lead to overindulgence in rich foods particularly, as well as the sometimes unregulated sex nature. Occasionally Scorpio natives have a certain susceptibility to conditions of physical disharmony in early youth. Children of this sign are not infrequently susceptible to asthma and various types of allergies. Very often, however, when there is a relatively delicate condition in early years it is overcome when the native reaches the period in life when his natural forces are brought into play. Early conditions often are overcome in later years so that the native becomes vigorous, in fact much more so than the average individual. It is the strong opinion of the writer that all physical conditions of so-called disease are the result of *inner disharmonies* and in the case of Scorpio natives asthma and the allergies to which they are sometimes susceptible are due to inharmonious conditions in their surroundings which may be very greatly resented.

The native of this sign who has allowed his negatives to develop strongly is always likely to directly attract, in the hidden world of vibration, conditions which bring about infections. In approaching a negative period in connection with health, the Scorpio native should strive particularly to condition his mind *first,* and then his body — by moderation in diet, in order to pass through the period without ill effect. This *he can accomplish,* if he will, because of his great natural powers of intense concentration!

1977 Sweeping elements are indicated as touching your income forcing "decisions" as to whether to "come or go" or to make a move that may be "chancy" but holds "the promise" of possible considerable benefit or to be satisfied to take less and be on solid ground. Especially in the months of April, May and October when the eclipse and the position of Mars will be felt are you likely to come "face to face" with a feeling of urgency which will be due to "a burning" desire *to excel.* Later things will smooth because of your tireless effort now, bringing not only "a peaceful" everyday existence later but security – not dreamed of earlier in your life, I am fully convinced!

1978 The mood for changing your circumstances will be powerful in 1978, I believe, and I encourage you, wholeheartedly, to follow a plan you may initiate in a channel of service "only you" can fulfill. Through uplifting emotions you will have a unique "know-how" for improving conditions for certain groups of people, I am sure. Distant places are likely to appeal to you, particularly as 1978 is apt to be a year when you can increase your learning substantially. Certain people may appear to ask more of you now than you would prefer. It might be a wise idea to continue to regard your resources of time, energy and assets, as enthusiastically as you usually have in the past, without going to extremes in any direction. "A turning."

1979 Now and then you probably will feel that some of your personal affections earn less satisfaction than your efforts to improve your position in "authoritative circles," as you may have moments during 1979 whereby you will gain greater happiness from acquaintances than from a few of your closer ties. You will receive evergrowing rewards, I am sure, when you endeavor to "attend to your personal responsibilities" and *also* fulfill other purposes you think will provide lasting contributions for the betterment of as many people as you are able to reach. Through your "soul-searching" you are now apt to make discoveries that will benefit you always. I anticipate you will have a deeper understanding of past "complications" at this time.

1980 The pattern of your life is now moving toward one of the dramatic and sudden changes which will probably color every phase of your life. There will be great demands on you most likely (I mean situations pressing for your personal attention and actual physical efforts). There are apt to be times when you feel extremely tired so your need for more rest will be considerable. Major planetary positions indicate the likelihood that another person will be a vexing problem . . . and that you may not find responsible or trustworthy people to "fill in," so your hours of carrying on certain obligations are apt to be long. You may be called upon to demonstrate the strength of your character as well as your courage by fighting a real "battle." There could be a tendency to suspect the motives of other people and to question their judgment under this cyclic trend. You are apt to feel it is wise to examine financial matters closely, particularly ventures that arise having a "get rich quick" appeal; however, straightforward methods are almost certain to help you improve your finances now, I believe.

SCORPIO

1981 You are apt to "close yourself off" from old friends or associates at times during this year and go through moody spells, because of feeling you do not have the affection or regard necessary from those who mean a great deal as an inspiration to put forth your best efforts. A particular person or some older individual may appear a "drag" upon you mentally or a temporary hindrance to your happiness and achievement. As this forecast period draws to an end, I feel some old set pattern of your life is likely to be closed out, and a doorway of fuller expression is opening to you. At times you are apt to think that you are being held like a caged lion, while waiting for particular events to occur so that you can start certain plans in motion. This is apt to be a cycle when you will consider unloading useless burdens you have carried in the past, in order to "free" yourself of entanglements that no longer seem necessary for your security. Health concerns might briefly touch you, but taking time to rest when your pace is tiring will prove to be unusually beneficial now, I am certain.

1982 Around the middle of this year, your aspirations and indeed some of your strongest beliefs are indicated as undergoing a "transformation" that will mark a definite "turning point" in your life. A sense of confinement or a need to work under confining circumstances will be burdensome at times, but an easing of these restrictive elements is clearly shown as this yearly cycle draws to a close. I believe you will be heartened and encouraged by the growth of a more positive self-image, so that some of the uncertainties and doubts which have cluttered up your mind in the recent past will now begin to fade. Money matters are apt to "fluctuate," with both unexpected reverses and surprising gains this year. Assets in which others share will demand close attention, probably in connection with insurance, taxes, or an inheritance. A watchful "eye" upon expenses so as to avoid pitfalls that could undermine you will pay handsome "dividends" later on.

1983 This is likely to be an exceptionally active year with respect to money and other financial matters. Changes in this area are strongly indicated, and there will undoubtedly be some "tricky" situations you will need to maneuver through before reaching a "safe harbor." On the other hand, 1983 is marked by a planetary cycle which usually brings financial benefits, sometimes in a providential manner. During this trend, I think it a wise idea for you to display the utmost integrity, not only in your personal management of expenses and income, but in *any* affairs involving possessions touching your close relationships or "group enterprises." A very welcome benefit is apt to contribute to your sense of security.

1984 Mars makes a significant station of about seven months duration in your birth sign this year. Such influences recur only at long intervals, and it will be of great importance to insure that the dynamic energy generated by this planetary influence is put to constructive use, in order to avert making mistakes that could trip you later and to avoid restlessness with no apparent direction. I feel your energy and vitality will be stronger now, and many of your efforts will be centered upon improving the economic climate of your life. It

110

may be difficult at times, but when you "bend over backward" to insure harmonious relationships and refuse to be involved in any questionable affairs, I think you will be surprised and gratified by the heartfelt warmth and helpful response you inspire from others!

SUMMATION (Scorpio)

Seldom in your life will there be a period when money and resources will be so subject to unusual factors as are likely during the time covered by this forecast. You may tend to manage your financial affairs more secretively than usual, and others will probably find it difficult to "pry loose" any information about what you are doing with your money. However, I feel your motives for keeping moves involving money "under your hat," so to speak, will often be based upon an effort to clarify "clouded" matters related to security before you speak out or answer the questions of others. It will be extremely important to guide all your maneuvers as realistically as you can during this cycle, because you might be misled by circumstances that appear before you as mirages — seeming to hold for you vast new prospects, but which could disappear at your "touch!"

Radical changes will probably appear which may alter the familiar pattern of your life. The dropping of "old friendships" and the establishing of "new contacts" are both outstandingly indicated, particularly until around 1981 or 1982, at which time a more settled series of conditions is likely to stabilize your relationships. On many occasions during this cycle, I feel you will be inclined to sacrifice security for the sake of new or exciting experiences. Impatience or unorthodox or erratic behavior frequently accompanies this kind of planetary influence, to the detriment of truly gainful accomplishment or the maintaining of satisfying personal relations.

I believe you will "talk over" the serious issues of life to an unusual degree, such as actual "life and death" problems, in order to arrive at conclusions that can advance or consolidate your affairs sensibly. Something that has been hanging "mid-air," so to speak, for a long time will now come to a terminal point for your benefit, in my judgment. It appears that a particular matter you will accomplish alone (or under somewhat confining circumstances) will open a door financially later although started during this cycle. You may have opportunities for increasing your assets through an affiliation with a "foundation" or large institution that attends to the needs of people whose circumstances are temporarily "limited." Quite definitely, I feel there will be a noticeable "turnover" in your alliances, because a different "set" of friends and acquaintances seems to surround you. This will be a challenging period of "inner" awakening, I am certain — with tremendous benefits following!

As with the other cusps, the solar vibrations were transmitted to those born at this time through two separate signs of the zodiac — Scorpio and Sagittarius, and the vibrations of these two signs were blended. The first of these is *"ruled"* by the planet Mars and the second by Jupiter. Both these planets are strong in the formation of characteristics and they continue so in the working out of destiny. The same being true of this as of other cusps, the combination brings about a certain amount of complexity but it is very *fortunate* in some respects. Natives usually possess a considerable degree of determination and courage. They have a strong tendency to throw themselves heart and soul into anything they undertake, but as a result of doing so, the mental intensity with which they attack problems tends to *wear out* their nervous energies. One born under predominant vibrations from this cusp is often disappointed in others and sometimes feels that the burdens of the world are resting upon his shoulders, as associates do not seem sufficiently dependable to carry things through as the native thinks they should.

He has a marked tendency to take on more burdens than he can really carry. Often he finds the characteristics of the two signs in conflict within him. Scorpio imparts qualities which make one a natural supervisor and inclined to see that other people do their duties. Sagittarius is executive, but it imparts characteristics which tend toward allowing other people to do things *on their own*. The full Sagittarian is inclined to devote his energies to that which is his own business and he usually allows others to do the same. In these respects, the native of this cusp finds the blend of the two influences not in harmony, as he sees the shortcomings of others and the ways in which they fail to measure up to that which is right and proper for them to do and he has, at times, a tendency to correct them and insist upon their doing their full duty — but again his instincts prompt him to let them alone.

He has remarkable powers which can be brought to a high state of development. The combination of these influences gives him a great deal of natural occult force and certain clairvoyant qualities. He can usually succeed in any occupation which requires a knowledge of finance and of merchandising. He is, however, not limited in his choice of occupations, as he has an inherent quality which enables him to duplicate almost anything others do. It is to be noted that the women of this influence become splendid wives and mothers, but sometimes they are quite outspoken and they possess strong characters. Natives of this cusp have qualities which inspire considerable confidence on the part of other people. This is a very valuable trait and can benefit them greatly. It isn't their natural tendency to violate confidences. If they feel that someone else reposes a great deal of confidence in them, they are quite likely to go to great lengths rather than to cause disappointment. The native of this cusp has very clear ideas of what is right and wrong, especially as applied to other people. It is sometimes difficult for him to restrain his tendency to bring others to task for violating his ideas of what *he thinks* is proper for them to do.

112

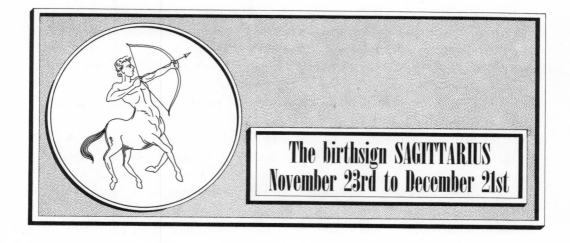

The birthsign SAGITTARIUS
November 23rd to December 21st

f your birth occurred between November 23rd and December 21st, you are a native of the sign Sagittarius — the sign associated with hunting, the out-of-doors, and animals. In essence the fundamental psychological reactions of this sign have a rather intimate connection with those sportsmanlike qualities considered a part of the hunting season. These aspects are depicted in the early Greek symbol of Sagittarius, which was Chiron, the wisest of the Centaurs. In mythology, Chiron was educated by Apollo and Diana and became the mentor of the most distinguished heroes of Grecian mythology, instructing them in hunting, medicine, music, and the art of prophecy.

It is considered to be masculine and fortunate. The gem which has vibrations most nearly harmonious with the basic vibration of Sagittarius is the turquoise, and the flower is the goldenrod. This sign is representative of the tribe of Joseph, one of the twelve original tribes of Israel, or one of the fundamental types of human beings. Jupiter is the ruling planet. This means that the qualities which were ascribed to that god of the ancients, and whose character was illustrative in story form of the inherent vibrations from the planet, are those which dominate the sign. Sagittarius is referred to as fiery, common, flexed, choleric, double-bodied, hot, dry, southern, motive, and of long ascension. The first fifteen degrees of the sign are called human, and the last fifteen degrees bestial. In a measure, the positive and negative qualities are conveyed therein. As with the other signs of the zodiac, we will describe as fully as possible, all the qualities of character and the psychological traits which are part of this fundamental vibration, considering them in both the positive and the negative forms. One who received a strong vibration from Sagittarius at birth will, unmistakably, recognize in himself all the qualities of the sign, though some may be quite minor in the extent to which they are expressed. Since this sign contains positive qualities on an extremely high plane, it also has equally strong negative qualities. A properly erected natal chart will indicate the state of evolution a particular individual has attained, and as a result the extent to which either the

113

positives or negatives will be expressed by him. The pure Sagittarius influence produces people who are quite symmetrical of feature. Among the most handsome of human beings are those who came into the world under a strong influence from this sign. They have "open" countenances, vigorous constitutions and a freshness of complexion which are a clear mark of this fundamental vibration. The eyes are quite expressive, large, and have a penetrating quality when the Sagittarius influence is strongly predominant at birth.

The native of Sagittarius is basically an optimistic, jovial, happy individual. A marked characteristic is his generosity in dealing with others. He is possessed of a great amount of foresight, and a high sense of justice and consequently is able to develop a truly lofty form of wisdom. An outstanding quality of this sign is the ability the native has of moving swiftly, capably, and at the same time audaciously in emergencies. When he takes the time to deliberate he will in all probability exercise more caution. The true Sagittarian will frequently see things in a light that is completely different from that of natives of other signs. It is not unusual for his outlook to be *widely divergent* from others of this human race. Perhaps more consistently, and to a larger degree, the native of this sign will be more successful in what he undertakes than those of other signs, since his mental reactions are rapid, and at the same time he is capable of quickly grasping the basic significance of conditions or problems facing him. In his mind, the very essentials involved stand out clearly.

You probably have a strong tendency to look into the future. It has often been said that the Sagittarius native who received a predominating influence from this sign at birth belongs among the prophets of the world. The searching quality of the Sagittarius mind is not limited. Those who were born in the sign and who are more evolved than others, develop their naturally remarkable gift of foresight, becoming advanced metaphysicians. The tendency of the Sagittarius native, in fact, is to peer into the future. He is fundamentally a student of the occult sciences, and can develop a knowledge along those lines far above that which is possible to most of the rest of the world. A strong fundamental reverence is present in most Sagittarians, although they might not be religious in what is called the "orthodox fashion". Even though not professing one particular creed, the evolved native will in all probability provide an inspiring example for others. Should he follow his inclination toward spiritual development, he will make great progress and frequently scale the heights of understanding.

Loyalty is a strong characteristic of this sign, together with a deep sympathy not only for close friends, but for the troubles of all mankind. Once friendship is given to another, that person can count himself a friend for life, unless a really extraordinary reason arises for a change. Should such a change occur and one lose the friendship of a Sagittarian, it is difficult to regain it, even though the native may still regard the transgressor with affection. More than once it has been said of a native of this sign that he will grieve almost endlessly over the loss of a friend. He attracts many friends to him, but due to the fact that he is often misunderstood, his intimacies may be few. He is, in fact, usually better off when he has comparatively few close friends. Widening his circle of friendship often brings him disappointment, and because of his generosity and warm-heartedness, he is apt to be imposed upon by others, and particularly his confidences are quite likely to be violated. He speaks with such frankness at all times that he naturally reveals to his intimates more of his innermost thoughts than most people do. The true Sagittarian is never envious of the success of his friends, often being an *inspiration* in their endeavors.

The person who was born under a strong influence from Sagittarius is quite fond of travel and likes *variety*. In common with the other two fire signs, he dislikes monotony and routine. His mental capacity is large, and his mind extremely active; capable of running much ahead of any subject under discussion. Sometimes, this trait causes him to *jump to conclusions*. This frequently happens in conversation when he anticipates what is going to be said, and fails to pay close attention to details. In such cases, his conclusions may be erroneous, for the simple reason that he has actually failed to grasp *all* the facts.

Many of the other signs (especially the air and fire signs), impart a tendency for the natives to scatter their energies in too many undertakings. Sagittarius is an exception among the fire signs. Seldom is it necessary for the native to remind himself of the necessity for concentrated effort. His inclination is to give anything in which he engages his undivided attention until it is completed. This ability undoubtedly accounts for the great accomplishment possible to those born in this sign. They have a strong tendency to tend to their own business; seldom having any desire to pry into the affairs of others. The secrets and confidences of others are treated with the utmost respect by the Sagittarian and anything disadvantageous to another person is seldom revealed by him.

Because the influence of the planet Jupiter is powerful in this sign, there is a strong likelihood that the native will be fortunate. In the working out of cosmic law, there is always a quite definite reason for success and good fortune which is never the result of chance. Always, the true Sagittarius native tends to look upon his affairs optimistically. He is seldom a pessimist, being much more inclined to look upon the bright side of everything rather than the dark. This is particularly true when it comes to financial matters, and as a result it is quite unusual to find a Sagittarian who in later years of life is not independent. The inherent good business sense and balanced judgment of these natives causes them to be economical and good managers, to the extent that it is not at all unusual for them to become wealthy. Their ability to pursue an objective single-mindedly is, to a considerable extent, responsible for the fact that a large number of them continue unswervingly upon a path which ultimately leads them to financial success.

Almost all Sagittarius natives are fond of animals. They also love the out-of-doors, and if their interest in that direction is aroused, they are good walkers and love to stroll through quiet countrysides or actively engage in the sports which are associated with outdoor activities. Many (both men and women) have a great love for horses and have become expert riders and jumpers, and they derive great benefit from such exercise when they are so inclined.

As previously expressed, and in common with the other signs of the zodiac, the native of this sign has extremely powerful positives which are inherently a part of the basic Sagittarius vibration, but on the other hand equally powerful negatives. Words which describe the positive qualities of Sagittarius are: frank, generous, honest, optimistic, foresight, just, buoyant, charitable, hopeful, persevering, jovial, sincere, logical, companionable, genial, restrained, steady. Words expressing the negative characteristics inherent in the sign are: blunt, rash, brusque, defiant, speculative, boisterous, argumentative, impatient, uncompromising, hasty. It remains, however, for the native of Sagittarius to recognize the desirability of developing the *positive phases* of his character, and to understand the results which may be accomplished when he does so. Then he becomes a human being of the *highest type* in the present state of human evolution.

An outstanding characteristic of the sign is the tendency it imparts to the native to *speak the truth* under all conditions. One who received a predominating influence from Sagittarius seldom sees any reason *why* the truth should not be spoken at all times, and being honest and truthful himself, he expects the same thing in others. This trait of frankness is carried to an extreme by the *unevolved* individual who was born in this sign. He is blunt to the point of being almost wholly inconsiderate of the feelings of others. Being quick mentally himself, he is inclined to speak without giving thought to the possible effect of his words, and often says the first thing that comes into his mind, without consideration for any possible views of others. Due to the faculty the people of this sign have for *anticipating* what others are going to say, and of jumping to conclusions, as well as their tendency to speak without giving full consideration to their statements, they often make unintentionally contradictory statements. This not infrequently gives a Sagittarius native the reputation of being untruthful. As a matter of fact, that is as far from being the case as anything could be. Their *intentions* are so completely opposite in nature that ordinary evasiveness and untruths are the farthest things from their minds at any time.

The undeveloped or unevolved native has a marked tendency to become angry over trifles, and often extremely impatient. Frequently he is in such a hurry to accomplish results, because of this impatience, that he works himself into a condition of flaring temper and ragged nerves. Most of those born in this sign *are* possessed of a *quick temper,* and are apt to be easily aroused to anger when they are directly opposed. Often the unevolved native is intolerant in certain respects. He is quite inclined to view with disdain those who are less active and energetic than he, as well as those who cannot speak their minds clearly and precisely. Sometimes this works rather a hardship upon individuals with whom he is associated. Whenever the native of Sagittarius asks someone a question he expects a completely truthful answer, *regardless* of the fact that every dictate of diplomacy would indicate a certain amount of tactfulness. In such case, the questions of the native may be so directed as to

116

be quite embarrassing.

The true Sagittarius individual has a very penetrating quality of mind, and he usually can probe deeply in an effort to bring out the truth from another who may be attempting to evade him. The evolved native of this sign can almost invariably detect an effort at evasion, and is quick to discover a falsehood. Above everything else, he despises deception and any kind of trickery.

While the native of this sign is seldom deliberately selfish, his instincts being of an entirely opposite nature, he sometimes is so, without fully realizing the fact. He can become quite self-centered and, in such case, he takes services performed for him as a matter of course. He fails to see that he doesn't give a great deal in the way of service in return. Although his instincts are completely generous when it comes to going to the rescue of a friend, with money or other resources, in case of extreme emergency, he is often neglectful in the ordinary affairs of life. A choleric temper is the particular downfall of many people who came into the world under a strong Sagittarius influence and who are unevolved. The negatives of this vibration are of such a nature, however, that the native can usually overcome them when once he is awakened to the desirability of doing so.

The Sagittarius individual who is in a lower state of development is very apt to be boisterous and lack restraint in his speech, and has a marked tendency to boast and perhaps even to "swagger" a little. As opposed to the evolved native, who tends to find coarseness and vulgarity repulsive, the one who allows the negatives of this basic vibration to control him, will show a tendency to go to the opposite extreme. In justice to him, it should be said, however, that this is more a form of "braggadocio" than it is a basic instinct.

The true native of Sagittarius has tremendous capabilities. In fact, there is no sign of the zodiac that imparts to the natives more of the qualities for potential good in the world than does Sagittarius. The truly evolved native can give without stint to others, and never notice a lack for himself. Not only he, but those around him will share in his generosity, his judgment, his intellect, and his capacity for doing the greatest good for the greatest number. The calmness and inner poise of which the true Sagittarius native is capable brings him extraordinary power and an unshakeable character which, combined with his natural wisdom, lend him unfailing aid in the most ambitious endeavors. In such case, the happiness, peace, friendship, and security he enjoys are much above the average. A study of world history reveals the fact that many of the outstanding leaders of humanity in science, public affairs, and religion were born under a predominating influence from Sagittarius.

WOMEN OF SAGITTARIUS

Women who came into the world under a strong influence from the sign Sagittarius are sparkling and witty conversationalists. They have keen active intellects, are invariably well-informed on matters of general interest, and are seldom left out in any conversation. They are fond of human contacts, being seldom inclined to live a secluded life. The true daughter of Sagittarius is fond of the outdoors; she is hospitable, vividly alive, and intrigued by all matters of a progressive nature which affect her country and the world as a whole. She is fond of her own home. It is rare to find a true Sagittarius woman who is a *"busy-body"*, unduly interested in the affairs of her neighbors and friends. She is not at all inclined to pry, being occupied with her own concerns, and willing to let others lead their own lives as they choose.

The undeveloped or unevolved woman of Sagittarius has some tendency to be reckless and impulsive, but she never means any harm by the reckless decisions she makes. While she is not of extremely sensitive nature or inclined to be neurotic, the tragedies which she sometimes encounters in life make a deep impression; and, as a result, she may give way to negatives which increase her reckless tendencies. Also, few women who came into the world in Sagittarius escape the tendency which is imparted by this vibration toward displays of temper. It is usually necessary for them to learn to control these outbursts. The woman of this sign has a strong sense of justice and when she feels that another has acted unfairly toward her, or toward another in whom she is interested, or when she believes that unreasonableness is being manifested, her temper quickly comes to the fore. Under such conditions, she is quite likely to speak her mind with unrestrained frankness.

Like the man of the sign, the woman who came into the world under this vibration is almost invariably fortunate. Sometimes she gets herself into difficulties because of her recklessness, but when she finds herself involved in a troublesome situation, the woman of Sagittarius is usually able to extricate herself; or some fortuitous circumstance arises which enables her to come out of the difficulty unscathed. The true daughter of Sagittarius has a strongly marked quality of companionship. Women of this sign are perhaps the best all around companions for the men they marry, because of their wide interests and their capacity for understanding. The Sagittarius woman is keenly and intelligently interested in the business affairs of her husband. Often she is of great assistance, as her foresight is marked, and her judgment is shrewd.

Any woman who was born under a predominating influence from this sign should be given a constant outlet for her energy; she should be actively busy. Lacking such an opportunity for expression of her constructive instincts, she becomes fretful. In commercial occupations, the Sagittarius woman has capabilities comparable to those of the men. She has financial abilities of a high order. Real estate is fully as favorable for her as it is for the man. Women of Sagittarius are quite successful as teachers, become particularly efficient secretaries and stenographers, and they are often highly successful modistes. The woman of this sign who goes through life depending upon her own efforts entirely, almost invariably obtains a competence; seldom in later life being a burden to others. Women of Sagittarius are extremely loyal and devoted and they rarely go back on a bargain.

Children who are born under a predominating Sagittarius influence are affectionate, sensitive, normal, and truthful. They are likely to be quick-tempered, active, and restless. They need appreciation, understanding, and praise for their endeavors. They thrive on love and an atmosphere of affection and sympathy, becoming a great source of satisfaction to parents and to others who are close to them. The youngster of this sign is encouraged by understanding and kindness. He finds no work too severe or task too irksome to carry through, for the sake of those whom he loves. Praise .and a caress will stimulate him to the greatest effort. They are extremely lovable children and are by nature unselfish, kind, and affectionate toward playmates and toward their parents. They are seldom, under any circumstance, cruel, and rarely give evidence of vicious tendencies in early years.

The true Sagittarius youngster is extremely sensitive and is wounded far more deeply by criticism and harsh words than most people realize. He may have tried to do something with extreme loving attention and when he finds that his efforts are met coldly, he is often aroused to unruliness. Frequently, however, he simply withdraws within himself; the natural sunshiny quality of his nature is dimmed, and his sweet temperament and cheerfulness are over-shadowed.

There should be a constant effort on the part of parents to stimulate the interest of these youngsters in constructive, congenial tasks. Frequently, they are at a loss to know how to occupy their time. While they have a natural interest in building and, in fact, all constructive endeavors, they may not know how to do these things and rarely ask, though they may yearn to be engaged in them. All youngsters of this sign should be stimulated to put forth their best efforts but, to the greatest extent possible, they should be allowed to choose their own endeavors. *Life work* without exception should be left to the choice of young people who were born under a strong influence from this sign. Rarely do they choose unwisely. Their qualities of intuition invariably guide them aright when they are not too greatly influenced by the arbitrary rule of parents or guardians. The true Sagittarius vibrations impart a splendid quality of thoroughness. Youngsters of this sign seldom have to be taught the necessity for carrying through something once started. They have a remarkable ability to concentrate.

Parents of these children should especially avoid deliberately deceiving them in any matter. When once the youngster of this sign learns that he has been told an untruth his confidence is greatly shaken, and it usually takes him a long time to overcome the effect. While these children have confiding and trusting natures, they are not as easily led or deceived as one might assume. Certainly the higher qualities of sympathy and affection which are inherent in the Sagittarius nature should be developed. Careful cultivation of these qualities will be repaid a thousandfold. Adults who have charge of the destinies of Sagittarius children should strive to use as much tact in dealing with them as they would with an older person and, in fact, to treat them more as adults than as children. It will readily be seen that tactless remarks, and thoughtless criticism, will leave an indelible mark on the youngster of this solar vibration which he may perhaps never overcome. Sagittarius imparts really splendid qualities and these children are capable of becoming *shining lights* in this world.

119

MARRIAGES OF SAGITTARIUS

It is not at all unusual for natives of the sign Sagittarius to marry early in life, often upon impulse. It is extremely important, however, that the matrimonial partner of the person who was born in this sign be on the same level spiritually and intellectually. The natural tendency of the Sagittarius vibration is to produce intentions of the most loyal and faithful sort in matrimony. As a matter of fact, the native of this sign almost invariably has very definite ideals in that connection. Conditions of life, however, frequently cause those ideals to be lessened greatly or sometimes destroyed completely. The Sagittarian, when he is greatly disillusioned or disappointed in life, tends to become embittered. The true son or daughter of this sign dislikes all that is gross or vulgar, and particularly turns away from obscenity and vulgarity. The inclination imparted by these vibrations is toward an unusual purity of mind in that connection. Not infrequently, however, their minds are conditioned by disillusioning experiences in life, and they *"let down"* in that respect.

When the true Sagittarian is disappointed in love, or when his marriage is unhappy, he is often too proud to show it and, as far as the outside world is concerned, there is never any indication that things are not exactly as they should be. Not infrequently, the person who came into the world under a strong influence from this sign goes through his entire life in an extremely unhappy matrimonial situation without, of his own volition, revealing the fact to the outside world.

Gemini (May 23rd — June 22nd) is the opposition sign, which means that it is directly opposite Sagittarius in the zodiac. Always in signs which are so opposite each other, there are *complementary* qualities of character, and a certain degree of harmony is to be expected from matrimonial alliances between people born in such opposing signs. This is perhaps more true of Sagittarius and Gemini than of others. There is an intellectual parity and companionship which often manifest themselves between people who were born in these two signs. For that reason it is to be considered that Gemini is the most matrimonially harmonious of all the signs. Leo (July 22nd — August 22nd), and Libra (September 24th — October 23rd) are also quite harmonious, perhaps the latter just a little more so than the former. Among those of reasonably high development, marriage between a man and woman both of whom were born in Sagittarius, is likely to be harmonious; but there is a lack of balance in their union which has a tendency to produce less strong and vital children.

A great deal of unhappiness, to fully as great an extent as may be said of those who were born in any other sign of the zodiac, has been brought about in the lives of people who were born in Sagittarius, by unfortunate matrimonial alliances. A large number have come to middle life before they experienced upheavals in their affairs, but then have encountered dissension in their relationship, and often complete disruption of family ties. Certainly one who was born in this sign should seek a partner in marriage who has congenial tastes and who is, especially, of companionable nature, for certainly there is no sign in which the qualities of companionship are more strongly marked than in this one. The true native of Sagittarius is completely at a loss when real companionship is lacking in his life, and should make a determined effort to find a congenial partner in order to achieve that state of unity so necessary to him.

Natives of Sagittarius are seldom limited in their fields of endeavor and can successfully engage in a wide variety of undertakings. Essentially, because of the influence of Jupiter, true Sagittarians are capable along financial lines. They are likely to be most successful in a vocation which requires them to handle money. Real estate is usually a very profitable field for the native of this sign, especially when he concentrates on the buying and selling of land. He is not apt to be so successful in dealing with the products of that land. While business ventures are usually most appealing to the Sagittarian, he is by no means limited in choice. His fondness for animals and the out-of-doors, for example, may lead him to breeding and handling dogs or horses. The true native has an almost uncanny ability in training animals. The fields of forestry, athletics, and physical culture are also favorable.

While, as mentioned, the religious tendencies of the Sagittarian are more apt to be general than specific, many fine priests and ministers were born in this sign. The highly evolved native is invariably a powerful speaker upon such subjects, and being completely sincere and honest, he often has an extraordinary power to convince others. Although not fond of a monotonous routine, he has the innate capacity to master detail and essentials, and thus might find a solid position in the legal profession. His obvious sincerity and honesty will make an excellent appearance and impression in court, and his clients will depend on him, and his associates respect him. The sign Sagittarius is extremely well represented in the theater. The field of drama is indeed a favorable outlet for the abilities of the native. Musical talent, however, is perhaps the most outstanding ability possessed by natives of this sign. Some of the greatest of musical geniuses were born under predominating influences from Sagittarius. They are forceful and imaginative in their rendition, and as a rule perfect unusually fine techniques. Natives of this sign are capable of great *singleness of purpose,* and are apparently able to pursue an objective steadily and persistently without ever becoming weary of their work.

Sagittarius natives are, in fact, great workers. Their instinct is to seek the *greatest possible opportunities* for development and achievement. Invariably, the true native of this sign will gravitate toward the most active fields of endeavor and in which there is the greatest degree of growing interest. The evolved native of this sign is very painstaking in working out the details of a business. While he is usually strong physically and has the capacity for great physical exertion, he believes in doing things with his mind rather than his hands; consequently one finds the business undertakings of the Sagittarius native well organized and efficiently operated. The sign is ingenious, being inventive to a considerable degree. Both the men and women of Sagittarius are likely to develop ideas for convenience in homes, or otherwise in their personal lives, of the greatest practical value. They are apt at creating appliances of various kinds. The pure Sagittarius vibration imparts a particular ability for these natives to furnish the driving ability and the leadership necessary to make practical, and bring into usage, the ideas and inventions of others. The Sagittarian, when he is engaged in a stimulating activity, is able to absorb himself fully in his endeavors and, as a result, is likely to be happy, optimistic, and progressive.

DISHARMONY OF SAGITTARIUS

The negatives of the sign Sagittarius exist in a prominent form coincidentally with conditions in the physical organism which are referred to as disease. Frequently, the native of this sign is reckless in his mental expenditure. Agitation, excitability, irritability, haste, and impatient drive are always outward manifestations of inner uncertainties. Often the Sagittarius native who has allowed the negatives of anxiety or apprehension to become prominent, drives himself ceaselessly to accomplish a purpose. He comes to think it is absolutely imperative for him to finish whatever he is engaged upon, without relaxing for a moment his intense application. This grows to become an extremely powerful negative. It impresses the subconscious deeply and, as a result, under negative planetary vibrations his actions are guided in directions which are outward manifestations of this strongly developed negative.

While it is quite necessary for the true native of Sagittarius to be active and busy to the extent that his mind and his energies are fully occupied, his activities should be without apprehension, strain, and worry. The constant tension of unrelaxed effort when nervous strain and apprehension are present, sometimes breaks down the wonderful physical equipment with which most people of this sign are endowed. Walks, or other activity, in the open air are extremely valuable to the native. He is usually fond of such exercise and, as previously expressed, he is also attracted by all sports. Frequently, however, he becomes so absorbed in his undertakings that he feels he has no time for such relaxation. Usually this is a mistake, as the mental effect of exercise along these lines is extremely beneficial. The temperament of the Sagittarius native undoubtedly requires almost constant activity; but, in common with other signs, natives should realize the necessity for constantly searching their mental processes to be certain that they express positive thought forms.

It should be frequently recalled to mind that outer expressions of irritability and of striving in agitation express negative thought vibrations which are growing without the conscious recognition of the individual. Sagittarius has particularly to do with, and exercises a more direct effect upon, the thighs than any other part of the body. Indirect results of negatives are traceable in their effect, directly to these parts. The negatives of the Sagittarius vibration result in conditions of disharmony in the body which are referred to as feverish ailments (often resulting from infections caused by cuts), disorders of the blood (which quite frequently manifest themselves in various forms of rheumatism), difficulties in connection with the hip joints, sciatica, enteric disorders, nerve troubles, and other conditions of inflammation in the thighs and legs. As an indirect result of the negatives most often given expression to by the native of Sagittarius, he also sometimes suffers from infections of the throat, the ears, bronchial tubes and other parts of the lungs. He is much more likely to be susceptible to invasion of the cold virus in those parts than in the head.

The negative of irritable impatience often results in minor accidents. Also, any individual who was born under a strong influence from this sign, should avoid eating too rapidly. Conditioning the mind to expressing positives will invariably guide the native of Sagittarius to the choice of proper foods, and to a state of perfect harmony in the physical organism.

1977 A "long desired" wish may be on the road to fulfillment now. "Pleasurable events" that are connected to entertainment and possibly "youth" will be of significance. Some form of conveyance may be expensive to you around this time. I suggest that you be alert to possible "accidental" situations all during this year, but particularly in April, August, October and November. If you are careless you might find circumstances stemming from "an unseen" but explosive source which could cause you to "lay up" for a period or would be "restrictive" in nature. As I have said before, this is not said to alarm you — but to caution you to be "alert" and thereby to avoid such a likelihood. The promotion of something "new" is very likely. A wonderful later period I believe lies ahead in your future!

1978 It will be oh, just so tremendously important for you to notice all the things you have to be thankful for every day of 1978, in my opinion. You are apt to have such great dreams that your true position in your world could seem disappointing from time to time, but this may provide your special opportunity to *reorganize your aims* quite constructively. Instead of seeking your fulfillment "in the background," I think you will earn far greater happiness through a policy of facing up to conditions around you, even when it appears that your progress is less swift than you really prefer, as it surely will seem sometimes. I believe you will acquire something from someone this year that will increase your assets.

1979 Your thoughts are apt to turn to distant places so often in 1979 that it seems hard to keep your mind on other important considerations now and then. You are likely to be in the mood for taking decisive steps to increase your knowledge and enjoy the fervor of newer surroundings and associations. Because I feel that you will let your own TRUE convictions lead your thoughts, words, deeds and actions this year, I believe you will arise steadily up the ladder to the greatest accomplishment your desires hold. One of your strongest assets now will be humility, no question, even in a situation where "important people" forget to "praise" you, in my opinion. 1979 will provide an opportunity to show that your undertakings are your gift to Mankind, I feel.

1980 Your entire outlook on life is being reshaped, so that in later years you will look back on this period as one when a new viewpoint was responsible for the changes which marked your future from here on, as a great turning point. I believe your urge will be centered seriously upon attaining a strong financial position or standing among people who know of your special talents. You are apt to experience what would amount to a windfall in the form of financial gain, either as a gift, a bonus you had not expected or the support of someone who is influential in your affairs. "Hidden" matters that emerge suddenly might spring into the open because of dissatisfaction on the part of another person, but your patience and sincerity will be the deciding factor as to how these matters will affect your inter-

1981 I feel this year will be highlighted by the growth of constructive and helpful friendships, which could bring an expansion to your circle of acquaintances that is strong-

123

ly indicated as bringing benefits later. Some of the results you expect from efforts you make to progress are likely to result in success to a lesser degree than you hope for temporarily, but energies you devote to a particular long-range goal seem wisely expended during this forecast period. Discussions and plans for "big things" are outstandingly indicated, filtering from someone who has your interests at heart. "Background" efforts are shown as causing you to increase your knowledge in order to find better uses for special information you have acquired, which will be of particular advantage later, I am sure. Unexpected occasions to be "on your own" for brief periods will help you resolve questions which have been pushed aside in the recent past. Daily pressures on your time — and the breaking of uncongenial ties or former close associations may figure in your considerations at this time. This will be a busy, changeful cycle.

1982

The cycle stressing "behind the scenes" maneuvers which began last year is likely to increase in scope this year. You will need to be alert to moves which could be disadvantageous, coming from sources that perhaps you haven't questioned up until now. I feel this will be a period of exceptional emotional sensitivity, so that your outlook will tend to be highly colored by your feelings of the moment. Some nervous tension leading to temporary health concerns could filter down and touch your relationships and money interests. This brief tendency will require control, through constructive outlets (by means of inventive, imaginative, or scientific pursuits) which in some way will penetrate through your quite idealistic impressions. A climaxing point with respect to money or interests in which others share is indicated near the middle of this year. Avoid entanglements and thereby protect yourself from expensive situations.

1983

It is likely that you will have a strong inclination toward independence, and this may touch at least one of your close associations. There are apt to be temporary restraints which you may regard as being unreasonable. "Avenues leading nowhere" will seem to surround you from time to time, especially those you will be tempted to follow. I feel, however, that you will *face up* to a certain situation and see it through loyally, as well as pursue a *definite* goal, particularly regarding "life and death" matters such as insurance, inheritance, and similar areas of serious concern. Jupiter's new position is likely to influence your confidence and assurance, so that greater strides toward material security can be gained, provided overconfidence does not provoke ill thought out or hasty steps, causing you to be involved in "hidden" plans.

1984

A great deal of personal integrity and attention to "rules of conduct" are advisable during this planetary cycle. Otherwise "bending" to desires of the moment or a willingness to take "shortcuts" that are not considered acceptable or aboveboard could be costly. You might be more subjected to "hearsay" or gossip during this phase, and "secrets" should be kept out of "hands" which might use them to your disadvantage. Burdensome situations involving close ties, possibly someone older, may be counterbalanced by almost peculiar "lucky breaks" or through strange people. A very exciting period with a "turnabout" in your

SUMMATION (Sagittarius)

Your longing to rid your life of the dull, monotonous, or routine is likely to be exceptionally "close to your heart" during these especially significant years of this forecast period! Gradually, through the years of this cycle, I believe you will shed many ideas that have previously played an important role in your thinking, but I do not feel that the "bedrock" which underlies your nature . . . and I am speaking of your instinctive independent outlook . . . will be anything but strengthened. At the 1980's open, I am certain that strange, unusual, and highly different varieties of people will begin to assume greater importance to you. Sidestep quicksands that may come through other people involving you emotionally in their plans. Hidden or confidential matters could mire you down for a time.

Superficial changes will "come and go" as this cycle moves forward, but I anticipate significant development in that "private world" which is really only known to you — your awareness, the inner pattern of your thinking, your knowledge, and your outlook. You may not always be conscious of this transition "within," but it will be perpetually at work, I know! These new planetary cycles may take you through several phases which seem to you somewhat peculiar . . . but as I am convinced betterment will be your motive always, in my opinion this should be for you a *time of preparation.* The eclipse patterns indicate that financial considerations will frequently be your first interest. One entanglement involving a piece of property or valuable possessions is likely . . . and this may keep you on "pins and needles" for a while, owing to restraints toward settlement of the matter, combined with a great deal of "output" on your part.

Something you prefer to keep quiet may present obstacles, particularly toward the close of this period. Throughout much of this cycle, I definitely feel you will gather strength in background areas of your life, which will result in new achievements later. Around 1983 and 1984, I think you will tend to be more "retiring" in your manner so that you will need to make a special effort to reach out to other people, by displaying a sense of humor, using tact, and showing that you *are* concerned with the happiness and well-being of close ties. One particular person, in whom you have confidence, will have an influential role in certain future undertakings, I am sure. I feel that the "turning point" toward a happier and more fulfilling life will emerge during this far-reaching cycle!

Sagittarius and Capricorn are, of course, the two signs of the zodiac which are important in forming (or symbolizing) the characteristics of those who were born in this cusp and which have to do with the working out of their destiny. The first is *"ruled"* by the planet Jupiter, and the latter by Saturn. Natives are essentially well balanced and not at all inclined to be upset or disturbed over things of no real importance. They are usually *good mixers,* having an easy conversational ability and the quality of being able to make themselves at home in almost any company.

The native of this cusp is fond of the *good* things of life and particularly admires those who occupy positions above the average. He is quite inclined to regard wealth with a great deal of *reverence* and feels a strong desire to occupy a position of importance, and is usually willing to sacrifice a great deal in order to attain such a position. The native is almost invariably fond of music and many who were born in this cusp become accomplished musicians. This combination of planetary influences is, in fact, favorable for the development of musical talent, being extremely likely to produce outstanding *natural* ability. The native is quite likely to be fastidious in dress and to particularly like *nice things.* He is quite fond of freedom and it is a difficult situation for him to be tied down by binding chains; in fact, he is not likely to *tamely submit.* Due to the influence of the sign Sagittarius in his nature, he likes to do things in his own way. It is frustrating for him to be directly under the supervision of someone else and to feel that another person must tell him how to do his work or how to conduct his affairs. He is very much better able to proceed when he can do so on his own initiative.

Women who were born under this particular combination of influences become splendid wives and mothers. They are especially happy to be with their children. They display a remarkable understanding of young folk and have unusual patience in dealing with them. They are exceedingly loyal to those whom they love, but as do the men, they require considerable freedom and are quite independent by nature. Due to the influence of Sagittarius, the native has considerable ability to understand finance and through the influence of Capricorn, a great deal of conservative business judgment. The man of this cusp is a good trader. In any business undertaking which involves trading, he is quite likely to achieve a considerable degree of success.

The individual who was born in the full sun sign Capricorn is likely to be relatively diplomatic and restrained in speech but the Sagittarian is more than likely to be frank and outspoken. In fact, he may be explosively so. These tendencies are in conflict among natives of this cusp. They sometimes repress their inclination to speak out for a long time, but when their pent up emotions are released, the eruption may be tremendous. The sign Sagittarius is a spiritual sign and because of the vibrations which come to natives through it, they have extremely powerful and immediately available natural forces upon which they can call. Their fundamental possibilities of achievement and the reaching of any goal they desire are remarkably good.

f you were born between December 22nd and January 20th you were born in the sign Capricorn. The basic vibration of Capricorn is distinct in its qualities. The *"horn of plenty"* or the cornucopia was derived from its qualities and is an emblem of occult significance. Its symbolism was part of the legends of ancient peoples. The sages of ancient Greece gave the stories and legends about the god *Pan* to the people, as a symbol of this sign. He was horned and goat-footed and ruled over the rural scenery, but over wooded country in particular, and he was referred to as the *God of Plenty*. Today the symbol of Capricorn is the Mountain Goat. It has been assumed that the symbol was given for the reason that the constellation looks like a goat, but as with the other signs, that is not the case. The intent has always been to express graphically in each case, the innermost psychological qualities inherent in the sign. In association with the Mountain Goat, one would naturally assume obstacles, or peaks to be scaled. It is a fact that the average Capricorn native encounters more obstacles than do others, but, carrying the analogy further, he has the ability of the Mountain Goat to surmount the obstacles which bar his path. The gem which has vibrations possessing a relationship to those of Capricorn is the garnet, and the flower is the snow-drop. Saturn is the ruling planet. Vibrations from Saturn in their essence, play the greatest part in this basic vibration. Capricorn is representative of the Bible tribe of Zebulun, one of the original tribes of Israel, or one of the twelve fundamental types of human beings.

Capricorn is a feminine sign and cardinal. It is earthy, cold, dry, southern, movable, tropical, negative, serving, melancholy, quadrupedal, of short ascension. As in all signs, the vibrations are both positive and negative in character. The extent to which the native has evolved, and consequently the degree to which he will commence life expressing the positives of the sign, are indicated in the positions of the various planets at birth, harmonizing with heredity. The fundamental psychological characteristics of the sign are described in both their positive and negative phases. The true native of Capricorn will recognize the qualities as being part of his innermost thoughts and feelings, though some may be minor in his character while others are more predominant. The Capricorn nature in its higher attributes is quite moral. The native has strong instincts which prompt him to desire a position of respectability and substance. The true Capricorn has a strong sense of responsibility and he is extremely conscientious in all his undertakings. The power to reason and to formulate clear and consecutive plans are outstanding qualities of the sign.

You are not very demonstrative and you have some tendency to prefer seclusion, or even solitude, to active mingling with many others. You are peaceable by nature, but you have an inclination at times to be obstinate. You have a great deal of respect for the opinions of your neighbors and associates. You do not like to be conspicuous and, if you should come into the limelight, you prefer to do so in a very dignified manner. You feel that you are fitted to occupy a place of responsibility in the world and you would be very dissatisfied in a subservient, menial position.

The strong tendency of Capricorn natives is to believe that financial independence or even wealth is their rightful due. They are not at all inclined to feel that the position which this signifies should be presented to them without effort on their part, but feel that they are fitted to occupy such a place and their intention is to reach it. Capricorn is an extremely brilliant, intellectual sign. Some of the finest minds the world has known were possessed by people who came into the world under a strong influence from this sign. There is an ability for clear, keen, and detached analysis. The Capricorn vibration imparts a strong tendency toward extreme moods of depression, however. The true Capricorn native, unless he has definitely learned to control and direct his thought processes, is susceptible to these moods, and when they come upon him he is likely to feel that nothing in the world is worth while. That is partially due to the fact that he is usually well-informed, being a wide reader. One whose approach to human problems is wholly intellectual and worldly, comes often to the belief that *effort* is futile.

The pure Capricorn vibrations produce a definite type. The individual who receives predominating influences from this sign is of average height or below. He is slender, his neck is rather longer than the average, his chest is not wide (usually being the opposite), and his complexion is dark. Except in extremely low types, the tendency of Capricorn people is to be very conservative in dress, as well as in their undertakings. The native is never *flashy* in his appearance. He demands the best of materials; but to satisfy him clothes must be of a dignified cut and a conservative color.

The true Capricorn is by instinct and ability a leader in commerce. He is calculating, and capable of exercising the greatest shrewdness in business dealings. His conservativeness causes him to give the most careful consideration to any change or business venture before taking a step. The ability to manage business undertakings is a marked quality of this sign. It has often been said that the people of Capricorn are the backbone of the economic and business systems. They are well-balanced and often exert a restraining influence upon others who would go off at a tangent. They are among the best managers in the world. The Capricorn native has a great deal of confidence in his own ability to achieve success in business ventures and he believes greatly in his capacity to manage his own affairs; but when it comes to a large and important undertaking, he usually lacks self-confidence, unless repeated successes have built up his assurance. Even then he is extremely cautious. He is quick to see opportunities in business, however, and unless there is a question involved of adopting a new policy, he is capable of taking prompt advantage of them. He has a great deal of foresight in financial matters, and is a good organizer. This sign produces people who are more efficient, orderly, and methodical in their business habits than does any other sign of the zodiac.

The true native of Capricorn is extremely trustworthy and he may be depended upon to methodically carry out the details of any undertaking which is entrusted to his care. He requires responsibility in order that his real abilities be brought out. When he *is* placed in such a responsible position, he invariably bears the load, living up to the best that may be expected of him. When he works under the direction of others, his natural talents are often not apparent, and sometimes they are never developed. He may not be fully aware himself that he possesses them.

This is an Earth sign and there is a tendency on the part of natives to regard the mysteries of life and death from a material point of view; yet it is an occult sign, and frequently the native is led, from an intellectual standpoint, to extensive reading in philosophical and occult fields. Many men of Capricorn, in fact, have distinguished themselves as philosophers. As a rule, however, they are more intellectual and scientific than emotional and spiritual. The great scientist, Sir Isaac Newton, was a Capricorn native. The person who receives a strong influence from this sign at birth depends upon his judgment and his mind, rather than his physical equipment, to achieve success. He is highly studious by nature. He applies to any problem upon which he turns his mind, an intense power of intellect. He has great admiration for attainments of an intellectual nature, and often seeks to emulate the example of those who have been extremely brilliant mentally. Not infrequently he succeeds in doing so. The average individual in fact, who was born under a strong influence from this sign, has a great desire to learn, and he constantly adds to his store of knowledge. It is seldom that a true Capricorn stagnates mentally. With the attainment of broad intellectual development, he becomes extremely liberal in his views — tolerant and understanding. It is of the utmost importance for the native of this sign to be given an *opportunity* for education.

There is a marked tendency on the part of the Capricorn native to feel that he is taken advantage of, and imposed upon, more frequently than are others. Often that is true. In fact, natives of Capricorn often accomplish things for which they never receive credit. They are frequently taken advantage of by associates, or someone above them in authority, who will assume credit for what the native has actually done. Due to the fact that the true Capricorn has an extremely strong desire to occupy a position above the average in life, he strives, often desperately, to maintain a prosperous appearance and to keep pace with those who occupy positions which he believes should be his. Sometimes this causes him a great deal of difficulty and when he is unable to keep up appearances, he becomes very distressed. When the true Capricorn comes into the world under conditions of poverty and there is very little opportunity for advancement, his surroundings may condition his mind to a very low order of life and he becomes a completely frustrated, bitter and despondent individual. In such case, when he is not at least partially successful which would inspire him to envision the possibility of real achievement, he feels that any effort he may extend will be useless and consequently that his life is entirely wasted.

The native of this sign who becomes engaged in public affairs is inclined to be extremely conservative and positive in his opinions. He may be dogmatic. He pursues his course and his ideas, regardless of opposition or the arguments of others. It is seldom that the true native of Capricorn who engages in affairs of public nature can be induced to change his mind about anything, though he may alter his opinions as a result of his own reasoning. Regardless of how difficult the affairs of life may be, he is likely to win the battle of gaining a secure and respected position because of his ability to plan and manage. The negatives of the sign, however, tending as they do toward deep moods of despair at times, and working in harmony with other natural forces, will, if given way to, inevitably bring about difficulties in material affairs. The affairs of Capricorn natives often do not operate smoothly except for very short periods of time. Despite all these conditions, they usually gain at least a position of financial independence, although the climbing is almost invariably in spite of many reverses and the greatest of difficulties. The true native of this sign is able to carry burdens without complaint, however. His energy and particularly his ability to manage money, usually bring him through.

The very qualities of mind which bring the Capricorn native eventual success, cause in his affairs the difficulties he encounters. The individual who receives a predominating influence from this sign at birth is in the process of evolution, and has reached a stage during which he is required to learn certain lessons, as we all are. Words which express the positive qualities of the sign are: profound, particular, prudent, reverent, thoughtful, organizing, serving, practical, cautious, faithful, steady, dependable. Words which describe the negative qualities are: suspicious, gloomy, avaricious, miserly, selfish, vain, scheming, haughty, austere, cold.

To a considerable extent, the unevolved native is likely to be his own worst enemy. That is true, in the final analysis, of people who were born in any sign of the zodiac. Yet the immediate negatives of Capricorn are responsible for direct results in this plane of physical being. They bring delays, difficulties, and hindrances. The most pronounced negatives of the sign are a combination of vanity about certain things and, on the other hand, distrust of self. Psychologically, the vanity of Capricorn, which not infrequently concerns the intellectual development of the native, is a form of compensation for other imagined shortcomings. He is quite likely to be what is termed an introvert, and frequently he dwells at too great length upon himself and his own inner reactions. Because of this tendency toward self-analysis, he often comes to center his mind upon his own being and he may inwardly become a merciless critic of himself.

The native of Capricorn is extremely sensitive, frequently to the point of being abnormal in that respect. It is not at all unusual for people who come into the world under a strong influence from this sign to dwell upon their own worries and anxieties at length, and to spend a great deal of time in talking with others about their own perplexities and problems. Because of the tendency this basic vibration imparts toward great sensitiveness and self-consciousness, the native is often *super-sensitive* to slights or to imagined snubs and is, more or less consciously, always on the look-out for them. The natural coldness of the sign comes strongly to the fore when the native has been hurt, or when he feels he has been slighted. The mistakes of judgment which are made by Capricorn people often live with them. They are quite likely to look back over the past, and to regret errors and mistakes they have made to the extent that they become extremely melancholy and filled with self-censure. They are prone to worry about the opinions of others as far as their own conduct, their appearance, and their home surroundings are concerned. If the native were less concerned with the opinions of the world, he would be far happier.

The great lesson unevolved natives of this sign need to learn is the *elimination* of worry and anxiety. They must learn to *dwell upon* and *speak with* OPTIMISM. There is no other way in which they can achieve a true state of happiness and assure themselves of the greatest degree of accomplishment. Their usefulness to society is potentially great; but they need to apply themselves to real *cultivation* of the positive qualities of their natures, perhaps to a greater extent than do natives of any other sign. Due to the inherent tendency toward anxiety, and for the reason that there is a strong instinct for thrift in the sign, natives often become extremely calculating in their financial transactions and sometimes they allow that trait in their characters to become actual miserliness. Under such conditions the unevolved native is likely to be hard, cold, proud, austere, and have few or no intimate companions. His life is then, of course, quite unhappy and, for the most part, unsatisfactory. In the extremely unevolved native, the *earthy* nature comes to the fore and there is a tendency toward vulgarity in dress; and, due to inner conflict, he becomes boastful and frequently drinks intoxicants to excess. Instead of being extremely fastidious, neat, and conservative, he comes to be quite the reverse.

The powers of the *evolved* native of Capricorn are inferior to none. He is capable of the greatest achievement, and is especially gifted with spiritual qualities of the highest order. Aspiration toward the higher things of life and an *earnest desire* to cultivate the positives of his nature will bring the spiritual forces of Capricorn to the point of being extraordinarily powerful factors in his *own* life, and in the lives of those with whom he is associated as well!

WOMEN OF CAPRICORN

Women who came into the world under a predominating influence from this sign are invariably good managers in money affairs, being prudent and discreet to a marked degree. It has often been said that the man who marries a Capricorn woman seldom makes a mistake if he allows her to manage the financial affairs for both, as far as savings and handling mutual living expenditures are concerned. She is extremely thrifty, not only in a financial way but she feels additionally that *time is money,* and has a strong tendency to arrange her activities so that she does not waste her time in useless or frivolous activities of any kind.

The Capricorn woman is invariably quite sensible, efficient, and able to plan carefully. In commercial occupations, she is especially fitted to become the manager of an institution or a managing housekeeper. She is able to acquit herself creditably because of her inherent ability to be painstaking in details, and to know where she stands financially, as well as to be economical in purchases. These qualities also make her extremely efficient in the management of her own home. Her judgment as to the practical affairs of life and the conduct of her domestic life is excellent. The true Capricorn woman, however, is almost invariably possessed of a strong business sense, and she frequently finds a purely domestic life rather confining and without sufficient breadth for exercising her abilities. A large number of Capricorn women have business interests, and their undertakings are usually successful financially. In common with the men however, they frequently encounter obstacles, and experience reverses which their purely intellectual judgment fails to foresee. The Capricorn woman has a marked tendency to regard everything which comes within the scope of her experience from a material, intellectual viewpoint; and if she is to find happiness she must have an outlet other than domestic for her abilities.

Women who were born under a strong influence from this basic harmonic are extremely devoted to those whom they love, yet they have a strong tendency to form conclusive opinions, and consequently they may exercise a great degree of firmness and express an inflexible positiveness of viewpoint. They have a marked tendency to be undemonstrative, though may be capable of the utmost loyalty and devotion. When a native of this sign is outwardly emotional or demonstrative, there were powerful vibrations from signs other than Capricorn at birth. It is rare for the native to have more than a very few good friends. Women of this sign wish equality and recognition of their abilities rather than ardent or demonstrative affection. It is not unusual for them to feel intellectually superior, and to appear to be aloof and haughty.

These women often have fine minds, with a tremendous capacity for investigation and study along occult lines. Capricorn is referred to as the *dark* or *occult* sign, and natives have a marked ability to accumulate knowledge along these lines, and can be *a shining light* of spiritual knowledge and wisdom. Women of this sign become remarkably efficient secretaries, stenographers, and office managers; in fact, are capable executives in almost any commercial field. They almost invariably wear immaculately tailored clothes — strictly conventional with a tendency toward severity. They have the tenacity which marks both sexes and will work patiently, calmly, and with endless persistence to accomplish economic security and a position of respectability.

132

The child who comes into the world under a predominating influence from Capricorn is likely to have what is often referred to as *"an old head on young shoulders"*. These children quite frequently display wisdom far beyond their years and often astonish parents by their comments. (It might be noted that the adult native is likely to be extremely tenacious of life and to grow younger in spirit as he grows older in years. The slender, wiry, frail appearing person of advanced age who continues to be in good health and who lives *on and on* is typical of this sign.)

There is a strong tendency on the part of Capricorn youngsters to become quickly conditioned by their surroundings and associates. The higher attributes of the sign should be stimulated early in life. When once simple tastes and habits of reasonable reserve have been instilled into these children, those habits are never shaken during life. The earthy quality of this sign manifests itself when the child is thrown into contact with those who are vulgar, and who have tendencies toward loud, flashy dress. He may be quick to emulate such an example, and such habits once formed may be difficult to overcome.

It should be remembered that encouragement is a prime factor in the development of the positives which are rightfully a part of the Capricorn nature. Under no circumstances should the adult who has charge of a child of Capricorn display contempt for his endeavors, or lose his temper in dealing with him. The tendency of the true Capricorn is to lack confidence in himself; consequently, nothing but unfavorable results can be expected from belittling the efforts of any child who is a native of this sign. The youngster of Capricorn is capable of working tirelessly to complete a task. He has a strong desire to please and an unconscious wish to raise his own self-esteem. He will strive unceasingly to overcome any difficulty which besets him in the completion of a task which he feels someone else is depending upon him to perform. It is quite advisable for any child born under a strong influence from this sign to be allowed to complete his work after his own fashion. He should not be supervised any more closely than is absolutely necessary, as this is apt to lessen his self-esteem; making him feel that he is incapable of doing his work on his own initiative. It is extremely important also for the parents or guardians of a Capricorn child to *unfailingly* extend praise when any task has been faithfully completed.

The youngster of this sign responds amazingly to reason; and the parents of one should take great pains to *explain* the reason for things and to talk to the child as to an equal. These youngsters blossom under such treatment and often display astonishing wisdom. The Capricorn child is always greatly stimulated and aided when he is surrounded by those who are optimistic, not only about their own affairs but in connection with his as well. The example of cheerfulness and optimism is not lost upon him, and he should be carefully guided into channels of thought which will enable him in later years to overcome the strong Capricorn tendency to give way to depression and self-censuring analysis. Attention should be given to the cultural and educational advantages these youngsters receive; and the true Capricorn child should also receive a thorough business or commercial training. These children can be powerful factors in aiding humanity, as well as fine examples of *faithfulness* to duty and obligation.

It is important for natives of most signs to seek matrimonial partners who are on the same plane intellectually and socially, but it is true to a greater extent of Capricorn than to others. The native of this sign encounters a great many obstacles and reverses during life, as previously mentioned, and in this connection matrimonial affairs are not excepted. All people of Capricorn tend to be fastidious and to seek perfection and they are usually dissatisfied with anything they think is short of that ideal. This is applied intensively to themselves and their own efforts but it also comes to be applied to those with whom they are associated. Not infrequently the native suffers frequent disappointments, and this often comes about in marriage, of course. The standards of excellence which are set by the Capricorn native are likely to be rather high.

The native of this sign often finds himself encountering unhappy situations in his domestic affairs during middle life. To a considerable extent, this is due to the fact that his selection of a life partner has not been based upon the factors of harmony and understanding which are particularly necessary to him. All true Capricorns require encouragement, and they need expressions of confidence in them on the part of those who are their closest associates. This is particularly true in the marriage relationship. The native of this sign has a strong tendency to become despondent and discouraged at times, and while he is not likely to be enthusiastically encouraging in the affairs of another, he still requires such encouragement as far as his own affairs are concerned. This trait is naturally one which requires understanding.

The native of Capricorn is reserved to a degree that relatively few people get past that reserve. This is often extended to members of his own family; he is, in fact, likely to be considered quite *cold* by other people. The often deep loyalty and devotion of the native may be expressed very little or not at all, outwardly. Despite the reserve of the Capricorn nature, however, both men and women of this sign have a tendency to wish to have those whom they love entirely to themselves and seldom care to share their company or affection with anyone else. This tendency not infrequently brings about unhappiness in their lives. They are sometimes inarticulate in expressing the genuine love and devotion which they bear for another; consequently the marriage partner may feel that the native is demanding and unreasonable.

The signs Virgo (August 23rd – September 23rd) and Cancer (June 23rd – July 21st) are probably the most harmonious birthsign influences – the Capricorn individual being most likely to find congenial companionship and understanding among those who were born in one of these signs. Aries (March 20th – April 20th) is also, in a measure at least, harmonious, as is Taurus (April 21st – May 22nd); although the natives of the latter sign may fall somewhat short of the culture and niceties which an intellectual Capricorn desires in such a personal association.

It is obvious, of course, that a great deal of understanding may be necessary upon the part of the mate of a Capricorn. In fundamentals the Capricorn is likely to be very faithful and meticulous in discharging that which he conceives to be his duty, but anyone who marries a native of this sign and whose basic need is *demonstrativeness* is likely to be disappointed in this respect.

This basic vibration tends to impart a good intellect; and the native is balanced in his thinking along purely intellectual lines. He is methodical, orderly, and precise; and he has a marked ability to convey information and knowledge, which he himself possesses, to others. For that reason, probably more successful teachers and instructors were born under a strong Capricorn influence than may be said of any other sign of the zodiac. The instructor or teacher who is a native of this sign is unfailingly thorough, careful, and patient. In addition, he has the quality of inspiring his pupils with a desire to excel. Often this is the result of their wish to live up to the *expectations* of their instructor, and they strive for excellence to a greater extent than would be true if it were not for the *inspiration* which he has imparted.

The tendency of the evolved Capricorn is to go about the attainment of any objective in life in an orderly fashion, with a steady but quiet determination that is not to be shaken by vicissitudes of fortune or any difficulties he may encounter in dealing with material affairs. Sometimes his advance is slow to the extent that he may not appear to be progressing, but due to his persevering tenacity and the enduring quality of his determination he ultimately reaches his goal — perhaps to the astonishment of others who have not observed his unobtrusive progress. His caution almost invariably is a restraining factor, holding him to tried and true methods, or to plans which he has calculated with the greatest degree of thoroughness.

Because of the thoroughness with which the native deals with any problem, the legal profession is a favorable outlet for Capricorn abilities. The true Capricorn is capable of using the most exhaustive patience in preparing a case. This tendency toward careful preparation makes the public speaker who is a native of Capricorn frequently much more effective than those with greater natural powers of oratory, but whose statements are less concise, less careful, and therefore inspire less confidence. Capricorn natives have been highly successful in creative fields, but invariably upon investigation it becomes apparent in each case that there were strong influences from other basic vibrations at birth, due to the positions of planets in other signs. When there is inspiration toward creative endeavors, the Capricorn qualities of perseverance and patience are responsible, to a considerable degree, for achievement in that field.

Not a few natives of this sign have been possessed of brilliant mentalities, and have become outstandingly successful in literary fields. It will be found, however, that the true Capricorn is adapted particularly to commercial undertakings. Almost any management field is a favorable outlet for the energies of the Capricorn native, and business management is his forte. The true Capricorn will go to the greatest lengths to straighten out the most minor flaw in any work with which he is associated. As a statistician or an accountant, the native is extraordinarily particular. His work is invariably a very model of orderliness and efficiency.

Capricorn is an earth sign and there seems to be conditions of harmony between the natural qualities of the sign and earth products; meaning such products as are grown agriculturally, mined, or otherwise taken from the ground itself. The native of Capricorn has the ability to be successful in manufacturing spheres, as an executive; or as the manager of a public institution.

DISHARMONY OF CAPRICORN

The condition which is ordinarily referred to as disease is dealt with here in the light of negatives which are always coexistent with such conditions, and expressed in processes of thought, and as indicated, the Capricorn nature has inherent tendencies toward specific negatives. The knees come particularly under the Capricorn vibration. In other words, they are more directly affected either positively or negatively by this basic harmonic; the skeletal structure in general is also closely associated.

The epidermis comes directly under the Capricorn influence, and consequently the negatives express themselves in disturbances affecting the skin. Eczema is common among unevolved individuals who received a strong influence from this sign at birth. Cosmetics are likely to be particularly irritating to the skins of Capricorn women; often being quite injurious. Negatives of the sign, which tend to bring about extremes of melancholy and depression, as well as discontent, manifest themselves in specific disharmony or disorder in the bodily functions. Nervousness and worry are marked negatives to which the Capricorn native is susceptible. Conditions of disharmony in the physical body are never manifest except in the presence of, and in association with, those negatives of thought. Directly resulting from them, the native is susceptible to colds, to bruises resulting from falls, minor accidents, as well as dislocations in the bony structure of the body.

There is a marked tendency toward rheumatism and there are other inharmonious conditions of the body which occur in sympathy with the parts coming under the specific dominion of the sign. The native of this sign not infrequently notices weakness and trembling in the knees. There is a tendency to suffer from chills and from poor circulation. The system of the Capricorn native, this being a dry, barren sign, is quite likely to suffer from a lack of oil. While those who were born in some of the other signs should be at particular pains to avoid stimulating and heating foods, the reverse is usually true of the Capricorn native. He needs such foods, as the development of warmth is a necessity to his physical well-being.

The native of Capricorn is affected greatly by what other people say and by what he reads in the newspapers of a morbid or discouraging nature. He should be more careful than the average person of the kind of things he reads, whether they occur in the public prints or in various types of literature. He is subject to deep moods of despair, and this tendency toward morbidity should be noted particularly, and definite steps taken to counteract it. All the vital forces of Capricorn are likely to come to a low ebb succeeding or coincidental with periods of despondency. The influence of Saturn in this connection is powerful throughout the life of the true Capricorn. Transits of this planet bring particular tendencies toward extreme negatives when they are what is usually called adverse.

The native of this sign who is able to express in his thinking processes a continued *optimism,* and that faith which is a requisite for real achievement, leads a happy and extremely useful life, enjoying the best of health and tremendous vitality which in many cases belies his appearance. When once the true Capricorn applies himself to real cultivation of the *positive qualities* of his nature, the defects and the negatives which are inherent in the sign disappear like snow beneath the warm sun.

1977 An atmosphere of "uncertain nature" appears still to surround your dwelling or home-life, coupled with money matters. Your "day-by-day" thoughts appear to be set in the direction of sober "life and death" affairs such as wills, insurance or *the possessions of others!* BENEFIT APPEARS LIKELY TO DROP INTO YOUR LAP, and the strong probability of your seeking "a safe harbor" for *your valuable* holdings. Extremely "unorthodox" circumstances are outstandingly pointed to, as more than mere coincidence. Your hopes and wishes are in for "a queer" turn of events, which isn't to say that you won't achieve your goals, at least in part, but their achievement will be the result of "peculiar" elements. By using calm deliberation and sticking to "ecomony of movement" and in other ways, I do *not* believe you can fail to build a solid, secure place for your future happiness!

1978 During this year I believe you will be able to transform your daily endeavors into a pattern which resembles more closely the picture you originally held in mind. One of your close associations is likely to be exceptionally beneficial in your efforts to realize your goal, although a situation "at a distance" is apt to need your special understanding for a time. The mood for entering more actively into your world may lead you away from certain "withdrawing" tendencies you have had occasionally in the past. Because I think you are capable of approaching every moment of 1978 with a smile, inwardly and outwardly, I feel you will earn a surprising response from someone whose effect will be gainful for you.

1979 Due to conditions that give you another view of a "childhood ideal," your values are likely to be ever changing in 1979. I think you will have a stronger sense of "duty" to use your knowledge, capabilities and talents, for pursuits that will serve certain people's interests more fully now, even in instances where you consider that your "new mission" will require of you greater self-discernment. As you practice a regulated plan of conduct, I believe you will earn assistance from another source that will increase your sense of security. Entanglements in the courts of law may attract your attention occasionally under this cycle. Through your willingness to share your blessings a gratifying reward may grow.

1980 The strong planetary patterns this year indicate you can do a great deal alone and unaided if you don't make hasty moves which can prove expensive. On the other hand, a particular friendship or association with someone of considerable importance in your affairs will probably bring unexpected benefit or an advancement in the "business" or social world which you have long cherished as an especially desirable and rewarding goal. Great effort will probably be demanded of you for you are apt to be under constant pressures, but one of your strongest characteristics I believe is the ability to carry on an objective patiently and dependably. A happy frame of mind and steady "push" can take you far this year in my judgment.

1981 Your eyes will likely be trained upon a "peak" you would like to reach, involving a more secure position you hope to attain as a result of the planetary influences this year. The eclipse pattern shortly after the middle of this forecast period indicates a "turning point" when adapting your efforts to a significant change affecting your personal interests will take on added importance. Someone close in association may reverse a "stand" they have previously taken which could signal an advantage or opportunity to improve your position in a rather dramatic fashion, probably through the cheerful acceptance of minor shortcomings which have been a "bone of contention" recently. Your name is apt to be mentioned prominently or receive publicity in a manner that draws the attention of others more widely.

1982 Security will be of importance to you this year, because of subtle or hidden "movements" going on "behind-the-scenes" which lead you to wonder whether any "settlement" will ever be reached. Although this is a temporary cycle, I feel passing burdens will be weighty, giving rise to uncertainty or doubts that will be difficult to dispel. However, your natural inclination to move forward steadily will be aided by unexpected support from someone whose actions have proved themselves to be "tried and true." Those who have close ties with you may create briefly upsetting elements in certain relationships, but I urge you to advance your knowledge, because this is apt to be your solution to pressing problems which temporarily seem perplexing.

1983 For a short time you are apt to be the target for concealed conditions, of which you have had no hint or warning. In spite of "undermining" situations that are difficult to deal with because they are unseen, I am convinced after careful study that you will make good headway and will find a solution to each irritating problem. I believe that during this interval you should move warily and conservatively *temporarily,* not only "money-wise" but also in physical "outpourings" where you might overextend yourself. I am sure there will be a turnover in your personal interests during this cycle, and a younger person, or someone with whom you have affectionate ties, is likely to be helpful in a particular achievement.

1984 You are apt to take a rather "retrospective" view of your overall life purpose now, often preferring to carry through your undertakings in privacy . . . sharing your favored ideas only with confidants in whom you feel able to entrust knowledge which you do not care to share with just anyone at this time. A temporarily "confining circumstance" may lead you to surprising benefit. I consider this will be a planetary cycle of preparation for you. You are likely to be involved in "risky" ventures at times, but because I believe you'll approach these practically, gratifying results are indicated later on. Unexpected elements are likely to change a few of your close ties, but I feel you will accept calmly *passing* situations you cannot alter.

SUMMATION (Capricorn)

During these years, your natural ability to take one step at a time will enable you to climb to greater heights and to consolidate gains in a way that promises the kind of material security you believe you are entitled to through the steadiness of your efforts. Although it will be necessary to "work hard," I am certain you are no stranger to the idea that what is worth having is worth *working* to achieve. According to the planetary cycles touching your birth influences throughout this forecast period, there will be times when your way will seem blocked, probably in connection with a relationship you have formed in "good faith," but which later may prove unreliable. I am convinced that this *temporary* setback, while worrisome and disappointing, will be overcome through the unexpected intervention of circumstances that will seem almost in the nature of a "providential hand" . . . lifting you over burdensome conditions.

Throughout the years covered by this forecast, I believe a number of unusual (I might even say "unconventional") people will touch your life, sometimes in a startling or unexpected fashion! In at least one instance, I feel that you will form a relationship with someone whose background — and even "accent" — seems totally "foreign" to your previous experiences. Nevertheless, I am convinced you will benefit from this association in a quite surprising manner.

During 1983 and 1984, peculiar circumstances involving something of a "hidden" nature are likely to perplex you at first, but later turn out to be a "lucky" change of direction for you. I know that many times, as the cycle of these years moves forward, you will experience deep satisfaction from your sense of having given practical and consistent effort to your chosen lines of endeavor, because I am certain this is a trend when a "job well done" will help you lay a firm foundation for the kind of material security you long for!

The two signs of the zodiac which are important in the lives of those who came into the world during this cusp period, having a great deal to do with the formation of their characteristics (or symbolizing them) as well as their affairs of life are, of course, Capricorn and Aquarius. The first of these is *"ruled"* by the planet Saturn and the second by Uranus. Both are important in the working out of destiny in the operation of Cosmic Law. Natives of this cusp have widely varied talents. They are likely to be poised and to be *self-possessed*. They display a great deal of coolness and judgment in carrying through any transaction. Due to the influence of the sign Capricorn, they are likely to be careful and painstaking, but they are innovators and are quite likely to be unpredictable. In any work which engages their attention, they are usually quite methodical and strict, not only with others, but with themselves. They have, in fact, some tendency to be exacting. There is also usually some tendency to be obstinate, but when properly guided and directed that is a good quality, as it is the one attribute which leads to the reaching of a personal goal. One who has this quality is not easily diverted or swayed by the opinions of others.

Natives of this cusp are likely to be extremely good judges of people. They are not inclined to trust associates completely. The combination of influences gives them a great deal of sympathy for others, however, but a tendency to feel that human beings bring their troubles upon themselves. The native hasn't much confidence in the good intentions of many whom he meets. He is a good entertainer, in fact, he loves to entertain and is usually quite successful in doing so. He is likely to be a naturally good speaker and in many cases absolutely original. A great many of those who pursue several vocations were born under similar influences.

The individual who was born under predominating vibrations from this cusp has a natural pride and to an unusual degree enjoys his accomplishments, being proud of the things he is able to do. He is likely to be quite self-sufficient and not dependent upon others. He very rarely takes his troubles to associates, feeling that he can bear up under them himself. It is to be noted that women of this combination of influences yearn for some kind of personal distinction and are certainly not likely to be satisfied with their home surroundings and affairs unless they outwardly manifest success. They are less likely to be interested in housework than are most women. The right marriage partner is quite essential for people of either sex who were born under influences such as these, as they are likely to be deeply disappointed if their mates are not up to the standards they set.

These natives are particularly fitted to be successful in business undertakings. Their judgment of that which others desire is usually good; consequently they are often successful in retail merchandising and in anything which has to do with manufacturing. Especially those processes which convert products which have just come from the ground into some useful article are favorable. They are often successful in group activities. A high order of musical ability is to be noted.

140

The birthsign AQUARIUS
January 21st to February 19th

f you were born between January 21st and February 19th, your birthsign is Aquarius. This sign of the zodiac has a particular significance at this time. All people who came into the world under a strongly predominating influence from Aquarius have a potentially important part to play in the immediate development of the human race. Among the ancient Greeks, Ganymede, a beautiful shepherd youth, symbolized Aquarius. This youth was made *"cup-bearer"* of the gods by Jupiter. In those stories of the ancients great truths were illustrated. The portion of the sky which is occupied by the Water-Bearer was dealt with significantly in those stories, which might be compared to tales prepared for children, intended to convey important truths for the moral development of the child. Among early Christians, the sign symbolized John the Baptist. Again there is a strong occult significance, related particularly to the association between Aquarius and Pisces. The element of water appeared predominantly during the Piscean age, and the ceremony of baptism has been present in one form or another in every outgrowth of Christian teachings from that day to this.

Aquarius is referred to as a *fixed* sign. It is scientific, serving, intuitive, moist, airy, sanguine, human, electric, and of short ascension. It is additionally referred to as masculine and fortunate. The stone which vibrates most in harmony with the basic vibration of Aquarius itself is the amethyst; the primrose is the flower. The sign is representative of the Bible tribe of Reuben, one of the twelve original tribes of Israel, or one of the basic types of humanity. Uranus is the planet which rules the sign, the vibrations of that planet being most important in the formation of the Aquarius basic harmonic. Consequently, the character traits of people who were born in the sign, as well as the working out of their destinies in the operation of cosmic law are greatly affected by that planet.

In describing the fundamental traits of the sign, both the positive and negative qualities of Aquarius are dealt with, and the native will recognize these qualities in himself; though some may be dominant in his character and others quite minor. The planetary chart at birth indicates more or less that state of evolution which the individual has reached and the extent to which he will express either the positive or the negative qualities of the sign. This factor is in no way apparent in the birth sign alone.

The individual who received a predominating influence from Aquarius at birth, invariably has an extremely pleasing expression about the eyes, and the quality may be both penetrating and fascinating to the extent that it is hypnotic. The natural facial expression of the Aquarian is one of keen interest and alertness. The true native of Aquarius is intuitive, humanitarian, imaginative, sometimes inclined to be erratic, yet very quick mentally, and creative. The evolved native invariably has an inherent power to influence the actions of others with whom he comes in contact, and he may become a powerful leader in human affairs. He often has a great deal of financial ability, but is seldom calculating in matters which pertain to money. The mind of one who received a strong influence from this sign at birth is extremely receptive and quick. It is in particular, progressive. The Aquarius basic harmonic tends to produce an individual who constantly pushes forward into the realm of that which has hitherto been unknown. He is an inventor of the first order, and in many cases spends his life seeking to bring about changes in the established order of things.

The influence of this basic vibration instills an instinctive ability to judge others. Some of the best students of human nature are natives of this sign. Aquarius tends to produce an individual who is courteous, kindly, agreeable, and poised. He is not often quick-tempered, except when there is a strong blending of one or more of the other basic vibrations at birth which impart that quality. In any event, the native of Aquarius *usually* is able to control his tendency toward flashes of temper. The evolved native is always faithful in the discharge of his obligations, and is trustworthy. In whatever field his endeavors take him, or in whatever manner obligation is thrust upon him, he shoulders that which duty requires and usually acquits himself well. The true Aquarian is dignified and, unless he is quite unevolved, is rarely to be forced into positions which are undignified; and especially rarely in vulgar brawls or quarrels. The highly evolved native is invariably a brilliant conversationalist. Among the best, the most concise, and thoroughly convincing speakers, are those who were born under a strong influence from this sign. The native almost always has the fullest ability to explain any question comprehensively to others.

You probably remember personalities to the extent that your memory is almost unfailing in that connection, but you recollect a face much better than you do a name. As a matter of fact, names probably don't mean a great deal to you. You have an inquisitive mind which is very active, but you are not at all inclined to *pry* into the affairs of others, certainly with any intention to injure them. You are, however, much interested *constructively* in the problems of those who surround you, and particularly in those problems which confront humanity as a whole. You are by nature, a clear reasoner and extremely intuitive. Your judgment of what is right and wrong, and particularly those things which involve honor or dishonor, is very positive and strong.

The evolved native of this sign is able to get quickly to the heart of any matter which is presented to him. Additionally, he has the extremely valuable faculty of appealing to the kindly emotions of others, and can touch their hearts more effectively than those born in almost any other sign. The Aquarian is able to converse with an individual or group in a manner which expresses a great deal of understanding and sympathy. Sometimes he is not actually aware of the impression he conveys in this connection, but he usually arouses responsive warmth on the part of those with whom he talks. Even when there is considerable opposition to his views he receives credit for sincerity and is usually considered to have an intelligent mind.

The true son or daughter of Aquarius is *tactful* to an amazing degree. Both sexes are able to adapt themselves to almost any condition of life; but, as a rule, they rise above completely restricting circumstances. They usually have a keen sense of humor and are wide awake and interested in the lighter things of life. This is often responsible for their ability to carry the many burdens which they may be forced to carry. The hypnotic quality often possessed by the native of this sign may be almost impossible for the observer to either analyze or understand, but it often enables the Aquarian to exert a mysterious and amazing influence over others. When the evolved native has developed this power, and when it is used for the well-being of others, it may be an extraordinarily uplifting and inspiring factor in the lives of a great many. The Aquarius native is a natural healer of spiritual ills though often he is unaware of it. Great spiritual gifts are bestowed upon all people who were born under a strong influence from this sign, and they are often the means of bringing an inner sense of security and peace to those who are greatly in need of a morally sustaining force in their lives. They are invariably interested in the welfare of others, and often are actively engaged in helping them to discover unsuspected abilities and talents; and may be the means of imparting self-confidence and a desire to excel which would not have existed without their perception and stimulating encouragement.

There is a tendency for the Aquarian to give way to nervous strain, to lack self-confidence, and to be susceptible to moodiness at times. The nervous impulses they receive from hidden vibrations and from the conditions of mind expressed by many others with whom they come in contact, are often a source of great pain to the Aquarius native. Life is constantly tearing him to pieces inwardly, unless he builds a strong spiritual wall about his inner sensibilities, guiding and controlling his thought processes into those constructive channels which he is so well able to express. The Aquarian is attracted to ancient places, and is fond of antiques. He often feels an inner urge to seek lonely spots as a result of an inner seeking for calm and peace of spirit which his instinct tells him may be found in areas which represent a time that is past. His melancholy tendencies cause him to yearn for the most solitary state. He does not give way to these inner urges as a rule, being much more inclined toward active participation in the affairs of mankind.

Not infrequently, the native of this sign gives the impression of being vacillating or wavering in his ideas and opinions. This is not often the case, but if he is forced to give opinions or explain what he proposes to do in some particular matter when he has not yet decided himself, he is often evasive and seemingly uncertain. When he *has* decided, however, that a course of action is the right one, it is quite difficult to swerve him from it; no criticism, opposing ideas, or customs can change his determination. As a rule, the pure Aquarian gives little indication of his inner thoughts and often when he is in great turmoil and inwardly very agitated, there is no outward evidence of the fact. Frequently when he is under the greatest stress, he is at his calmest and appears to be unaffected by the nervousness of others.

The highly evolved native of this sign is invariably kind-hearted, extremely gentle in his dealings with others, and of equally honest intent, though he may sometimes be misunderstood. He seldom does a thing because it has previously been done that way, and is never bound by convention. The fact that a certain course of procedure has always been followed, is to him no reason why it should continue to be; in fact, it is likely to be a *challenge* to him. As a result of a tendency toward reforms, inventiveness, and originality, the native of Aquarius is often radical in his ideas and his opinions may be expressed in the face of the most determined opposition. Invariably, the Aquarius native who has developed the higher attributes of his nature is deeply interested in occult subjects. He is frequently a metaphysician of the higher type. Truth to tell, strong Aquarius vibrations are basically indicative of a fine, noble, humanitarian mind. While the native of this sign often becomes a leader, the fact is not, as a rule, due to his having *sought* to be, but because he has definite progressive ideas, and he furthers them energetically and consistently. Because of his natural qualities, he then arrives in a position of leadership due to the confidence he is able to inspire in others.

We have dealt principally with the positive qualities of the Aquarian nature to this point, but this basic harmonic also has, in common with the other signs, potentially powerful negatives. In some individuals, who are unevolved, these negatives are expressed quite fully. Words which express the positive qualities of the sign are: scientific, earnest, humane, refined, sociable, cooperative, patient, seeker, leader, philosophical, progressive, unbiased, poised, encouraging. Words which express the negatives of Aquarius are: irrational, sentimental, impressionable, radical, apprehensive, visionary, interfering, impractical, indolent, uncertain, procrastinating, unreliable.

One of the pronounced outward expressions of the unevolved Aquarian is the tendency he has to continually ask advice of his friends and associates, then completely ignore it and proceed according to his own ideas. The undeveloped native who has not come to the point of realizing the great powers which are within him often procrastinates, making decisions and engaging in actions only when circumstances compel him to. He is likely to spend a great deal of time in imagining great achievements, often of widely diversified nature, and consequently never comes to the point of concentrating on one sufficiently to produce the steady action and endeavor which would bring it to realization. In such case, he finds *dreaming* about his desires much easier than the active striving necessary to accomplish them. He is convinced that actual achievement is beyond him. This is partially due to the negative which suggests a lack of confidence in his own abilities. This condition actually exists within him subconsciously; he is, not infrequently, unaware of it.

The most pronounced trait of the unevolved native is a tendency to get into a rut. He may go along for many years in such a rut, until force of circumstances drives him out. The Aquarian is often benefited by association with those who are more adventurous than he, and frequently he is greatly stimulated when responsibilities are *forced* upon him. Though unintentional, the undeveloped native of this sign has more than a little tendency to break promises. This is mainly due to the fact that he so desires to please others that he agrees to do things, which at the moment he has every intention of doing, but which prove impossible to fulfill.

The Aquarius native who is in a low state of evolution is unaffected by the most constructive advice. Suggestions as to how he may improve his life are completely lost upon him, if they require him to exert himself. The unevolved native is apt to be rather boastful at times, and in such case there is a marked tendency for him to talk at length (in fact, far too freely) about his own personal affairs. As a result, he may place himself in embarrassing positions by revealing too much. The marked Aquarius trait of trying to help others, tends to become *interference* in the unevolved native. He constantly seeks to change everything with which he comes in contact, without regard for how well it may be functioning. He seems to think that any change, whether it is an improvement or not, is better than to allow matters to continue as they are.

This basic harmonic is not material in the same sense that some of the others are, but there is a tendency in natives to overeat. This is often a psychological trait; a manner of *compensating* for other lacks in life. Natives who are unevolved desire popularity to an excessive degree. They wish to create the belief that they are of importance, and try to give the impression of great deeds accomplished. They seek to impress others, often making exaggerated statements about their association with distinguished persons. All this is, to a considerable extent, due to a feeling of *lack* in themselves. While they desire to accomplish greatly, they have not learned to turn their energies into direct channels of achievement.

Development of the positive Aquarius traits will inevitably make the native of this sign capable of the most *lofty* accomplishments, which may be far reaching in their beneficial effect upon others. Some of the most remarkable leaders in public life as well as in spiritual fields were born under a predominating influence from Aquarius. Recognition of the *necessity* for developing his positive traits will, in itself, place the Aquarian on the road to genuine accomplishment.

WOMEN OF AQUARIUS

Women who came into the world under a predominating influence from this sign are invariably witty, companionable, and possessed of sympathetic, winning personalities. The woman of Aquarius who has reached a fairly advanced state of evolution often has a desire to become active socially. In particular, she wishes to associate with people who are on a high cultural plane and whose stations in life are established on a basis of intellect rather than worldly goods. She is not inclined to form close or intimate friendships with those who have wealth or position alone; on the contrary, her friendships are likely to be formed among widely varying types of people. She usually chooses her friends for what they know, rather than what they have. She herself is often extremely unconventional and cares little for the opinions of others. She prefers to be received on the basis of her own individuality, rather than upon what she might assume to be.

The evolved woman of this sign has a great deal of common sense, and an extraordinary degree of understanding and sympathy for those who are in distress. She is almost invariably a faithful wife and mother, being extremely devoted to those whom she loves; however, it is frequently found that women of this sign also have active interests in club life, some kind of social service, or public affairs. She is quite likely to be on the committees of various organizations, especially those of genuinely helpful movements that are intent upon the betterment of humanity.

In common with the men, women who were born in this sign have a particular fitness for public affairs and often are outstandingly successful along those lines. They have literary and inventive abilities. However, due to an inherent lack of self-confidence (combined with the fact that women have been permitted to engage in these fields for only a short time), they are often restrained from giving full expression to their abilities. Women of this sign, along with the men, sometimes give the impression of being vacillating, and among unevolved types that is actually the case. Most women of Aquarius, however, dislike being questioned closely about any of their future plans, and when they are constantly associated with someone who is prone to *pry* into their intentions, they may persistently refuse to be drawn into any admissions or even conversations, and they are extremely evasive.

In her personal relationships, the average woman of Aquarius has fewer negatives which are difficult to correct than do those who were born in other signs. When the negatives, however, have been allowed to grow she may, in a measure, *let down*; and in such case, she becomes careless of her personal appearance. This is seldom true except of those who are in a very low state of development. The most prominent fault she often develops is the tendency to be *unpunctual* and to forget promises she has made. She will, however, go to great extremes to be loyal to those who are nearest and dearest to her. Often, through her desire to protect and guard those whom she loves, her ambitions are aroused and her native gifts are brought forth into the light of day. Responsibility is always a tremendous incentive to the native of Aquarius and, when conditions force her to shoulder burdens, she rarely breaks under them. Some of the warmest, most magnetic, and most lovable among the feminine population of the world, indisputably came from the sign Aquarius.

It will be noted that a great many children who came into the world under a strong influence from the sign Aquarius have a pronounced tendency toward procrastination. Additionally, the trait of day-dreaming is often marked. The habit of promising things with the greatest degree of readiness, and then breaking the promises, seems to be very difficult for them to overcome, and in this connection they need the most careful of parental guidance.

Youngsters who came into the world under this sign are imaginative, restless, extremely sensitive, and likely to be either over-active or completely the opposite — indolent. The most important lessons for children who were born under a predominating influence from this sign to learn are those of being on time, and of fully facing up to realities. Young people of this sign invariably are extremely responsive to kindness and affection. They should be criticized only when absolutely necessary, and great care should be taken lest their self-confidence be lessened. It is almost invariably a mistake to deal with the Aquarius child harshly. The marked trait of Aquarius natives, as previously mentioned, is a tendency to neglect developing the natural gifts bestowed upon them by this basic vibration; because of failure to recognize their own talents or to believe in themselves. This tendency in the Aquarius child is one that should be noted by his parents and they should strive to encourage the youngster to develop his natural skills and aptitudes and to build up his confidence in his own abilities.

To an extraordinary degree, the true native of Aquarius loves freedom; he hates to be restrained and to have his actions closely governed by someone else. This is as true of the children of this sign as it is of the adults. Because they dislike revealing their innermost thoughts and feelings they may appear to be secretive at times. Youngsters of Aquarius often have amazing memories and they have an inherent ability to develop extensive vocabularies. The true child of Aquarius is modest in demeanor, and he often tends to be retiring in disposition. This is not always a good trait, as it may be an outward expression of a powerful negative which causes him to shrink from contact with others and to be overly conscious of himself in the presence of people. The youngster of this sign should be reared, to as great an extent as possible, in quiet surroundings. His life should be simple and well ordered. He should, however, be encouraged to do things in his own way. His natural inventiveness and scientific leanings will invariably be brought more fully to the surface when he is allowed to use his own mind in connection with the problems which confront him, even in early years.

Sometimes the youngster who was born in Aquarius is rather trying to adults with whom he is closely associated, because of his propensity to ask endless questions. As a result of association with those who are wise and understanding, however, he gains a great deal of understanding, and is often possessed of a wisdom far ahead of other children his own age. The Aquarius nature is rarely gross and coarse. On the contrary, *it is sensitive and finely organized.* Understanding of the positive traits of Aquarius makes it possible to guide these youngsters minds into constructive channels to the extent that they become splendid and noble adults.

147

MARRIAGES OF AQUARIUS

It has previously been said that the true native of Aquarius seldom does anything in a particular way for the reason that it has always been done that way. He is likely to rebel against every kind of traditional activity. For that reason it is quite important for both men and women of this sign to marry one who has a similar point of view. Essentially both sexes of Aquarius are likely to be unconventional. To be bound to a marriage partner who does things habitually by set rule, who is reluctant to change, and who is not adventurous at heart, is likely to be a painful experience for the native of this sign. Under such conditions, the Aquarian will sometimes come to feel that it is right to do things methodically and in traditional ways, though it is *not his nature* to do so. It is then that some of the negatives of the sign are likely to become prominent, for the true Aquarius native will inevitably be unhappy under such circumstances. His life becomes one of continual frustration.

Any person who came into the world under a strong influence from this basic harmonic should marry one who has *imagination* and who likes experiment and change. Certainly the marriage partner of the Aquarian should understand the loyal and devoted nature of Aquarius, as well as the tendency to be *airy*; which is to say that it is sometimes difficult for the person of staid and orderly habits to understand the mental gyrations which are often indulged in by the true Aquarian!

The husband of an Aquarius woman who expects to come home regularly and find everything in its proper place, and peaceful order prevailing, is quite likely to be in for a shock. In his absence, the beds are likely to have changed places with the cocktail tables, and his favorite chair may have found a new location in which he finds it only after a diligent search. This, of course, can be quite disturbing to someone who likes the order of things to be changeless, and who, having settled into a routine, is to be moved only by a major catastrophe. In marriage, women of Aquarius are quite likely to take the wedded state as a new leaf in the book of freedom. The man who marries a woman of this sign should not expect to have found a paragon of domestic virtues who will be completely satisfied to spend her entire time in the drudgery of homely tasks. A few will do it — and have, but they are rarely happy in the doing. They prefer to be actively engaged in more stimulating endeavors.

On the other hand, men who were born under a strong influence from this vibration do not take kindly to being tied to inflexible routines of domestic obligation. When something develops in the life of an Aquarius man which captures his interest at a time when he should dutifully go home for dinner, he is more than likely — not to go home! He should be married to a woman who will understand the often seemingly erratic courses he takes, and who can be intelligently interested in his activities as well as capable of being as unconventional as he is.

Both sexes of Aquarius are essentially loyal, and their marriages usually endure, even though the native may be basically unhappy. The sign Libra (September 24th — October 23rd), another of the air trinity, is basically harmonious matrimonially. An alliance with Leo (July 22nd — August 22nd) usually produces strong and vital children and can be relatively happy. Gemini (May 23rd — June 22nd) and Aries (March 20th — April 20th) are usually considered harmonious — Gemini probably more so than Aries.

148

Above all, evolved individuals who were born under a predominating influence from the sign Aquarius are designed for leadership in public affairs. They have been among the most renowned and genuinely constructive public speakers. Often the native is an extremely successful promoter of large ideas. It has been said that the Aquarian can raise capital for speculative ventures more quickly and readily than can those born in any other sign of the zodiac. That is due to the hypnotic quality which, though indefinable, is invariably present in the true Aquarian. A number of famous financiers came into the world under a strong influence from this sign but the natural field of the Aquarius nature is less in pure finance than it is in endeavors which have to do with public welfare or the problems of humanity.

Many scientists of wide repute were born in this sign, and in the fields of invention Aquarius is particularly well represented. The true Aquarian is not limited in his choice of occupation, but he is not particularly fitted for positions in life which require *plodding efficiency* rather than *imagination* and which fail to permit the development of inspirational opportunities. While the native often does get into a rut in which he performs the most ordinary and plodding tasks, he is far from realizing the full potentialities of his nature, and the great gifts which he is capable of using are dormant and unrecognized.

Literature is quite a favorable outlet for the talents and abilities of Aquarius. A number of extremely successful authors in our modern times were born in this sign, as well as many in the past. Salesmanship is a marked attribute. One would naturally assume that to be the case because of the ability the Aquarius native possesses to influence the actions of others. The legal profession is often favorable, the native having a sense of understanding and the capacity to acquire knowledge; combined with ability to talk extremely well and convincingly. He is frequently successful as a physician, though the true Aquarian is likely to be more successful in fields of research. Natives of this sign become splendid demonstrators, and of course when in an evolved state, extraordinarily capable public speakers. Every field of mechanics is favorable for them; they become capable engineers. In fact, all that has to do with technical matters of a progressive nature, provides a highly advantageous outlet for Aquarian abilities.

The tendency of some natives is to make plans of so gigantic a nature that they are unable to even properly begin to carry them through. Their own imaginations are too much for others and they are unable to gain the support which is necessary. The native who has not developed his aggressive qualities should be associated with someone who is adventurous and who has executive ability. The evolved individual who received a strong influence from this sign at birth is quick to see opportunities and he grasps them without hesitancy. Among those who are not so evolved, however, the tendency to dream comes into prominence and opportunities pass them by without being taken advantage of. In personal legal entanglements, the Aquarius native is more likely to get the worst of it than are those born in any other sign of the zodiac. He should, therefore, avoid any sort of legal controversy in his own affairs whenever it is possible for him to do so.

149

DISHARMONY OF AQUARIUS

In common with all the other signs of the zodiac, the negatives of this basic harmonic exist coincidentally with conditions which are customarily referred to as disease. It is utterly and absolutely impossible for those conditions, however, to exist without their like in vibrations of thought. It is equally impossible for negative vibrations in thought formations to long exist without reproducing on the material, physical plane of being, that condition which is called disease.

Indirectly, the effect of the Aquarius negatives may manifest themselves in any part of the body. It will be found, however, upon tracing the origin and progress of any condition of disharmony, that individuals whose negatives are those of Aquarius originated their physical disorders in the parts which are especially susceptible to the influence of this vibration. The calves and ankles are particularly associated with the basic vibration of Aquarius. Both the positive and the negative qualities of the sign, to whatever extent they may manifest themselves, are primarily associated with these parts. The negatives of this sign tend to produce ankle sprains, broken ankles, and falls. They are also responsible for nervous disorders and various types of disharmony in the physical body which are associated with diseases of the nerves. The nature of Aquarius that causes the native to appear poised and calm outwardly, even though he may be extremely upset inwardly, makes the native susceptible to a great deal of nervous agitation in the solar plexus. This, not infrequently, leads to an upset stomach.

There is a tendency on the part of natives to allow some of the negatives inherent in the sign, which produce disharmonies of a spasmodic nature, to grow. These are related to the nervous system, blood poisoning, or heart weakness. Swelling of the ankles and calves is not at all unusual in the Aquarius native. He is susceptible to sinus disorders and fevers, all of which is to say that when he suffers from these conditions, his rates of vibration are not in harmony with that state which we call health. The same being true of this as of all signs, the processes of thought and the consequent vibrations which are produced in the mind are of primary importance. Secondarily, the native should have plenty of fresh air and good water. An abundance of fruits and vegetables is necessary, and in many cases it will be found that there is a mineral lack.

While the native of Aquarius is inclined to be extremely active in the midst of other people's projects, he is benefited greatly by excursions into the countryside, or actually living in such areas. He needs to get away from the nervous pressures which are often pushed upon him by those with whom he is associated. He needs such conditions, at least at intervals, in which he can think alone and more deeply than may be possible otherwise. He can regain lost glandular balance through such means, and is often *born anew*. Greasy, fat, and heavy foods should be avoided by the native of this sign; candy and other sweets should be partaken of sparingly. Excessive use of these is an expression of inner negatives. Under conditions of constructive thought processes the *powerful forces* of Aquarius are brought into play, and the individual who was born under a strong influence from Aquarius achieves *absolute harmony* in his physical organism.

150

1977 Relatives seem to scramble "in and out" of your "day-by-day" world. A lot of "sorting out" of what may or may not be "useful" is indicated. A person who has shared the responsibilities you have known is likely either to prove an added burden, "walk out", or sever an old association. Communication or writings containing "UNUSUAL INFOR-MATION" will possibly reach you with surprising swiftness. Offers of strange nature having a financial undertone, will undoubtedly "come up" for your approval. Dreams you never expected to see realized are forming in such a manner as to bring fulfillment. I understand all the frustrations and weighty problems you have borne. Now I am convinced that "a time" of *easing* and *contentment* will be showered upon you as the future unfolds before you!

1978 You will be aware of so many fields of interest which seem attractive that it will be imperative for you to find reasons why the position you now hold in your world is serving gainful purposes for you this year, I feel. In a flashing moment you are apt to consider action you might come to regret, unless you make a policy of thinking every situation through clearly before you make more definite decisions. Your security is likely to be affected strongly by people around you now. Credit, estate, or insurance matters may become en-tangled for a time, but as you seek, I am sure you will find a particularly gratifying means of serving your world even more productively. 1978 will be a year for discovering your "real niche", in my opinion.

1979 Your personal relationships will be especially meaningful during this new cycle, I feel. Sweeping changes in influential circles may touch your source of income, but someone, in all probability, will enter your life who knows how to direct you to the realization of your most cherished goal. Money matters are apt to occupy your thoughts and influence your decisions more than in the past under your 1979 trends, but this should enable you to look more deeply into your "hidden talents" for gratifying solutions. Concepts that were precious to you once may appear less satisfying at this time. I believe a noticeable transformation will touch your ideals, leading you to "a changed set of values" you believe will give you far greater fulfillment.

1980 Matters of inheritance, insurance or similar "business" interests are likely to be uppermost in your mind for a time this year. Possessions which involve legal agree-ments or advice also may hold your attention during this planetary cycle, but unexpected benefits through the agency of another person seem to outweigh the burdensome elements that have possibly affected your mutual finances recently. 1980 and 1981 are apt to be marked by "faraway" or "foreign" people, or unusual avenues will be of interest which will increasingly take a stronghold in your thoughts . . . Discussions of religious or philosophical topics will be likely to provide stimulating as well as rewarding ideas that will help you transform some of your long-held beliefs into new concepts now, I believe.

1981   Shortly after the middle of this forecast period, sudden quarrels might flare temporarily, connected with a "hidden" element you will be disposed to keep "under cover." Toward the close of this year a somewhat strange and rather uncommon friendship with romantic overtones could become of prime interest as well as discussion, but sudden disruptions might arise because of differing opinions, as this planetary influence continues. New arrangements and the leave-taking of old associations are indicated now. Questions touching shared resources are apt to undergo close scrutiny, but unexpected good fortune will come to you through someone in a position to benefit you, I believe.

1982   I believe this year will be marked by an "about-face" of conditions that will alter the pattern of your life from one of confining or limiting factors to a very different one of astonishing freedom. I know you have experienced some very restricting elements that held you as though you were in a cage. Now the new planetary positions will, in my opinion, free you. Friendships that are nostalgic or have the power to "open" doors that have been closed will be instrumental in supporting some plan or desire you have had in mind for some time, in my opinion. In fact, where you have been puzzled by a stream of obstacles, even health concerns, I think now the aid of other people and probably one person in particular will be responsible for your name receiving prominent mention.

1983   During this forecast year, the new positions of major planets combine with the eclipse to lead you steadily upward on the "ladder of life," toward realization of plans you have long striven to accomplish, in my estimation. I am certain your efforts will be noticed, and I believe you will act with keen judgment that will attract the kind of attention you will be proud to claim as your own. Efforts you make to prevent irritations or dissensions which could react upon your health and well-being will be worthwhile, I am sure. I believe it will be advisable for you to avoid "risks" if you are around large objects or "pet" projects during this cycle. Changes are shown in your close relationships, particularly around the middle of this forecast period.

1984   New responsibilities are likely to be thrust upon you, particularly during the first six or seven months of this year. Feelings of restlessness will seem especially strong. There are indications that what *you* want personally will appear frequently to be at "cross-purposes" with another person's ideas. In the face of dissensions, you may now have a tendency to say things you really don't mean, or act in an unconventional manner which might prove less becoming than the impression you usually prefer to create. I believe, however, you will take time to "stop, look, and listen" throughout these cyclic influences and will thus realize highly beneficial results from your present efforts. Your circles of acquaintances are apt to take on unexpected and even hold quite unusual meaning for you, as this trend moves to a close!

SUMMATION (Aquarius)

"New beginnings" are outstandingly indicated as the major indication for you during this forecast period. I believe the pattern of your life will be turned toward a different direction, especially around the year 1982, with a surprising result which encourages you to enter a period of significant achievement for a long-cherished "ambition." I feel your sense of responsibility toward those you love and others who are held in affection will deepen throughout this cycle. I do not say this in a spirit of interpreting "responsibility" as something burdensome, but rather in terms of the joy and ease of heart that come from fulfilling obligations toward those who share the closest bonds with you.

Although significant adjustments will appear, I feel, as you undergo changes in relationships and other alterations which at times seem to turn your world "topsy turvy," I am certain that your natural ability to adapt or adjust yourself to even unexpected "uprootings" will assert itself. From these "moments of turmoil" will emerge a new set of conditions, encouraging you to use your abilities in an expanded and gratifying manner, I am certain!

To a greater degree than in the past, you will need to exercise patience and *control* the tendency to scatter your energies upon what could turn out to be "time wasting" activities. I believe your birth influences have gifted you with a great capability for directing your efforts in constructive directions. During this trend, particularly around 1978, strong planetary cycles will require that you give unusual attention to the practice of "double checking facts and figures" before you make commitments that might involve you "money wise."

Your intuitive powers are likely to reach "peaks" during this forecast period, according to my analysis of new planetary cycles touching your birth period. I believe you have the splendid faculty of instinctively "knowing" when a direction you are considering is "wrong or right." For this reason, I feel that during the coming years for each step "backward" that seems forced upon you, you will later take two "strides forward" in pursuit of the cherished goals which give purpose and dignity to your life!

The combination of influences under which those who were born in this cusp entered the world makes them much more complex and difficult to understand than the average individual. The two signs involved through which the sun's rays come in this cusp period are, of course, Aquarius and Pisces. The first of these, as we have observed, is an air sign and the second a water sign. Aquarius is *"ruled"* by the planet Uranus and Pisces by Neptune. The watery element, is quite marked in the sign Pisces and the psychic qualities are obvious. These two planets play an important part in the working out of destiny in the lives of natives as they play an important part in the formation of characteristics. They at least, symbolize them.

The natives of this cusp have unusual ability along executive lines. They possess a marked desire to accumulate money so as to give them substance and to place them in positions of independence. Particularly, the men of this combination of influences are guided by their own ideas. Natural forces are irresistible in helping them to attain their objectives when they have some knowledge of the rhythms of their own lives. The fundamental abilities of the evolved native are of such a nature as to permit them to achieve greatly.

The sign Pisces is inherently one of the most honest of any of the twelve. Natives are likely to be extremely faithful and loyal in the performance of allotted tasks and duties. Due to the strong desires of those who were born in this cusp period to occupy positions of independence financially, they are apt to be meticulous in the fulfilling of their obligations. They require harmony in their surroundings, however, and pleasant associations. If they are not in surroundings such as these, they are very likely to become extremely despondent and even bitter. By nature they are quite lovable, being generous and warmhearted. It is notable that women who come into the world under this particular combination of solar influences are not as inclined toward business ventures nor toward fulfilling exacting demands as are the men. There is a marked difference between the natures of men and women who were born within this combination of influences, more so than with other combinations. The problem of marriage is a very serious one for the native. He should by all means have a marriage partner who can appreciate his good qualities.

Occupations having to do with service to others are very favorable for him. Any occupation in which his qualities of being able to serve promptly and well is a good outlet for his traits of character. Public life is quite favorable for those who were born under this combination of influences as are things which have to do with retail merchandising. Development of new products is also a favorable medium. Pisces, which is psychic, imparts a natural ability to use the power of intuition. When these natives understand and use the forces available to them, in their own personal lives, their ability to achieve is remarkable in a business way. The achievement of happiness and proper home surroundings is much more likely under harmonious conditions. Women of this cusp are in many cases, great talkers.

154

The birthsign PISCES
February 20th to March 19th

f you were born between February 20th and March 19th, your birth occurred in the zodiacal sign Pisces. That part of the sky in which Pisces is located has been known throughout the period of recorded history as *"The Lea"*. This basic harmonic represents one of the twelve fundamental types of humanity which are referred to and illustrated in story and parable form in the Bible, and the original tribe of Israel which was called Levi is representative and illustrative of this sign. The symbol of Pisces is the two Fishes, and they are represented as swimming in opposite directions. The same is true of Pisces as is true of the other signs; the symbol was not derived from mere myth and folklore, but is intended to convey the fundamental, psychological qualities of this vibration.

The planet which is strongest in its influence upon this sign is Neptune. The spiritual, psychic qualities of that planet are strongly marked in those who came into the world under a strong influence from Pisces. This sign has always been the symbol of the Christian era. It is a feminine sign. Those who are students of cosmic vibration refer to it as watery, common, flexed, negative, emotional, serving, inspirational, lymphatic, fruitful, bicorporal, southern, and of short ascension. The gem which has basic vibrations similar to those of Pisces is the white chrysolite and the flower is the daffodil. As do all things, this basic vibration has both its positive and negative phases and the sign is described in a fashion which deals with both. One who was born under a strong influence from Pisces will recognize in himself, *all of the qualities* which are described although some, of course, are accentuated in the individual to a much greater degree than others.

To a marked degree, those who came into the world in the sign Pisces are very impressionable. They are greatly affected by the thought forms of others and are sensitive to cosmic vibrations. All the water signs are inspirational in nature and susceptible to psychic influences; Pisces perhaps somewhat more so than the other two. The individual who received a strongly predominating influence from this sign at birth, particularly one who came into the world at a time when the sign was also

155

rising, which means at daybreak, is of a definite physical type. The true Pisces has a rather large head. His countenance is full, his forehead broad with a tendency toward being dome-shaped. His complexion is pale rather than ruddy; his lips are full; his eyes frequently have a liquid appearance, and are often large and likely to have a soft expression. This is particularly true of the women, but is a noticeable characteristic of the Pisces native regardless of sex. The individual who tends toward the pure type has a very sensitive skin. He is of medium height, modest in appearance, and his demeanor is quiet. He has fine hair which is usually quite soft. The tendency of this basic harmonic is to produce rather short limbs.

You have strongly idealistic tendencies and you started life with many lofty ideals. You are not fond of that which is vulgar and lewd. Your nature is peaceful and you are inclined to be extremely patient. You can continue steadily in highly monotonous conditions of life, proceeding calmly and consistently. You are extremely good at detailed jobs and have the capacity for taking great pains with your work. You are not aggressive and have little inclination to force your ideas or your desires on others. You are not at all inclined to be boastful. You are fond of things which are scientific in nature and you have a love for the beautiful. Music affects you deeply, arousing you to heights or depths emotionally.

The true Pisces native has the capacity to *endure* much in the way of unpleasant conditions — without protest. He often allows himself to be imposed upon by others and is rarely quarrelsome, preferring to let matters work themselves out rather than to engage in controversy. He has a marked capacity for faithfulness to duty, and the ability to acquire efficiency. He desires to occupy a respected and secure position in life, but except in the case of the highly evolved native, is not likely to push his affairs aggressively. He often has a fine scientific and mechanical mind. He is inventive and has a great deal of ingenuity, but frequently these talents are not developed to the extent they could be. The true native of Pisces invariably has a great many noble and lofty instincts, but the *material* affairs of life often condition his thinking processes to an extreme degree. He is extremely loyal and faithful. He is sincere in almost everything he says and does. One rarely encounters a *shifty,* tricky and undependable Piscean.

The native of this sign is quite likely to be restless *inwardly,* but as a rule he does not give *outward* expression to this inner restlessness. Travel is quite beneficial, as this restlessness is satisfied, and when it is possible for him to realize his desire for change, the favorable effects are marked. He should, however, have his *roots* firmly fixed, as the true Pisces native is never satisfied to roam widely without a safe and definite anchorage. The person who came into the world under a strong influence from this sign is a *keen observer,* and if drawn into an argument is likely to reveal a surprising fund of knowledge. He is usually slow to give his opinion on any subject however, and thinks any question over at great length before expressing himself. As a result of his tendency to be quiet in manner and slow in speaking about matters on which he may be well-informed, he often gives the impression of being far less knowledgeable than he is. While the native of Pisces is extremely peaceable by nature, avoiding sharp speech or argument even under the most trying conditions, he may surprise others by his ability to defend himself in argument, or even physically, when he is finally pushed to the point of combat.

The individual who received a strong influence from this sign at birth is essentially romantic. He is often highly imaginative and may be a *dreamer* in the fullest sense of the word. In such case he is shy, retiring, and extraordinarily sensitive. The Pisces native of this type finds it almost an utter impossibility to cope with the harshness of life; and unless he is placed in a position wherein his talents can find expression, he may have a difficult time. Of all the signs, Pisces is perhaps the most reliable and honest by intention. One rarely makes a mistake when he entrusts the carrying out of business details or other matters to the native of this sign, providing a method of procedure has been fully understood *at the start*. He is naturally methodical in the practical affairs of life. He frequently has a capacity for research which is much above the average and his ability for painstaking analysis is also marked. When the true Pisces native is engaged in statistical work or in accounting, he is methodical to the ultimate degree, never being satisfied until his work is in perfect order. He is a detail worker *par-excellence*. The true Piscean will faithfully discharge every duty with which he is entrusted, and often goes through his entire life in complete faithfulness to a duty which may be almost entirely imagined. He has a strong sense of obligation, and for that reason he often gets the *short-end* in business as well as in his personal affairs. It is the Pisces native whom we find devotedly attending a neurotic, spoiled, and self-centered marriage partner. He may spend his entire life in such service, feeling that his obligations require him to sacrifice every personal inclination and desire. This attitude of mind is, of course, very worthy; and from the standpoint of *goodness* the Pisces native quite often has reached a state of high evolution.

Peculiarly enough, while the true native of this sign is greatly affected by psychic vibrations of all kinds, he is not inclined to believe anything which is not susceptible to *material proof*. He has a marked tendency to seek the reason for every condition that confronts him. He particularly wants a specific explanation for every act. He himself is always able to tell just why *he* has taken any step (because he invariably thinks it over carefully and plans it in detail), and he is equally insistent upon knowing exactly how another has reached a decision. All this is associated with his skepticism about anything which is not susceptible to clear and understandable proof. Due to the *meticulous nature* of the sign, Pisces natives often become faultfinding. They very often acquire definite *fixed* views relating to life. This is particularly true of religion. They tend to become materialistic and to disbelieve the tenets of all religions or, on the other hand, to embrace dogmas and creeds. They are seldom broadly philosophical, but tend either to reject all matters of a spiritual nature or to adopt a somewhat narrow perspective.

To a greater extent than perhaps any other sign of the zodiac, those who were born in Pisces lack aggressive self-confidence. Even when they have acquired a vast store of knowledge, or become highly skilled in some particular work, they are hesitant about displaying their abilities in any way, and they have a greater tendency to *"hide their light under a bushel"* than do the great majority of people. The evolved Pisces native has a fine intellect. He is a wide reader and almost invariably has an extensive library. He is especially interested in fine bindings and rare books. The great majority who are developed intellectually are constantly adding to their store of knowledge. Anything new immediately intrigues them and they avidly seek information. For that reason, they are prone to ask a great many questions. Sometimes this appears to be *prying,* but in the evolved native it is merely a desire to *learn* and to *know* about everything which comes within range of his observation. Education is quite necessary to the native of Pisces. The development of his intellect is an important factor in his ultimate success. Additionally the native of this sign should be launched early in life upon a career which permits growth and development. He is less likely to change when once engaged in an occupation than are those of any other group.

Due to the psychic qualities of this sign and the sensitivity to color, Pisces natives have a fine sense of color values. They have an instinctive judgment of that which is harmonious, and are greatly affected by vibrations of color. They are kindhearted, and easily touched by anything of sentimental nature. Frequently, they shed tears quite easily. This is almost equally true of the men as it is of the women. They make friends quite readily and are likely to be companionable and gregarious in their instincts. Due to the fact that they are unassuming and kindly, others are drawn to them strongly. The true Pisces native needs company. He is seldom satisfied to be alone and tends to become depressed when he is deprived of human companionship.

The true native of this sign has what really amounts to a *horror* of debt. He fears to incur obligations which he might not be able to fulfill. This is a pronounced Pisces attitude. He dreads the possibility of indebtedness, and particularly of poverty. He is apprehensive in almost every financial transaction. His greatest concern is to provide for the future and he wishes to be absolutely assured of independence. He is invariably more inclined to be boastful about his *freedom* from financial obligation or debt than about any other factor in his life. He wishes especially to be assured in his own mind and heart that he is justly entitled to everything he possesses and that he has fairly earned it.

This sign has within it, powerful constructives which are both practical and creative. On the other hand, it has inherent negatives which are extremely destructive when they are allowed to develop. Words which express the positive traits are: purity, service, inspiration, method, honest, friendly, psychometric, perceptive, generous, charitable, gentle. Words indicative of the negative qualities are: indecisive, dreamy, apologetic, timid, anxious, submissive, impressionable, defeatism, unassertive.

There is little question that to a greater extent than may be said of those born in any other sign, the negatives of Pisces *react immediately* in the affairs of the individual. One who was born under a predominating influence from this sign is the enemy of his own hopes and desires, though he does not realize it. Rarely is a native of this sign deliberately detrimental to the affairs of another, or revengeful, grasping, or self-seeking. Worry over money matters is perhaps the most powerful negative in the Pisces vibration. There is also a marked tendency for the native to become over-anxious, worried, and in consequence fretful over all the affairs of life. He is particularly likely to spend anxious hours because of the affairs of someone near him.

The true Pisces native is never found to possess vicious traits of character. His negatives are all related to his *lack of faith in himself,* and to his inability to fully believe that his affairs will prosper. When the native of Pisces allows the negatives of worry and over-anxiety to become strong, he reaches the point of being careless in his personal habits. He ceases to be particular about his clothes and he is quite inclined to neglect his own physical well-being. He has a marked tendency to worry about all those who are close to him, but does not worry about himself except along financial or business lines. The tendency toward self-censure and dwelling upon past failures sometimes has an extremely damaging effect upon the Pisces native. When the negatives are allowed to predominate, he is sure to encounter serious malfunctioning of the physical parts. Additionally, the sign being of the water element, susceptibility to psychic disturbances is great. The intense mental stress, and consequent despondency, which may develop in the native when these particular negatives are allowed to become strong, sometimes results in the breaking down of his mental faculties. The individual born under a strong Pisces influence, who observes a growing tendency in himself to become over-anxious and fretful, should definitely determine to cultivate a more optimistic and hopeful outlook. He should realize that this is an absolute necessity.

The Pisces native who is unevolved frequently becomes a *talker* to an excessive degree. He is quite likely to chatter along about trivialities, and it seems extremely difficult for him to cease. This is more true of the women than it is of the men. In this connection there is a tendency on the part of many Pisces natives to interrupt conversations, interjecting their own ideas at great length. The native who is unevolved is often a veritable *question box,* and can ask a tremendous number of irrelevant and unimportant questions.

There is no sign of the zodiac where the people are closer to powerful forces which they can call to their aid. When the Pisces native has conditioned his mind to *optimism* and a *clear knowledge* of what he wishes to bring about in his own affairs, he receives unmistakable *inspiration* through his mind which will give him the certainty within himself to bring about the realization of his constructive ambitions. The native of Pisces who goes about correcting his specific negatives can be a tremendous spiritual asset to all those with whom he is associated, and is broad, tolerant, and understanding. He *radiates* a spiritual quality which is an inspiration to others!

WOMEN OF PISCES

The women of this sign possess all of the qualities which are necessary to make completely faithful and devoted wives and mothers. One flaw in this connection is the tendency they have to become worried or anxious and the consequent *fretfulness* that may develop. Women of Pisces are invariably fond of their homes and everything connected with them. They have extremely fine conceptions of color, and their choice of combinations is always in good taste. They like bright shades, but, except in unevolved types, the Pisces women display skill and understanding of how to use them to achieve the greatest effect.

As previously mentioned, both sexes of this sign cry easily. The woman of Pisces is in particular easily driven to tears, and she may have protracted spells of weeping. While she is essentially sympathetic, kindly, and loyal, she has a marked quality of stubbornness. To a considerable extent this is present directly in relation to the sensitivity of the Pisces nature. The true woman of this sign is easily hurt, and when she has been so hurt she may sometimes not mention the fact, but take a stand which is difficult for anyone else to understand or to change. All women who were born under a strong influence from Pisces are extremely sensitive to criticism of any kind.

In business, Pisces women have the same quality of faithfulness in the execution of duties entrusted to them, as do the men. They are extremely capable office managers, bookkeepers, and accountants. A large number of Pisces women have remained in positions for many years, and are the type which is markedly always *on the job* — consistently capable and efficient. They are not usually efficient in the sense that some of those born in other signs are, as a result of being brisk and quick, but are much steadier. Women of this sign also become quite successful modistes, dressmakers, and beauty culturists. They are successful in banking institutions where skill and efficiency in figures are a requisite.

Often, as in the case of the men (this being a highly inspirational sign), women who are natives become successful in literary fields as well as in artistic endeavors. Not a few have been extremely capable in creative design, and a number have been illustrators, meeting with much success. They, of course, have the same ability with flowers as the men, finding occupations having to do with horticulture quite intriguing, if their interests are aroused in that direction.

Women of this birthsign are psychometric, often to an extreme degree. Their psychic flashes are often quite accurate and they frequently give strong evidence of extrasensory perception. They are apt to be good subjects for hypnosis and are very likely to pick up accurately what other people are thinking. However, when women of this sign allow some of the negatives to develop which are inherent in the sign they sometimes go to extremes in these connections. The women of this sign are capable of an extremely high form of development. This can be and is often due to their very inspirational natures. When there is harmony in their processes of thought there is no question about the fact that they can receive directly from the One Source (that is, the Intelligence of the Universe) the answer to any of their own problems in life. As a result they often are a tremendous inspiration in the lives of other people.

Youngsters who came into the world under a predominating influence from the sign Pisces should never under any circumstances know anything other than loving kindness and encouragement. The tendency of the sign toward self-censure and lack of self-confidence can be lessened greatly by proper parental guidance. These children are shy and timid. They display extremely generous traits early in life, but their inclination to give to others is sometimes an outward expression of an inner feeling of inferiority, and such giving is done with an idea that *liking* may be purchased in that way. Most people of this sign, and of course young people especially, are unaware of the fact, but they do have the feeling that they lack qualities which would draw others to them, and this is a psychological form of recompense for those imagined lacks. This tendency to give away possessions should be carefully guided by the parents of the Pisces child as it may be carried to extremes.

Every effort should be made to bolster the self-confidence of these youngsters and to make them believe in themselves. It is usually difficult, however, to impart real aggressiveness to a child who was born in Pisces unless he received strong influences from another sign at birth. Youngsters of this sign are often extremely brilliant, sometimes to the point of precocity. Frequently, however, due to their inherent shyness they do not give as much outward evidence of the keenness of their minds as do those who were born in other signs. As a matter of fact, children of this sign often get credit for being much less brilliant mentally than they really are. They are, in common with the adults, not inclined to be overconfident and they often are not very self-assured when it comes to expressing the things they really know. One can readily see that this trait may cause them to receive much less credit than is their due and it can be a considerable drawback in the fulfillment of their highest potential throughout life. These youngsters do not react happily to any sort of ridicule and some of their mental brilliance may be considerably dulled if parents make light of any of their constructive interests. They can be aided to much greater accomplishment in any field when they feel they have the thorough support and understanding of their parents.

While children of this birthsign need encouragement and the support of parents and those close to them in their endeavors to give expression to their ideas, an *overprotective* attitude is likely to be more damaging than beneficial. These youngsters need to feel greater *inner* assurance of their own capabilities, and an overprotective attitude on the part of parents is likely to take from their own self-confidence — particularly in their associations with other children and people in general. Parental guidance is perhaps more important to children of this particular birth period than it is to any others. They should be encouraged and praised for their efforts, but led to *depend upon themselves* rather than upon others.

When children of Pisces are discovered in wrong-doing, they require particularly careful guidance. They should be made to feel that such wrong-doing is completely forgiven, and never should they be reminded of errors committed in the past. The sins of these youngsters weigh heavily upon them and often leave a mark in later years. Pisces children are capable of the most lofty and constructive good, and with proper guidance and understanding, they blossom into splendid adults.

MARRIAGES OF PISCES

In marriage, as in other affairs of life, the native of Pisces is inclined to be faithful and loyal. Once the true Piscean has entered into matrimony he rarely — of his own volition — disrupts the partnership, even though he may be disappointed in his choice of a matrimonial companion. It may be stated quite definitely that the true native of Pisces is less likely to sever the ties of marriage than are those who were born in any of the other signs.

The pure Virgo vibrations (August 23rd — September 23rd) are very harmonious with those of Pisces; therefore, a matrimonial partner who was born in that sign is likely to prove to be quite congenial. Tastes and general outlook on life are usually quite similar. The sign Cancer (June 23rd — July 21st) is harmonious, as is Pisces itself. The sign Cancer is of course a water sign as is Pisces. There is some indication, as a matter of fact, that Cancer is the most harmonious matrimonially of all the signs. General observation without absolute statistical information points up the fact that a marriage between a native of the sign Cancer and one of Pisces almost invariably endures. In the observation of the author, one almost never encounters the severing of matrimonial ties between natives of these two signs. Both signs have a tendency to be patient and home-loving, and neither is likely to be particularly aggressive in self-assertion.

To some degree, Scorpio (October 24th — November 22nd) is also harmonious, but when the native of Pisces marries an undeveloped native of that sign it proves necessary for him to submit in almost every factor of life to the domination of the strong Scorpio nature. The fact has often been noted that there seems to be a strong attraction between the sign Pisces and the sign Libra (September 24th — October 23rd). There is, however, a fundamental difference in approach to the affairs of life between people who were born respectively in these two signs. The native of Libra acts upon his *intuitive judgment* to the extent that the Pisces native finds him quite difficult to understand. As previously mentioned, those who were born in Pisces are inclined to ask a reason for everything, and as the questions they formulate frequently remain unanswered by the Libran, there is likely to be considerable friction. A marriage, consequently, between people who were born in these two signs is not often completely successful.

Pisces men are as fond of their homes as are the women, and are devoted to their wives and families and are likely to spoil them to a considerable extent. They like comfortable surroundings but may not expend much effort to achieve them, and are, in fact, apt to be of little *active* assistance as far as the practical duties of the home are concerned. Women of this sign have been known to guide their matrimonial partners into channels which brought about the greatest degree of success as well as the avoidance of unhappy experiences — even extending to accidents.

Both the men and women of this sign are extremely adaptable to any condition in which they find themselves and are frequently able to make a go of marriage — even if it is not just to their liking. The native of Pisces who develops the higher qualities of the birthsign, certainly never has need to worry about any condition of life which seems to *pose* a threat but really doesn't — in marriage or otherwise.

162

The true native of Pisces, because of his sense of responsibility and fairness, will usually shine as a member of the legal profession, and, in particular when sitting as a judge. As a trial lawyer, he will believe so implicitly in the case he is representing that he will invariably make a simple, direct, and highly effective presentation. Indeed, unless he is so convinced in the truth of his case, he will probably refuse to handle it. Particularly when the native receives some of the Aries vibration, he has a knowledge of how to appeal to juries and how to present his case, taking advantage of the impression he creates of simple and rugged honesty.

Agriculture is another field for which the native of Pisces is suited, in particular the raising and handling of flowers. When strong influences from air or fire signs were present at birth, he may well develop into an excellent artist or writer. Pisces is represented by a number of very successful illustrators. The stage, also welcomes such natives, since they possess what is called *"heart appeal"* for an audience. Seldom is the native fitted for sales occupations which require aggressive self-assertion, unless he received strong vibrations from one of the signs which impart aggressiveness. The person who receives a predominating influence from this sign at birth is always extremely hesitant about converting others to his own way of thinking, which of course extends itself to anything he may attempt to sell. Since he will be the last person in the world to enforce payment of a debt, he is rarely suited for the role of bill-collector. His tendency is to believe everyone is as honest as he knows himself to be, and thus he may trust them to a greater extent than is justified. In this connection, he may often be taken advantage of in the matter of debts.

In selecting a field of employment, the Pisces native should look for a place that offers ample opportunity for advancement, since it is rare for him to make a change. He is most likely to succeed in a business or field wherein his trustworthiness, his capacity for work, his faithfulness and honesty will inevitably lead to the advancement he deserves. The true Pisces is not inclined to have an exaggerated idea of his own abilities. He is far more likely to underrate them, and to feel that he is receiving his just deserts when he is required to do voluminous amounts of detailed work. This is true even when a great deal of responsibility is thrust upon him and his financial compensation is small. In any position, the native of this sign is likely to fear that he is not measuring up to all that might be expected of him; and he often comes to believe that his work is unsatisfactory, despite its efficiency. The tendency toward *forebodings* of all kinds is a marked characteristic of this sign, and one who received a strong Pisces influence at birth can imagine obstacles, hindrances, and disasters for which there is absolutely no basis.

All *practical* business occupations are favorable for the Pisces native, particularly accounting and office management, or positions in which his faithfulness to duty and efficiency are received at their true worth. Whatever position he accepts, however, it is extremely necessary for the true native of Pisces to guard against mental anxiety and stress. He is never reluctant to take on burdens of work and these frequently produce a great deal of worry. He needs to learn, above all, how to direct and control his thought processes in order to achieve his most ambitious goals.

DISHARMONY OF PISCES

It has been said that natives of this sign have less robust physical equipment than do those who were born in most of the other signs. There is a tendency toward ill health or lack of vitality, but as in other conditions which are ordinarily referred to as disease, these invariably accompany powerful negatives in thought processes. The self-negation and anxiety to which the native of this sign is susceptible has its inevitable effects in the physical organism, consequently real effort to overcome these tendencies is necessary.

The sign is referred to as lymphatic, torpid, cold-blooded, and humid. The torpid nature of the sign is such as to produce considerable tendency toward softening of the tissues and is productive of mucous disturbances. The native, due to particular negatives in thought processes and in association with them, is especially susceptible to dropsy. Tumorous growths have a direct association with the watery, lymphatic, and plastic nature of the Pisces vibration in its negative phases. In certain of the negatives there is a tendency toward bowel troubles and particular susceptibility to contagious diseases. The use of drugs is especially unfavorable for the native of this sign, as is the use of intoxicating liquors – perhaps more so than for any other group.

The vibrations of the sign have a particularly close relationship to the feet. In its negative phases this sign tends toward deformed conditions of the feet. It induces callouses, bunions, corns, and all other manifestations of imperfection in those parts. Gout is indirectly a manifestation of Pisces negatives. When those negatives lead the native to overindulgence in rich foods the result through the Pisces vibration is likely to be that condition. The positive phases of Pisces produce quite agile and active feet and tend toward imparting an ability to dance.

The immediate relationship between negatives of the sign and disharmony in the physical organism manifest themselves in colds (contracted because of wet feet), resultant mucous discharges and all the conditions which naturally come about in association with colds. As a result of the feeling of inferiority and anxiety which is felt by the native of Pisces he is often extremely careless of his physical well-being. He does not take care to *avoid* catching colds and he exposes himself needlessly otherwise. All of these are manifestations of the powerful negatives which are inherent in the Pisces vibration.

It is absolutely impossible for disease organisms to invade any human body when the thought processes are sufficiently positive and balanced. Such a balancing of thought processes invariably is accompanied by an equal balance in glandular functioning. While the native of this sign is susceptible to the conditions as mentioned above, when the thought processes are brought to harmony – balanced glandular activity follows, and the native is immune to all of the conditions which are ordinarily referred to as disease. It is often quite difficult, however, for the native of this sign to overcome certain of his negatives in thinking which lead to disharmony in his physical organism. Certainly the Pisces native should make every effort to cultivate positives in habitual thought patterns. He should certainly employ the law of substitution, which means that he should constantly substitute thoughts of conditions he *wishes in his own life,* thereby *shutting out* the negatives of fear and worry.

1977 A wavering or speculative element is likely to come to the forefront, coloring both your home life or place of abode in connection with a distant spot. A journey as well as "a *means* of conveyance" will highlight this period. It is very likely that someone who speaks "a foreign language" or has come from such a place will be responsible for unorthodox situations or an "explosive" condition. Arguments or severances due to considerable difference of opinion will be apt to prove costly unless "you guard against" uttering even one careless word. This is the time for you to take "advantage" of "secret or confidential" information that might come your way. Even a secret telephone communication is shown as a strong likelihood of proving to be of enormous value, placing a certain "know-how" in your hands at the luckiest possible moment. I consider yours to be a good birthdate for "a turning point" that may place your life, for years to come, on a very solid foundation!

1978 When you would prefer to enjoy the assistance of another person, you are apt to find that it is necessary, now and then, to choose your own path in 1978. A changeful cycle is indicated in your outlook toward your security, temporarily. Someone will need your tender understanding, I am certain, but your circumstances will improve substantially as you center your life toward a particular goal and consider fleeting restraints your stepping stones to a more fulfilling future. Distant places are likely to offer pleasing opportunities, and your experiences probably will change some of your past attitudes. A "new tie" is indicated for you now, in my opinion. Your creations may earn praise this year.

1979 Sometimes you probably will feel that you could carry your plans through more successfully if people around you would offer greater cooperation in your efforts, but actually someone's restraining influence is apt to provide the helpful rein you can use. During this year of personal changes, a realistic approach will be imperative for you, I think, but people, devices, and contrivances that will assist you greatly will be close at hand, I know. As you earnestly endeavor to give your devoted service toward betterment in your world, you will earn ever-growing help from those around you, I am sure. Your explicit honesty in every undertaking will be your key to a door leading to your own fulfillment, in my opinion.

1980 The year ahead may stand out in your memory as one holding great achievement, but entirely because of the cooperation you gave to those who were closely associated with you. Your business associates as well as people with whom your home life is closely tied are indicated as being influences of protection, bringing welcome benefit. From the position of Saturn, I believe you may have an important decision facing you this year — I'd say a choice between "two" separate pathways, each one touching your income or "partnership" affairs. You might feel a need for a change of location because of a health problem or a desire for greater peace of mind. Hunches or dreams are apt to impress themselves deeply in your mind at unexpected times, for they are likely to be quite unusual. You will probably have to accede to the wishes of others during certain phases of this cycle, but later you can gain as a result of cooperating, far beyond any expectations you have now!

1981 This is a forecast period when your thoughts will frequently center upon the more serious aspects of the "here and hereafter," in my opinion. Because of present strong planetary influences, I believe it will be highly advisable to concentrate upon specific, long-range goals which should enable you to find inspiring answers to the "questions" you have had concerning your future course. Very unexpected new plans or pathways are indicated now, leading you toward an entirely different "philosophy of life" — a "turnabout" which may also bring surprising opportunities to travel or meet interesting people from faraway places.

1982 It appears that this cycle will be similar to a "spring housecleaning" where you will reorganize your concerns while discarding associations, ideas, or enterprises which once served important purposes in your life, but no longer have a helpful place with regard to your future accomplishments. You might have a tendency to cling to relationships (or undertakings) because you feel reliant upon them (or want them to rely upon you). The new positions of Saturn and Uranus indicate that it will be necessary to accept changes in complete faith of a better future. I am certain that even "strange happenings" will be stepping stones to major change, possibly touching your home life. I think a close tie or an attachment you have for a certain location, possession, or idea will have a restraining influence over you, for a short time.

1983 This is a year when the general pattern of your life will probably be marked by "complete changes," as though you had "wheeled around" in direction so that new people and new situations surround you. The sweeping away of past familiar ties as well as burdensome conditions is strongly indicated in connection with your "home life." I believe you are going to be "uprooted," so to speak, and there will be an "ending" to a path you have followed for some time, where possibly someone you consider important in your affairs (or several persons) was a strong factor in what you did or planned. I believe you will have surprising help or benefit from someone in a position to favor you who will be a loyal friend.

1984 The eclipse patterns, combined with new planetary positions, indicate to me that this will be a year of "new beginnings" for you. Opportunities for increasing your knowledge will abound, in my opinion, and whether you choose to further your learning along "formal lines" or more independently, I feel your "overall" understanding will grow into a deeper insight. You are likely to be in the mood for travel, although it would be advisable to take into account the possibility of unforeseen delays while doing so. This is a cycle of possible mishaps that can be averted by special care as you "come and go." Keeping a balanced frame of mind will be especially important to your happiness now, and I urge you to follow faithfully your highest principles, because I know this way will guide you toward betterment!

Ties with people who share bonds of affection with you are indicated as growing ever closer and deeper during the period covered by this forecast. As you look back upon this cycle in later years, I am sure your fondest memories will linger upon a "drawing together" which involves someone who has a special place in your heart! There will be frequent times, as this phase moves forward, when you clearly perceive a need to set aside some of your own interests and spend more time and effort helping other people. Although in one sense you will be sacrificing time and energy when assisting those who are close to you, I feel you will do so willingly, with a gratifying knowledge that you are "doing unto others as you would have them do unto you!"

Particularly during 1977 and the early months of 1978, being alert to your physical well-being will be of great importance. I interpret this period as a time when "overdoing," both mentally and physically, should be carefully watched so that you keep your efforts within reasonable limits and avoid excessive strain.

Unexpected opportunities to broaden your horizons are likely to offer pleasing and profitable experiences throughout this cycle. I think on several occasions you will find yourself absorbed in studying subjects which intrigue your interest quite suddenly. Far-off places or people at a distance are likely to attract your attention very strongly, and the prospects of travel will stimulate your desire to see "new faces and new sights." 1983 and 1984 will be marked by powerful planetary configurations that will lead you toward a completely different direction, in my opinion. Many of your "concepts of life" are apt to undergo dramatic revisions during this forecast period. I am certain you will emerge from these changes with a stronger grasp upon the "realities of life" as well as an advancement in your position!

In common with other people, those who were born in this cusp receive vibrations from a number of different signs, due to the presence of planets in them, but in addition the solar vibrations are divided between two separate signs. The two signs which are particularly important in this cusp, playing a part in the formation of character as well as in the development of destiny, are Pisces and Aries. The *"ruling"* planet of the former is Neptune, and of the latter, Mars. The two planets have a strong effect upon the lives of those who were born in this cusp. This particular combination of influences almost invariably produces a brilliant mind with some tendency on the part of natives to be too imaginative and at times quite unpredictable. Those who were born in this cusp have remarkably good foresight, however, although they do not always use it. They are extremely quick and usually skillful with their hands. This cusp combines two extremities, the head and the feet. It is considered to be a *favorable* combination of vibrations.

The native possesses considerable ability to understand human beings as well as practical problems with which he comes in contact. He has naturally strong mental capacities, but not infrequently some tendency to overwork his mental powers, due to the intensity of the Mars influence. As a result he may wear himself out needlessly. He can evolve brilliant projects and schemes of all kinds and he also has a natural ability to understand finance. His mind is likely to be constantly engaged in the working out of these plans or in devising new enterprises. He is quite fond of anything which is novel or new. He is particularly fitted for creative fields which combine necessity for appreciation of the artistic with practical application. He invariably has extremely powerful natural forces which he can call upon to aid him. In fact, these natural forces are irresistible when he has learned to clearly visualize his objectives in life and to hold his ambitions to a few things — and when he has gained ability to think constructively with *faith* that they will be realized. This enables him to work closely in harmony with these forces.

It is to be noted that while women born under this particular combination of solar influences become splendid wives and mothers, they frequently are more inclined toward the state of *single-blessedness*. It is to be particularly observed that people who come into the world under this combination of influences are extremely loyal in marriage, but they require a considerable degree of understanding on the part of their matrimonial partners. They are extremely sensitive and sometimes imaginative. They usually need to be occupied most of the time. The busier they are, the better. It remains for them only to bring out the constructive qualities they are given, to achieve almost any reasonably accessible and constructive goal. The native of this cusp is quite creative. At times his mind can be induced to produce ideas brilliantly. He may, however, experience difficulty in adjusting himself to the affairs of life and is sometimes disappointed in people and in conditions which he encounters. The true native has a good moral character, but is likely to be impulsive at times.

PREDICTIONS ABOUT OUR FUTURE

A few years ago a number of inscribed stones were discovered in Iraq, estimated to date from circa 1500 B.C. These relics were identified with the ancient Sumerian culture which flourished several thousands of years ago. One particular inscription caught my eye. Translated into modern language, it read: "There is nothing new under the sun!" So here were the words of a scholar or philosopher, speaking from the past of almost 3500 years ago, apparently sure in his belief that his civilization had reached a peak which encompassed total knowledge . . . in other words "there was nothing new to be discovered under the sun!"

For years I have at times thought about this provocative idea, going over in my mind all of the miraculous achievements mankind has made since 1500 B.C. And yet, there is a kernel of truth in these ancient words. Human nature is essentially the same as it was when man was created, I believe. In each of us there is the potential to be as great and to achieve as much as we can envision. Change is a vital part of all living creatures, indeed of Nature itself. The cells which comprise our skin renew themselves, or die and are replaced by new cells, so that every seven years we can said to be enclosed in entirely new skins! So it is with other parts of the body . . . each minute, each day momentous changes are going on within us, so that the intricate functioning of our being can meet and cope with the multitude of adjustments which make up our daily lives.

Planetary aspects recur with a frequency which can be and is calculated with mathematical accuracy. However, when a major planetary configuration comes into being, other planetary influences are different, so that a very long passage of time occurs before exact aspects return. For example, when Uranus and Saturn are in a square position to each other, as happens every 22 to 23 years, the other planets will occupy changed locations with respect to Uranus and Saturn. From these altered positions comes the change of influence which indicates what universal forces will be exerted.

My point in this discussion in that there is literally "always something new under the sun," and changes are always to be expected. During the years ahead, exceptionally powerful aspects are likely to be the harbingers of both immense changes in our physical world and a great out-reaching to new horizons in our mental outlook. I am absolutely certain that the next few years will be filled with astounding developments that will turn each of our minds toward exploring our "inner being" . . . the world of the mind and human spirit — the "mainspring" animating every thought or deed that has inspired mankind's noblest achievements since the dawn of time!

Neptune, representing spiritual forces, will remain in Sagittarius, the sign associated with truth and high aspirations, until 1984. I believe this influence will reinforce a religious revival that will lead countless millions to new paths in search of those eternal "truths" for which each of us hunger! There also will be "offshoots" that are likely to be manifested in strange or weird beliefs, embracing concepts quite violent in nature and in conflict with generally accepted religious "truth." Nevertheless, I feel this period will encourage a "swelling forth" in the minds and hearts of a great number of people that will encourage them to seek for fulfilling beliefs, bestowing meaning and substance to their lives.

Energy, especially the need for *new* sources of energy, will continue to spur the minds and efforts of scientists, researchers, and industrialists throughout this forecast period. There are likely to be unusual "breakthroughs" in areas related to liquid fuels, possibly in the nature of "recycling," which enable us to use existing supplies of oil with greater economy. In addition, Uranus in Scorpio until 1980 will undoubtedly influence a more diligent search for undiscovered sites containing oil in out-of-the-way parts of the world, particularly ocean beds.

Solar energy is strongly indicated as "coming into its own," as this cycle moves forward into the 1980's. Scientific studies have shown that the energy poured upon the Earth by the Sun in a *single day,* if convertible to use for power, heating, or cooling, would be sufficient to supply the needs of the world for thousands of years at present levels of consumption! I believe greater impetus will be given to research in this area, both from the use of government funds and from money for development from private sources. I do not think solar energy will completely replace other kinds of energy during this period, but tremendous strides will be made in its usage, in my opinion.

For at least one-half of the earth's population, a daily struggle for food is a grim matter of "life and death." Although I do not "see" an immediate alleviation of this overwhelming problem, I am certain significant improvements will be made in the area of developing plants for foodstuffs which are more disease-resistant and capable of surviving adverse weather conditions. In the 1890's, when Uranus was in Scorpio (as it now is until 1980), the noted plant geneticist, Luther Burbank, startled the world with numerous discoveries of improved plant life. I believe this cycle of Uranus through Scorpio also will be remembered as a time when vastly important experimentation and research led to the production of hardier plants and larger crop yields. New kinds of fertilizer are indicated as helping raise crop levels throughout the world.

We are entering an age when micro-computerization is likely to revolutionize certain areas of business, such as information storing or accessibility. By 1980, micro-computers will be commonplace in both large and small businesses as well as in many homes. The number of new satellites launched to speed the flow of information around the world is likely to increase, under this planetary influence. As a result, "tight-knit" communication between nations of the world should encourage both economic and political cooperation, especially in what is referred to as "Western civilization."

Our concept of entertainment may undergo radical change with the continued development of video discs or tapes. Large business concerns, notably RCA, Phillips, and MCA, are presently pouring immense funds into the improvement of these devices. They might be compared to phonograph recordings, because they are similar in the sense that a disc or tape is prepared for usage by the customer. However, the discs or tapes can be played through your television set, adding the visual to the aural. Manufacturers envision many varieties of discs or tapes, such as musical shows, plays, educational programs, or sports events, which will be sold much as phonograph records are now. Large "libraries" of these entertainments or educational material can be "built up" in the home, and it is likely that a rental service will be developed which makes available, at comparatively small cost, an enormous variety of subjects that appeal to almost any taste or interest. Particularly in areas of education,

I believe it will be possible to offer greatly enlarged programs which reach many who have the desire for new knowledge, but have previously lacked a convenient means for satisfying their longing.

Until energy problems move closer toward resolution, I believe during the next few years we will be "bombarded" by proposals from both government and industry to improve the way we use heating energy and gasoline. Some curtailments in this area are indicated, and we are likely to find restrictive burdens for larger cars as well as higher gasoline taxes. Some people will be "forced" to alter their practice of "coming and going," but I do not foresee actual hardships on a large scale. Nor do I believe sizable segments of our population will "freeze" in cold weather. However, for the time being, I think many of us will be forced into changes in accord with energy requirements or the availability of fuel.

Despite dire warnings, especially with respect to cancer, I feel that our reserachers and medical authorities will be able to uncover "secrets" of healing which will be in the nature of a new concept "born of old concepts!" In other words, it is my conviction that "rediscoveries" in the area of medicine and healing practices will open the way to undreamed-of improvements in the physical well-being of humankind. A powerful impetus will be given to research and new techniques that promote better health, while Uranus remains in Scorpio. In particular, surgical techniques could undergo unexpected developments in the years ahead.

A "happier home life" will be the goal of a great number of our citizens as this cycle continues. I know that this is a "wish" that is not confined to any particular time or area, but this is the kind of planetary influence which encourages one to "do something about it." I feel many people will seek unusual places to live, perhaps changing a lifetime pattern. The "sun-belt" — areas in the south, southeast, and southwest parts of our country — will have unusual appeal because of its climate. Already these areas have reported significant population growth, and I believe this trend not only will continue but also will be strengthened in the years to come. Locations which offer unusual features, such as natural beauty, cleaner air, or privacy, will have particular attraction as well, in my opinion.

RUSSIA — Startling, revolutionary changes are indicated as touching both the Soviet government and the lifestyle of people within this Communist land. The birth sign of Russia is represented as Scorpio, the sign through which the planet Uranus will be transiting until 1980. The last time this planet passed through Scorpio was in the 1890's — a period which saw the sudden rise of violent opposition to the then Tsarist empire. Political assassinations on the part of Anarchists as well as the surge of Bolshevik opposition troubled the imperial government during that cycle of Uranus.

Although we have not heard of political assassinations, in the last few years dissidents who spoke out for greater freedom in Russia were harassed, exiled, and imprisoned. Nevertheless, Soviet policy seems unable to crush the dissenters, particularly among the so-called "intelligentsia," notably writers and some scientists. I attribute this unsettling influence in part to the forceful passage of Uranus through Scorpio, awakening an impulse for greater freedom and desire to live with more individual rights among the Russian people. I feel dissatisfaction with the "regime" will intensify during the next three years.

In 1974 I wrote: " . . . the Russians appear headed toward capitalistic thinking." I repeat these words, and believe the world will hear more and more of attempts by prominent Russians to force their government to concentrate greater effort upon satisfying "consumer" needs of the people in this Communist land.

Also in 1974 I said: "Nations within the Soviet bloc will increasingly be desirous of breaking away from Russia's dominance, bringing the need for 'electrical' decisions." Between 1977 and 1981, I estimate that allies or "partners" will loosen the grip which binds them to the Soviet Union, sometimes in an "explosive" manner.

Relations between China and Russia are in the nature of an "uneasy truce," in my opinion. In 1977, indications point to a "confrontation" or time of critical disagreement between these giants of the Communist doctrine. In 1955, I stated: " . . . Someday Russia will have to fight a 'two-front war' — a war at her front door and another at her back door." I have not changed my prediction in the twenty some years that have followed these words, because powerful planetary influences that are long-range in nature still point to this outcome.

CHINA — Armed violence and a power struggle followed the death of Mao Tse-Tung in the summer of 1976. I believe there will continue to be resistance to the new Premier, Hua Kuo-feng, in the next year, although he seems to have a firm grasp upon the government. After 1980 I interpret the planetary influences touching China's birthchart as indicating that a somewhat more settled period, politically speaking, will begin. However, "high-minded reforms" are likely to be set in motion during the years following 1980. From the changes initiated I anticipate a "new" China is apt to emerge, with programs which have a strong appeal to other Asiatic nations.

AFRICA — A period of turmoil, political change, and restlessness is likely to characterize the future of many of the new nations of the "Dark Continent." Particularly in Rhodesia and South Africa, I feel there will be strong forces at work to change the racial policies of these nations. Violence in the streets will probably continue in South Africa as it has in the past few months. I see no easy settlement of the thorny problems besetting both Rhodesia and South Africa which are presently (spring of 1977) ruled by white minorities. Within the next year to two years, Uganda is likely to undergo a change of leadership with Idi Amin falling from power.

FRANCE — In late 1977 or 1978 a dramatic "change of purpose" could turn France and her government in a different direction. There are strong indications a "shaky" economy will hold serious threat for the present ruling party of France.

THE MIDDLE EAST — There is a tiny glimmer of "light" which may eventually lead to temporary easing in the tensions that have long plagued this troubled area of the world. I do not expect peaceful solutions, although there is a likelihood that for the first time Egypt and Israel will sit down together at a conference table, probably in late 1977 or 1978. However, this area presents such "impossible problems" that it will be long time, if ever, before threatening conflicts are resolved, in my opinion.

DRAMATIC WORLD PREDICTIONS RECENTLY FULFILLED

Editor's Note: Those friends of Miss Carter who have utilized her services in the past have been amazed over a period of many years by the uncanny accuracy of her predictions of coming world events. These predictions have been published, and copies of them as well as their verification through the public prints are on file. For her new friends, who may be reading her words for the first time, we list below, with dates, some of her predictions and verifications!

In 1975, over a year before the presidential elections, Miss Carter wrote: *". . . I am strongly of the opinion that Mr. Ford will turn out to be a short-term President."* Despite the overwhelming advantage that being an incumbent President insures, on November 2, 1976, President Ford went down to defeat at the polls!

In the summer of 1976, three months before the election, when President Ford seemed to be gaining in popularity, she stated and published in the Financial Forecast: *"Mr. Carter has the 'edge' over his Republican opponent to achieve victory at the polls this November. There are strong indications that this election will not be a 'runaway' win for Mr. Carter."* President Carter won the election by one of the narrowest margin of votes ever recorded.

At a time when China seemed firmly under control by the Communist Party, Miss Carter said in 1975: *"This period may witness an outburst of 'warlike' anger with strong repercussions . . . "* On September 8, 1976, headlines in the Communist Party's Paper acknowledged "armed conflict in China, unleashed by a power struggle to succeed the deceased Chairman Mao Tse-Tung."

On several occasions, President Ford stated categorically that money of the Federal Government would not be used to "bail out" the financial crisis of New York City. Miss Carter in 1975, however, took a different view when she said: *"Despite denials by the Administration, I believe New York City will not be allowed to become 'bankrupt.' Moves will be made to assure creditors and banks holding New York City bonds that they will not suffer loss through default."* Less than three months later, newspaper headlines disclosed "Check Written for Needy N. Y." The Federal Government's first check to help stave off bankruptcy had been sent to the city!

On September 23, 1975, in Miss Carter's Financial Forecast, at a time when many leaders of other countries might have been chosen for predictions, the head of India's government, Mme. Indira Ghandi, was selected as the one to dramatically make her exit. The following prediction was written when Mme. Ghandi's downfall appeared impossible, due to her strong grasp on the reins of Indian government: *"I believe her (Indira Ghandi) birth position of Saturn indicates she may be 'out of power' abruptly in the coming year to two years. Her position of Saturn takes the individual to the top and then tends to sweep everything away."* On March 21, 1977, Prime Minister Indira Ghandi was decisively beaten in the election and the next day resigned as leader of the government.

*A TREMENDOUS IMPRESSION MADE
WHEN THIS REMARKABLE PREDICTION
BY MARGUERITE CARTER
CAME ABOUT IN SUCH A STARTLING WAY*

The Times Herald   *Dallas*

— FRIDAY, JUNE 22, 1945 —

Stars Foretell

Astrologer Sees Early Jap Defeat

Turkey came into the war early this year. A few months later Germany surrendered, V-E Day was declared—and up went another chalk mark on the horoscope record for Marguerite Carter, astrologist.

Miss Carter, who has just returned to Dallas for her annual engagement at Titche-Goettinger Company where during the coming two weeks she will give horoscope readings on the first floor, brought with her a clipping from The Times Herald's files of 1939. It quotes this prediction from her writings for the Amalgamated Press in England in 1939:

"England, France, Germany and Russia will engage in a great war. Germany will defeat France, then turn her back to fight, and when she does, England will come through the northern part and defeat Germany. There's one way to time the ending, and that is when Turkey enters the war it will be over in a few months."

Miss Carter's 1944 predictions, while here last year, came through to maintain her high batting average. Roosevelt, for example, was re-elected and the subsequent "change in the White House" is naturally interpreted as his succession by Truman.

Truman's Future.

As for the new president, Miss Carter has consulted her charts and vouchsafes the opinion that the advice of others and the opinion of others will have a far more important role in the administration than in that of Roosevelt, and upon them will rest his success or failure.

She sees an early end for the war in the Pacific, predicting that Japan will give up before some of the men being transferred to that combat zone have reached it. In this she reiterates last year's prediction that Hitler and Hirohito will go down almost together, since they both are under the same astrological influences.

After the war, Miss Carter believes this country's greatest problems will be food, labor and intolerance, and the world's attention for a long time will be focused on the Far East—Persia, India, China. On the home front a short period of adjustment will be followed by a gold rush to manufacturing and the launching of many small businesses by returning servicemen who want to be their own bosses.

"There will be both good and bad influences but out of it all will come a revitalized religion, a new understanding of religion in a broader sense, brought into being by its blending with science," she said.

174

ASTROLOGY TODAY

I feel these writings would be incomplete if I failed to point out some of the most recent discoveries by our scientific researchers, which show beyond question the effect the Moon and Sun have, not only upon the Earth, but on living creatures as well.

One of the most dramatic proofs of the Moon's influence can be witnessed at the Bay of Fundy in Nova Scotia, where the tidal bore, *advancing against the natural flow,* reaches heights of 46½ feet due to the Moon's gravitational pull at certain periods. Precise measurements made over a long period of years have shown a *direct relationship* between the Moon-Sun influence and tides all over the world. In fact, not only are bodies of water affected by the Moon-Sun, but "Earth tides" have been measured in the very crust of the Earth, as well.

How are living organisms affected? Biologists have shown in recent years that energy variations in various organisms as well as changes in the electro-magnetic field occur *in harmony* with Moon-Sun cycles. These proofs have come through carefully controlled laboratory experiments, as well as through direct *observation* and *calculation.* For example, oysters shipped from Connecticut to a laboratory in Illinois responded to the Moon's cycle occurring in Connecticut for two weeks, by opening and closing their shells. After two weeks, they gradually adapted to the Moon's pull in *Illinois.* The potato has been shown to alter its metabolic rate from the lowest point (under the New Moon), to the highest point (under the Third Quarter) -- and, in addition, predicts barometric changes two days in advance!

The Grunion (a small fish found in California) cast themselves on the beaches at predictable times of high tide to bury their eggs, which are in turn swept back to sea as "fingerlings" by the next *high,* high tide. During a predictable hour in October and November the Palolo worm's posterior breaks off, filled with reproductive cells, and at this time reproduction takes place. Samoan natives time their particular expeditions by the Moon for gathering these bits of anatomy, which they consider quite a delicacy.

Dr. Frank A. Brown, Jr., who conducted two of the experiments mentioned (among many others along the same line) has stated: *"It has become increasingly evident in recent years that all living organisms are ryhthmic systems."* Dr. Leonard J. Ravitz has written: "...despite profound differences that exist between human beings, longitudinal field studies revealed periodicities similar to those which had been found in other forms of life." Rene Dubos of the Rockefeller Institue says: "However primitive, *all cells perceive cosmic forces and respond to them through mechanisms which are not yet understood."* (Italics are mine)

The findings are far too many to list; but more and more the teachings of scholars over thousands of years, that the effects of the Sun and Moon on life here on this whirling body we call Earth, result in "rhythm attunement", are being proved by *our modern-day scientists.*

I cannot doubt the truth of the ancient teachings, in the face of such evidence!

Alan R. McConnell

STELLARUM
INERRANTIUM
CATALOGUS BRITANNICUS,
Ad Annum Chrifti Completum, 1689.
Ab Obfervationibus GRENOVICI in OBSERVATORIO Regio habitis.
Affiduis Vigilijs, Cura, & Studio
JOHANNIS FLAMSTEEDII, Aftronom. Reg.
Deductus & Supputatus.

GREAT MEN OF HISTORY

Have Upheld Astrology!

Alan Carter once wrote: "...*All* are PART of ONE!" He said that this "one-ness" which he emphasizes in Unitology exists because there is a *single* source, a FIRST CAUSE, of all that has happened! Known by many names including that of God, this First Cause set in motion the chain of events that never ceases — the very *continuity* of life. "This sublime metaphysical truth," wrote Mr. Carter, "has been illustrated by mystics of all ages, in many different languages and in numberless ways. It is a broad but changeless law."

Viewed from one point, Unitology is the ancient science of astrology *extended to* and *based upon* this ONENESS of all. It teaches that while the universe and our world were "originated", in one sense they are STILL being *created!* Only man, on this plane of being, has the freedom to *choose direction,* and to participate in creation. To arrive where we are today, at this particular point of awareness and knowledge, great men have worked through the study of planetary influences upon human life, *knowing* that everyone is influenced — "impelled" — along certain paths. Thus it has been and thus it always shall be!

As Professor Don Cameron Allen stated, in *The Star-Crossed Renaissance* (1941), "My inference now is that everybody who lived during the Renaissance believed to some extent in astrology." He could also have said that in *all* civilized ages, there have been countless thinking people who believed in the significance of astrology; for civilization has traveled hand-in-hand *with astrology's development*. Indeed, at times the burden of human advancement was borne by men who were authorities on planetary influences. The term "astronomy" reaches to antiquity; but, until the 15th Century, it dealt specifically with what has *become known* as *astrology*. Prior to that time, astronomy as it is NOW used -- as an investigation into the orbits, motions, distances or physical construction of celestial bodies -- was an auxiliary part of the primary analysis of planets' *influence*. Therefore, when you see the word "astronomy" alluding to *pre*-15th Century endeavors, use the word "astrology" in your mind; they were *referring to astrology*! It is helpful to remember another comment by Prof. Allen: "...The defenders of astrology were *not* ignorant and superstitious men. Some of the *greatest scientific minds*...believed in the art of the stars. As we look over these books, we notice to our amazement what *intelligent* writers most of the *astrologers* are; on the other hand, we are only too often confronted with an *anti*-astrologer who is both ignorant and dull" (italics supplied).

In the 700 years before Christ, we find the earliest *established* records of man's great studies: philosophy, mathematics, physics, medicine -- and *astrology*. (To locate the ORIGIN of these subjects, one might have to go beyond the ancient Babylonians.) In Greece, this was a humanistic period; a goal was *improvement* of man's lot. Hence, the high esteem in which astrology was held. Hippocrates, "father" of medicine, wrote: "A physician without a knowledge of Astrology has no right to call himself a physician." This golden Age was remarkable for the *coordination* or *organization* of *data*. It was an age of "lampposts", of brilliant lights in the wilderness; a time when a small number of amazing men began to LIFT mankind -- and carry it forward.

Pythagoras, responsible for the harmonic progression of the musical scale, studied under the astounding Thales. Thales (of Miletus, one of the prosperous cities of Greece) was a merchant who used astrology (it is recorded) to *corner* the olive market, retired early, and began to work on other intriguing matters, particularly mathematics. He contributed to logical reasoning and geometry. Called one of the 7 Wise Men, he used his study of Babylonian astrology to predict a sun eclipse -- in 585 B.C.! Thales' reasoning led to the development of many mathematical concepts; without his kind of logic, it is said that we would not have mathematics today -- nor calendars, cartography, meteorology, architecture, or electronics. Thales, the teacher of Pythagoras (who gave us the TERM "mathematics", as well as "parabole", "ellipsis" and "hyperbole") was an *astrologer*! And Pythagoras was probably the first to theorize that the earth was not square or rounded but spherical.

During the Golden Age, Democritus (with his pupils) developed a theory of small invisible units or "building blocks", called -- *atoms*! This was approximately 2400 years before the Atomic Age. Democritus spent many years of study in the *east,* unquestionably encountering *astrological instruction*! He also is said to have *predicted exact dates* of earthquakes and correctly theorized that there were planets *beyond* Saturn. (In 1963, Nobel prize-winning genetics expert George W. Beadle was to state that we now know the principle by which ALL elements may evolve from *one* "primordial universe" of hydrogen! "All," said Alan Carter earlier, "are PART OF ONE!")

Ptolemy, the astrologer, presented (in the first two decades after the birth of Christ) an explanation of mathematics which was a *device* (of epicycles) by which it was possible to calculate planetary positions in the solar system. It has proved to compare favorably with modern findings. He also developed trigonometry to a higher state. His life proves, again, the *universality* of astrology and, in a time of limited communication as well as transportation, the continuity and "range" of astrology in providing knowledge for advancement. Ptolemy corrected Hipparchus' catalogue of fixed stars and formed tables for the regulation and calculation of the sun's and moon's motions. His system was accepted by all centers of learning throughout Europe for twelve-hundred years. In his *Tetrabiblos,* Ptolemy discussed the influence of stars, saying: "A mind apt in knowledge will discover truth more readily than one practised in the highest branches of science.....A skilful person, acquainted with the nature of the stars, is enabled to avert many of their effects, and to prepare himself for those effects before they arrive." Keep in mind that the astonishing Ptolemy was an *astrologer* -- of over 1,900 years ago!

Between 340-350 A.D., one of the first attempts to *unite* the Christian religion with other factions was made by Julius Firmicus Maternus, born in Sicily and of senatorial rank. At the request of a friend, Maternus wrote the *Mathesis* in which he insisted that there was *one* supreme deity who acted as "the rector" of the planets and "who composed all things by the arrangement of everlasting law", making man, the microcosm, from the four elements. In this early work, Maternus expressed an *astrologer's prayer* which stated, in part, "Thee with trembling supplication we venerate; grant us grace to attempt the explanation of the courses of thy stars; *thine* is the power that somehow impels us to that interpretation. With a mind pure and separated from all earthly thoughts and purged from every stain of sin we have written these books for thy Romans." It is not unreasonable to assume that Maternus, who in these pages declared that those who have not tested astrology are *unfit* to pass upon its merit, and who admitted to casting horoscopes with successful predictions based on them, was *also* an ASTROLOGER!

Tycho Brahe (1546?-1601) contributed major improvements to "astronomical" instruments. He added greatly to the knowledge of the stars and the solar system through observation. At left, you see one of the two observatories where Tycho taught, in Hveen, an island off the southwest coast of Sweden. Uraniborg (pictured) was the prototype of modern observatories. It is seldom said of the Dane that he was, first and foremost, an *astrologer:* "The stars," said he, "rule the lot of man."

You may well have studied Albertus Magnus in school; he still is revered for the *universality* of his knowledge: he was a scientist, philosopher, theologian — and *astrologer!* He taught, also, and his greatest pupil became St. Thomas Aquinas, who shared his teacher's appreciation of astrology to the extent of writing, later: "The celestial bodies are the cause of all that takes place in this sublunar world."

Johann Kepler (1571-1630) is one who will live forever in the annals of science. His work, in effect, paved the way for the work of modern astronauts; for Kepler succeeded in establishing the *size* of orbits and their speeds. Through Kepler, Newton's physics had a foundation and Copernicus' ideas were retained, not discarded entirely. Kepler may be regarded as the father of modern astronomy, for he turned men's eyes once again to the stars. Harassed by ill health and poverty, Kepler courageously continued his lonely investigations and found the actual orbit in which Mars travels through space -- a problem which had evaded Eudoxus, Tycho, the Alexandrian astrologers and every earlier thinker! He wrote: "An unfailing experience of mundane events in harmony with the changes occurring in the heavens, has instructed and compelled my unwilling belief."

Since the time of Kepler, astronomy has leapt forward; yet *astrology* has continued to engage the attention of "the great". John Donne (1572-1631), who spoke of "for whom the bell tolls", penned poetry replete with references to astrology. In 1603, Sir Christopher Heydon penned his *Defence of Judiciall Astrologie*. Sir Walter Raleigh, too, bowed to planetary influences in his *History of the World* (1614). Earlier, Roger Bacon -- philosopher, scientist, educational reformer -- is considered to have been an *astrologer*. Sir Francis Bacon (1561-1626), essayist and philosopher, has been called the father of *modern science*. He vigorously disputed certain tenets of astrology but, in *De Augmentis Scientiarum,* wrote: "But for my part I admit astrology as a part of Physic ..." and urged various improvements which he claimed would enable man accurately to predict acts of nature, variations in health, revolutions and wars. Said Sir Francis: "The natures and dispositions of men are, not without truth, distinguished from the predominances of the planets."

Another great Englishman, John Flamsteed (1646-1719), classmate of Sir Isaac Newton at Cambridge, used *astrological data* in his work -- which became very helpful to Newton (according to the best available evidence). Flamsteed was appointed Royal "astronomical observator" in 1675. His published observations contained the first Greenwich star catalogue (shown at the start of this section).

When Sir Isaac himself (1642-1727) was asked what he desired to study at Cambridge, he is said to have replied: "Mathematics -- because I wish to test Judicial

Astrology.'' Here was a priceless scientific mind. At 23, he asked questions few people had dared consider. Since he lacked a mathematics needed for the type of calculations he wished to make, Newton devised his own system of differential and integral calcu-

lus! He found that the moon, sun and earth can be treated as *points* in space. He defined inertia, mass, force; established the laws of motion; and is credited with developing physics to a *pure* science. He explained the puzzle of tides and comets. And there is ground to believe that never in his 84 years did Sir Isaac abandon *his interest in astrology*!

When we go forward to our times, we find that similar concepts to those which, throughout history, have been held by great creative thinkers in support of planetary influences, *continue*. Here lies the essential *"oneness"* of ALL, the chain of circumstances reaching from FIRST Cause!

John Hays Hammond, Jr., born in 1888, devised a system of radio control of ships, selective radiotelegraphy, a torpedo for coastal defense. A remarkable inventor, Hammond married an astrologer; he studied astrology himself, regarding it as one of the ''vital'' subjects.

J. H. Nelson, R.C.A. engineer, one decade ago searched for the cause of magnetic storms. He found that planets disturb the sun, that the sun disturbs electrical conditions of the earth's atmosphere. R.C.A. *admitted* that they *successfully predicted* radio reception with 93% accuracy -- by the study of PLANETARY MOTIONS! Dr. Robert O. Bates, a surgeon, mapped out the human electro-magnetic field, incidentally indicating that the fluctuations (to which organic things react) *synchronize* with the positions of the Sun, and planets, and phases of the Moon! The president of Tensitron, Inc., Dr. Erwin J. Saxl, theorized in April 1964 that ''G'' (gravitational constant), felt to be an *unchanging* value in the universe, VARIES. *What* does it vary *with*? Seemingly, with eclipses, geo-magnetic alterations, and planetary conjunctions. Dr. Saxl believed that magnetism, electricity, gravitation and inertial mass are therefore *related*!

Recent research by Dr. F. A. Brown of Northwestern University revealed that while succeeding in measuring metabolism in animals and plants (among them, potato plants), he found that the metabolism varies with the LUNAR cycle, being *highest* at the *full moon*! Under scientifically-controlled conditions, eliminating all local influences, the variations *continued* to *correspond* with the lunar cycle! Dr. Brown declared that there was ''incontrovertible evidence'' that ''there is a cyclic *information* in the form of radiation'' which *''impresses all living things corresponding to atmospheric and lunar periodicity.''* (Italics supplied) Thus, dear friend, do our greatest FREE MINDS *continue* to establish the verity of the ancients — and of *astrology,* itself!

HISTORICAL HIGHLIGHTS OF ASTROLOGY!

This page is VISUAL proof of the world-wide respect held for the belief that the stars influence our lives and to point out the dignified position astrology held—the dramatic part it has played from the earliest period in history to our present day!

The great universities in Europe taught astrology—the courts of justice were guided by it. Here is a picture of the Zodiac clock in the world-famous Hall of Justice in Venice, Italy. Originally the jury of twelve men for a trial were carefully selected, *one from each of the twelve signs of the Zodiac.* Thus a "fair and just" decision could be reached. Today, we *still* have twelve jurors!

This mysterious city in the clouds is a centuries old ruin of the Inca civilization, high in the Andes Mountains of Peru. Miss Carter considers this one of her favorite areas of research into knowledge of the ancients. Not only a place of breath-taking beauty, it contained astonishing evidence of high engineering achievement and a great degree of astronomical knowledge!

The faint traces of these people still intrigue and puzzle archaeologists. One of the most baffling of all the bits of evidence is the huge figures, covering square miles, marked on the ground that only become legible when viewed from a plane at an altitude of several thousand feet. Who was intended to view these massive representations?

From the halls of highest learning in Europe we travel back across the ocean to the land of the Mayans who lived in Yucatan before the time of Christ, and WHO BELIEVED IN ASTROLOGY. THEIR CALENDAR IS THE EQUAL OF OURS IN ACCURACY. Here is one of the world's great archeologists, Senor Alberto Ruz, whose recent discovery of A MAYAN KING-PRIEST'S TOMB is considered as important as the finding of King Tut's burial place. Senor Ruz (at the left) has received world-wide acclaim and his discoveries have been taken to Europe for all the world to view!

Stonehenge, in England, has been the object of much conjecture for centuries. The origin and purpose of its varying sized stones, arranged in circular patterns have intrigued scientific minds. Modern apparatus was used to analyze various artifacts and establish the time of its building at 1,800 to 2,000 B.C.

The architectural refinements and extreme accuracy of placement are unequalled in prehistoric northern Europe. The gigantic size of some of these stones is illustrated by Miss Carter's figure at left of photo.

Recently, the plotted positions of still standing stones and astronomical data were fed into a computer and the result proved that Stonehenge itself is a computer—a computer that can accurately predict the positions of the sun, moon and eclipses up to 300 years in advance!

Great Minds Throughout Recorded History Have Used ASTROLOGY

When you visit St. Peter's Cathedral in Rome where a zodiac is imbedded just outside of the entrance you are overwhelmed by the beauty left by the master hand of Michelangelo, the painter. The very year which closed the curtain upon this great man and marked his passing, strangely brought another genius into the world, Galileo—the year 1564.

It was at the Leaning Tower of Pisa that Galileo sought to prove to a large gathering of doubters that any object would fall at the same rate of speed regardless of its weight. Previously it had been taught that if a 10 lb. weight were dropped from a certain height it would fall 10 times as fast as a 1 lb. weight — and to even *question* such a teaching was heresy! On the appointed day the crowd gathered, old college professors and young students. The crowd jeered as Galileo lifted a 100 lb. weight and a 1 lb. weight and dropped them from the top of this famous tower. They plunged to earth *together* and in spite of the proof they had witnessed of Galileo's theory, the university professors declared — "Galileo is wrong" — and refused to accept a new concept even though it has been proved correct. He believed in Astrology!

The same fact emerges from investigation of all the great civilizations. As soon as man learned to employ his tools and mind in calculation, his attention turned to the heavens. Invariably, evidence of highly complex and advanced forms of Astrology, dating back many centuries, are found. Examples from China date back to the fifth century B. C.

At the edge of China's bamboo curtain lies Hong Kong. Here, side by side, stand the ultra-modern and ancient structures in which the beliefs and rituals of antiquity are still carried on. Miss Carter was privileged to be the first American to visit the Castle Peak Buddhist Temple where the centuries old religious rites remain untouched by the outside world. The Priest, pictured with Miss Carter, had not been beyond the Temple walls in twenty years!

Marguerite and Alan Carter having breakfast outside their hotel in northern Italy preparing to leave for Vienna, Austria, behind the iron curtain, after receiving their gray permit cards. At this time people were disappearing constantly never to be heard from again in this unprotected territory — but Marguerite Carter believed in a safe return!

How many tourists have fed the pigeons before St. Mark's in Venice just as Marguerite Carter is doing and loved it! But few know that Casanova made his escape over the adjoining roof and down these walls. Here astrology played a major role, as it did in Rome where under the very wisest rulers the finest universities taught astrology, as a subject of first importance — while closeby, the city of Florence, Italy, maintained a city astrologer very much like our health officers today!

CONCLUSION

The science which deals with cosmic influences upon human affairs and which has been known during the ages as Astrology, is traceable in its practice throughout the recorded history of mankind. All civilizations of which we have any record used it but some were, of course, more skilled and possessed a higher knowledge of its implications than did others.

It is perhaps well to state at this point that while the material herein contained is partially based upon astrological textbooks of long ago, it is not to be considered *solely* as Astrology, for the reason that the factors which deal with *higher spiritual meanings* are a quite *definite* part. The subject is not dealt with as a wholly material science and the foretelling of future events is considered only in the light of a knowledge of human negatives and the manner in which individuals as well as nations and races fail to harmonize with the *constructive* laws of nature — or divine law.

In order to avoid needless and boring repetition throughout the text, of the fact that much of the material relating to planetary influence is unproved from a wholly scientific standpoint, the statements made concerning birthsigns are of definite form and made as being conclusively and unchangeably so. Those statements are based upon many years of experience as well as upon wide research in the lore of the ancients. They are subject to change however as *no* human knowledge is complete or expressive of ultimate truth in fullest degree.

Each person, according to every student of the subject, combines the qualities of many basic birth vibrations, or birthsigns, in varying degrees. It has been the experience of the authors, however, that at least eight people out of every ten have so many of the characteristics of their birthsigns that there is no mistaking the fact. It is our belief that the cultured intellects of the past who have occupied themselves with the subject were, as individuals, aware of the higher spiritual meanings, and in the majority of cases did not regard Astrology as a wholly material science.

Dealing with the birthsign alone can never be completely scientific for the reason that there are many modifying or altering factors in the birth chart of an individual as well as fine shades of meaning which play a part in the life of that individual as he treads the path of living. There are no doubts in our minds that the vibrations as the planets move have a part in the formation of human character and it does, on the other hand appear that the order of the universe is so complex yet so perfect in its functioning that every living thing enters this plane of vibration which we call life, at exactly the time allotted, not a moment before nor after. It is further our opinion that cosmic influences at that moment actually, in minutest detail, express that individual, and that the universe in which one comes to *live* is actually a reflection of the individual, rather than the opposite.

It is an incontrovertible and startling fact that in all the civilizations of the world, including our own, the subject of planetary influence upon mundane affairs was almost never used or accepted by the *ignorant*, excepting in the form of a "mulligan stew" of superstition, bearing no real relation to its truths, as well as general misinformation about the subject, which led those who might be termed *skeptics* to scorn it. On the contrary it has, during the course of every civilization which developed a relatively high intellectual state, been a cultural background of the most outstanding intelligence which arose in that particular civilization. There is completely conclusive evidence of this. There is much to indicate that the Chaldeans had records of planetary movements or of the "stars" for a period of nearly 400,000 years.

It may be surprising to those who tend to regard "astrologers" and those who read material relating to the subject as either charlatans or ignorantly superstitious, to learn that a very large proportion of those who have been outstanding in world history as intellectuals in every field, were either avowed astrologers or earnest students of the subject. Among them were such greats as Ptolemy, Pliny, Aristotle, Hippocrates — the father of medicine, Vitruvius — the great architect, Virgil, Galileo, Goethe, Genghis Khan, Kepler, Byron, Flamsteed — the founder of the Greenwich Observatory, Pope Leo X, as well as many other popes, Sir Isaac Newton, Julius Caesar, Copernicus, George Washington, Benjamin Franklin (Poor Richard's Almanac), Tycho Brahe, and many others of like calibre. There is conclusive evidence that a considerable number of those who had a hand in drafting the Declaration of Independence were possessed of much knowledge relating to the subject. Astrological books in the Library of Congress which have written notations on the margins, made by the men of this period, attest the fact.

It has been stated by authorities that no race of the long dead past rose to a high level of civilization without having developed a belief in this science as well as methods for its use. It was used among the most cultured of the Greeks, Romans, Chinese, Egyptians, Chaldeans, the Toltecs and the Mayas, as well as others. The Mayas had developed their calendar over five thousand years ago. It was, according to to reliable researchers, possible for them to tabulate and identify any specific day in 370,000 years. They worshipped one god as the creator of all things. There is conclusive evidence that instead of being accepted by the ignorantly superstitious, or on the other hand used by practitioners who without real knowledge or a sincere desire to attain it, had the desire to play upon the fears of the credulous, not a few of the ancient civilizations had a greater knowledge of planetary movements than we ourselves do — or certainly more than we had until quite recently.

There is much evidence to support the claim that the Babylonians kept the nativities of all children born in that country for thousands of years and used the evidence thus obtained in arriving at scientific deductions. Al Hakim, a Persian, was one of the earliest known astrologers and philosophers. He predicted astrologically the birth of Christ as well as the fact that Mohammed would be born. All of this is by way of stating that we would do well to gain a more completely scientific knowledge related to the functioning of cosmic forces in order that we may perhaps come more clearly to understand, as intelligent beings, the requirements for successful and happy lives. The one thing that any human being should bear in mind is that no matter how trying, how discouraging, or how unpromising his life may be at a given moment it is but a CYCLE which WILL PASS and that there will be IMPROVEMENT unless he allows his mind to be unchangeably grooved with the pattern of hopelessness.

The startling predictions and unique writings are the culmination of many years devoted to research and study by this fascinating woman. In the '30's, she had already attracted a large following across the country with lectures to packed houses in most of our major cities. In the '40's, her fame grew as her writings appeared in the nation's leading newspapers as well as Canada and England. Her astrological counseling included "the greats" in the entertainment world, business and government leaders. Before our entry in the war, Miss Carter's predictions concerning Italy's course in the War, Russia's role in Germany's downfall and Hitler's suicide were on the front page of The Tulsa Daily World. In the 1950's, she made trips to many points of the globe to study the knowledge of the ancient scholars and the true meaning of Astrology. It held a most important part in the earliest civilizations as well as the centers of culture and learning in the old capitals of Europe! The extraordinary background and experience in personal counseling reveal themselves in the writings of this woman. The warm sincerity, thoroughness and straightforward manner in which the problems of the individual are approached have brought letters of gratitude from people in every walk of life. Many thousands have found the **guidance** they need in her Forecast with Special Notations!

The Unitology Forecast

Thousands of people have found their own Forecast a constant source of help, inspiration and guidance—the guidance you will find in Miss Carter's Forecast with her Special Notations for the year ahead. You'll find "the key" to a better understanding of your personal life, relations with others, the path to happiness and success. TEST HER. Send for Miss Carter's Forecast with Special Notations showing outstanding indications covering your financial outlook, changes indicated, etc., for a full year! Make the next twelve months the most rewarding of your life. Send $4.75 for your FORECAST plus 25¢ toward mailing costs, with your birthdate; month, date, year, place and hour of birth (if known). Each Forecast is individually assembled based on birthdate information. Please allow 3 weeks for receipt of Miss Carter's Unitology Forecast.

Price _____$5.95

(Plus 50c mailing cost)

There IS a Shortcut to Success!

Not just a theory, not wishful thinking, but a practical, tested and proven method. Would you follow simple instructions which would actually change your life and turn it toward the fondest desires of your heart? You can! And, Marguerite Carter will show you every step of the way in her book "There IS a Shortcut to Success!"

She will demonstrate to you that success—in romance, social, home life, friendship, wealth and business can be yours. Over thirty-five years of personal contact, counseling and case studies of thousands of men and women all over the world are responsible for the development of this formula. Now, these experiences and discoveries are given to you in one easy-to-understand plan. For those who will follow these instructions honestly, it will be a living magic with unbelievable rewards!

Price each copy _____$3.25

(Plus 40c mailing cost)

"The Greatest Five Years of Your Life"

Her writings in books, magazines and newspapers, both here and abroad, have made Marguerite Carter an internationally known authority. A lifetime of research and study has drawn her to the remote corners of the globe and brought to light the intriguing information in this wonderful book.

THE GREATEST FIVE YEARS OF YOUR LIFE discusses thoroughly the characteristics of your birthsign, those of family and friends—in fact, everyone you know. Miss Carter gives predictions for each five years. Changes are described, new opportunities, employment, income, home affairs and they are startling in their accuracy. In addition to the description of every birth period and five years of predictions each, you will find: a history of Astrology that brings to light little-known facts from the past—explanations of cycles, birthsigns, cusps—method of self-help and an abundance of illustrations, many in color!

This amazing Forecast, assembled in book form, will provide you the rare opportunity of better understanding of your life as well as the ability to more fully comprehend others. You will find it the most helpful guidance you have ever known. A beautiful and lasting gift for a friend or member of your family.

Price each copy _____$5.95

(Please enclose 50c toward mailing cost)

"Rich Rewards Revealed By Your Birthdate"

This is guidance to **understand** the problems, needs, "drives" and desires of marital partners, young children, "teen-agers" and relatives; in addition to **specific** suggestions for successful career vocations, areas from which money may come, happy marriages; even hobby interests, and dozens of other VITAL areas. Here, with descriptions of each birthsign, is the thoughtful analysis of "day-to-day" problems confronting **you** as well as loved ones! Included is a section written for **"the teen-ager"** to read—simply, **understandingly** put, in their language!

Price each copy _____$3.00

(Please enclose 30c toward mailing cost)

The Time When Your Luck Will Change According to Your Birthdate

The most important events and changes in your life, even to radical turnabouts, can occur under the major cyclic influences. These cycles are covered by your individual decan at birth. This phenomena is rarely presented as it is here relating to the individual. The explanation will highlight the bright and danger spots indicated and matters relating to your most intimate wishes for your lifetime. Perhaps, nearly as important, you can gain "a vital" understanding of the innermost conflicts and desires of those you hold dear.

A thorough discussion of the most important and powerful element in planetary positions at your birth; the decan of your sun sign! You'll find your very own segment in a delineation of all 36. Your decan, endowing the elements of character and ability, is "the key" to your distinctness as an individual. These revealing keys can be of special value in assessing potential harmony or friction in your most important relationships.

A deluxe hardbound edition.

Price each copy _____$6.50

(Please enclose 40c toward mailing cost)

Alan McConnell & Son, Inc.

Publishers

546 South Meridian St., Rm. 602   Indianapolis, Indiana 46225